W9-ARG-268

On *CULTURE* and
LITERATURE

BOOKS BY MARVIN MUDRICK

Jane Austen
Conrad: A Collection of Critical Essays (editor)
On Culture and Literature

On CULTURE and LITERATURE

by MARVIN MUDRICK

Horizon Press   New York

To Hugh Kenner

PREFACE

The earliest of these essays was published in 1955, the most recent in 1970. They are all reprinted here very nearly as they first appeared, with the exception of the essay on Hemingway. This was published in 1964 as a review of *A Moveable Feast*, which no longer seems to me so wonderful a recovery of Hemingway's powers as it did then; but I still admire the book, and I hope that the revised essay published here hasn't entirely filtered out my original enthusiasm. The essay on Mailer and Styron and the one on Malamud, Bellow, and Roth, which appeared six and four years ago respectively, continue to represent my impressions of those writers; and I have updated each by adding a "Postscript 1970" to deal briefly with their later work.

I am grateful to the periodicals in which these essays first appeared: *Art News, The Denver Quarterly, The Lugano Review, The New York Review of Books, Shenandoah, The Yale Review,* and especially *The Hudson Review*, which published eleven of the seventeen.

MARVIN MUDRICK
University of California
Santa Barbara, California

CONTENTS

I. Politics and Science

HERZEN AND ORWELL:
POLITICAL ANIMALS

George Orwell,* who was a brave man and a patriotic Englishman, didn't flinch from the job of defending Shakespeare against the often ridiculed but seldom answered attack by Tolstoy:

> He objects, with some justification, to the raggedness of Shakespeare's plays, the irrelevancies, the incredible plots, the exaggerated language: but what at bottom he probably most dislikes is a sort of exuberance, a tendency to take—not so much a pleasure, as simply an interest in the actual process of life. It is a mistake to write Tolstoy off as a moralist attacking an artist. He never said that art, as such, is wicked or meaningless, nor did he even say that technical virtuosity is unimportant. But his main aim, in his later years, was to narrow the range of human consciousness. One's interests, one's points of attachment to the physical world and the day-to-day struggle, must be as few and not as many as possible. Literature must consist of parables, stripped of detail and almost independent of language. The parables—this is where Tolstoy differs from the average vulgar puritan—must themselves be works of art, but pleasure and

---

* *The Collected Essays, Journalism and Letters of George Orwell* (Vol. 1: *An Age Like This;* Vol. 2: *My Country Right or Left;* Vol. 3: *As I Please;* Vol. 4: *In Front of Your Nose*), edited by Sonia Orwell and Ian Angus, Harcourt, Brace & World.

curiosity must be excluded from them. Science, also, must be divorced from curiosity. The business of science, he says, is not to discover what happens, but to teach men how they ought to live. So also with history and politics. . . .

Late Tolstoy doesn't usually provoke such conscientious discriminations, which are not less interesting for being truer of Orwell himself. *Animal Farm* and *1984*, for instance, might be described, far more damagingly than *The Death of Ivan Ilyich* and *Hadji Murad*, as "parables, stripped of detail and almost independent of language." Orwell too, in his novels or in his literary and political journalism, subordinates "pleasure and curiosity" to the "business" of "teaching men how they ought to live"; for (as he remarks in his essay on Dickens) "every writer" has "a 'message,' whether he admits it or not," and, though "not all propaganda is art," "all art is propaganda."

Orwell's "main aim," like old Tolstoy's, is "to narrow the range of human consciousness," to persuade the reader that his options are few and his time is short, that "his points of attachment to the physical world . . . must be as few . . . as possible." Unlike Tolstoy, however, Orwell doesn't exhort or impose: what he does, he does because he plainly is what he is; his substance doesn't exceed or contradict, it isn't even conceivable apart from, his aim; he believes in belief; he is sincere. As for the old sinner Tolstoy, since he has so much of himself to keep down before he can settle for so little, he is as devious and uncomfortable as Shakespeare. Orwell, making lucid distinctions, fails to notice that Tolstoy's denunciation of Shakespearean exuberance is as exuberant as Shakespeare. Orwell is careful and sober (though not "the average vulgar puritan"), he is all conscience, and he can't imagine the level of principled insincerity at which such gigantic dreamers survive the wreckage of their dreams.

Tolstoy, moreover, was young once. In 1861 the young Tolstoy, full of projects, not yet the author of *War and Peace*, made a voyage to London, where he heard Dickens deliver a lecture on education and paid a visit to the famous exile, Alexander Herzen. Half a century later, speaking to a friend, Tolstoy remembered Herzen as a "plump little man"

. . . who generated electric energy. "Lively, responsive, intelligent, interesting," Lev Nikolayevich explained (as usual illustrating every shade of meaning by appropriate movements of his hands), "Herzen at once began talking to me as if we had known each other for a long time. I found his personality enchanting. I have never met a more attractive man. He stood head and shoulders above all the politicians of his own and of our time." *

Tolstoy at eighty had little patience with politics or revolutionary socialism, and he didn't care for Westernized Russians; so his enthusiastic recollection testifies to Herzen's charm and conversation. Herzen was born in Moscow in 1812, just in time to be there during the great fire and Napoleon's occupation: his father was able to obtain Napoleon's permission to leave Moscow with his household by agreeing to carry a message to the Tsar in Petersburg. Later, by means of his influential political journalism, Herzen helped more directly to make history, and he was friendly with the leaders of all the republican movements in nineteenth-century Europe. When he set about writing his memoirs, he recorded the events of his childhood and youth with as much flavor and delight as if he were not a politician but Tolstoy:

> . . . an exclusive sentiment of nationality never leads to any good; it led me to the following incident. Among others who used to visit us was the Comte de Quinsonas, a French *émigré* and a lieutenant-general in the Russian service. A desperate royalist, he took part in the celebrated fête of Versailles, at which the King's life-guards trampled underfoot the popular cockade and at which Marie Antoinette drank to the destruction of the revolution. This French count, a tall, thin, graceful old man with grey hair, was the very model of politeness and elegant manners. There was a peerage awaiting him in Paris, where he had already been to congratulate Louis XVIII on getting his situation. He had returned to Russia to dispose of his estate. Unluckily for me this most courteous of the generals of all the Russian armies had to begin speaking of the war in my presence.

* Quoted from P. Sergeyenko's book on Tolstoy, in Isaiah Berlin's Introduction to *My Past and Thoughts: The Memoirs of Alexander Herzen*, translated by Constance Garnett, revised by Humphrey Higgens, Alfred A. Knopf. 4 vols.

"But surely you must have been fighting against us?" I remarked with extreme naïveté.

"*Non, mon petit, non; j'étais dans l'armée russe.*"

"What?" said I, "you, a Frenchman, and fighting in our army?
That's impossible!"

My father glanced sternly at me and changed the subject. The
Count heroically set things right by saying to my father that "he
liked such *patriotic* sentiments.". . .

Or, with equal sympathy, he is a witness at the deathbed of his
lonely, perverse, Voltairean father:

Klyucharëv, an extremely honest man who at that time was
managing my father's business affairs and was more trusted by
him than anyone, bent down to him and said:

"All the measures you have tried hitherto have been unsuccess-
ful: allow me to advise you to resort to another remedy."

"What remedy?" asked the sick man.

"Won't you send for the priest?"

"Oh," said my father, turning to me, "I thought Grigory
Ivanovich really had some remedy to advise."

Orwell remembers a different kind of childhood and youth,
in the quite respectable boarding-school he attended:

It is not easy for me to think of my schooldays without seeming to breathe a whiff of something cold and evil-smelling—a sort
of compound of sweaty stockings, dirty towels, faecal smells
blowing along corridors, forks with old food between the prongs,
neck-of-mutton stew, and the banging doors of the lavatories
and the echoing chamber-pots in the dormitories.

"From a very early age," he begins an essay entitled "Why I
Write," "I knew that when I grew up I should be a writer.
. . . I knew that I had a facility with words and a power of
facing unpleasant facts . . ." He is at home among the unpleasant facts, and if they aren't altogether ubiquitous he will
go anywhere to hunt them down, in the filthy kitchens of
splendid French hotels, in prisons, in vile hostels for tramps and
itinerant laborers, in workingmen's lodging-houses:

The squalor of this house is beginning to get on my nerves.
Nothing is ever cleaned or dusted, the rooms not done till 5 in
the afternoon, and the cloth never even removed from the kitchen
table. At supper you still see the crumbs from breakfast. The

most revolting feature is Mrs F being always in bed on the kitchen sofa. She has a terrible habit of tearing off strips of newspaper, wiping her mouth with them and then throwing them onto the floor. Unemptied chamberpot under the table at break-fast this morning. The food is dreadful, too. We are given those little twopenny ready-made steak and kidney pies out of stock. I hear horrible stories, too, about the cellars where the tripe is kept and which are said to swarm with black beetles. . . .

"Disgusting" is a word he always has at hand:

One result of the breakdown of religious belief has been a sloppy idealisation of the physical side of life. In a way this is nat-ural enough. For if there is no life beyond the grave, it is obvi-ously harder to face the fact that birth, copulation, etc are in certain aspects disgusting. . . .

This sort of self-fulfilling nausea has its antecedents in Eng-lish literature: in Swift, for example, and—diluted with Wilde and water—in Shaw. Swift and Shaw were also cranks about language; as Orwell is, explaining how quantities of new words can be invented to enable us to make all our thoughts clear to one another:

The thing that suggests itself immediately is the cinematograph. Everyone must have noticed the extraordinary powers that are latent in the film—the powers of distortion, of fantasy, in general of escaping the restrictions of the physical world. . . . Properly used, the film is the one possible medium for conveying mental processes. . . . A millionaire with a private cinematograph, all the necessary props and a troupe of intelligent actors could, if he wished, make practically all of his inner life known. He could explain the real reasons of his actions instead of telling ration-alised lies, point out the things that seemed to him beautiful, pathetic, funny, etc—things that an ordinary man has to keep locked up because there are no words to express them. In general, he could make other people understand him. Of course, it is not desirable that any one man, short of a genius, should make a show of his inner life. What is wanted is to discover the now nameless feelings that men have *in common*. All the powerful motives which will not go into words and which are a cause of constant lying and misunderstanding, could be tracked down, given visible form, agreed upon, and named. I am sure that the film, with its almost limitless powers of representation, could

accomplish this in the hands of the right investigators, though
putting thoughts into visible shape would not always be easy—
in fact, at first it might be as difficult as any other art.

The really breathtaking looniness and ignorance of this paragraph should be pondered by anyone sympathetic to Orwell's
posthumous reputation as a distinguished writer and a paragon
of reason.

Orwell was brave, honest, and political, qualities that in combination are perhaps rare enough to help justify a monument of
four handsome volumes of miscellaneous writings. He detested
"humbug" (another favorite word) and was adept at spotting
it. He held, from at least as early as the Spanish War, to a set of
convictions which made him a standing target from left and
right: (1) that democratic socialism, though not inevitable and
in fact becoming less and less likely, was the only hope of the
world; (2) that "human society must be based on common decency, whatever the political and economic forms may be";
(3) that "common decency" was a function of bourgeois morality and of the civil liberties which have existed only under
the bourgeois state; (4) that imperialism was the slave-econ-
omy with which the bourgeois state indispensably enriched itself at a safe distance from home; (5) that the Soviet Union
was not Utopia or a degenerated workers' state but a monstrous tyranny. After World War II, especially once the Cold
War had started, these convictions became the articles of faith
for unaffiliated radicals, to whom Orwell seemed a tough-
minded patriarchal prophet. But Orwell has no density or resonance. It's not surprising that *Animal Farm* and *1984* were both
Cold-War Books-of-the-Month, runaway successes in America
as exposés of Godless Communism.

Even the most lumpish American readers, tipped off by
these unpuzzling fables, were able to ascertain that, for Orwell,
the Soviet Union was the enemy; and nothing else was necessary. All art, says Orwell, is propaganda. The purpose of propaganda is to establish a collective rhetorical advantage for our
side over an instantly identifiable collective enemy: the methods don't have to be very subtle, indeed if they're too subtle
they may cause the audience to wonder which side is which;

only the effect counts. Orwell is himself the very image of collective virtue ("common decency") and makes virtue seem easy if not exactly worthwhile.

Herzen is something else: what Orwell does by reflex Herzen must, out of his conscious choice of a political life, strain to do, learn to do, surrender his wit and vividness to do. Herzen was by right of birth and upbringing a wealthy and cultured member of the Russian gentry. His father was an eighteenth-century gentleman, a dandy of Catherine the Great's court, who survived with increasingly distrustful irony into the drill-sergeant reign of Nicholas I. Even a boorish despot like Nicholas, however, could not suppress the air of family, of domesticity and intimacy, which characterized the Russian upper-class attitude toward the Tsar, which is the element of boldness and freedom in the great ladies of Catherine's time as Herzen affectionately memorializes them, and which persevered even when the Tsar felt obliged to play the rôle of offended majesty against upper-class political refractoriness. A recognizable pattern for a member of the gentry was to spend his youth living on familiar terms with courtiers and government officials, going to the university to read Hegel and argue the need for political change with other well-born high-minded young men, being arrested by personal order of the Tsar and sent off to an isolated provincial town for a few years of punitive rustication, returning to Moscow or Petersburg for more familiarity and friendliness with government officials as well as more study and subversive night-long discussions under surveillance by informers and secret police, being arrested and sentenced to further rustication, and so on. This was Herzen's life in summary till the age of thirty-five; and in his memoirs his hatred of Nicholas is less striking than its tone of a bitter family quarrel:

> The government pardoned Passek, and never thought of restoring to him some part of his property. Wasted by exertions and privations, the old man took to his bed; they did not know what they should dine on the next day.
> At this time Nicholas was celebrating his coronation: banquet followed banquet, and Moscow was like a heavily decorated ballroom, everywhere lights, escutcheons and gay attire. . . . The two elder sisters, without consulting anyone, wrote a petition to

Nicholas, describing the situation of the family, and begged him to review the case and restore their property. They left the house secretly in the morning and went to the Kremlin, elbowed their way to the front, and awaited the Tsar, "crowned and exalted on high." When Nicholas came down the steps of the Red Staircase, the two girls quietly stepped forward and held up the petition. He passed by, pretending not to notice them; an aide-de-camp took the paper and the police led them away to the police station.

Nicholas was about thirty at the time and already was capable of such heartlessness. This coldness, this intransigence is characteristic of slight commonplace natures, cashiers, and tipstaffs. I have often noticed this unshakable firmness of character in postal officials, salesmen of theatre and railway tickets, and people who are continually bothered and interrupted. . . . They learn to look at a man without seeing him, and not to listen to him, although they are standing side by side. But how did this autocratic clerk train himself not to see, and what need had he not to be a minute late for a parade?

The girls were kept in custody until evening. Frightened and shocked, they besought the police superintendent with tears to let them go home, where their absence must have alarmed the whole family. Nothing was done about the petition.

Herzen broke out of the circle of surveillance and banishment by receiving permission to travel to western Europe: he left in 1847, and he never returned to Russia. (Herzen tells the delicious story of discomfiting Nicholas and saving his inheritance. After 1848, when he refused to obey an Imperial command to return home, he became officially a political exile, and Nicholas stopped payment on bonds Herzen had inherited from his mother. Herzen persuaded the French banker, Baron James Rothschild, to intervene; Rothschild informed Nicholas that a pending Rothschild loan to Russia might be cancelled unless Herzen's bonds were honored; and the Tsar backed down.) Nicholas did not die till 1855: during his entire reign, which began with his suppression of the Decembrist uprising in 1825, he did not attempt a single act of political conciliation or reform. Since Herzen's commitment to revolutionary causes is seldom unambiguous, since he often uses the words without seeming to be possessed by the spirit, it is tempting to guess that his commitment had something to do with his loneliness in exile and his continually exacerbated outrage over Nicholas's policies. Anyhow, the cultured Russian gentleman is never altogether at ease, as Orwell is, in situations that solicit gestures of collective virtue; at the time of his first political banishment, for example:

We stood with folded arms, making not the slightest sign that our hearts were touched by the Imperial and princely mercy.

Then Shubinsky thought of another dodge and, addressing Ogarëv, said:

"You are going to Penza; do you imagine that that is by chance? Your father is lying paralysed at Penza and the prince besought the Tsar to designate that town for you, that your being near might to some extent alleviate for him the blow of your exile. Do you not think that you have reason to thank the prince?"

There was no help for it: Ogarëv made a slight bow. This was what they were trying to get.

The good-natured old man was pleased at this, and next, I do not know why, he summoned me. I stepped forward with the devout intention of not thanking him, whatever he or Shubinsky might say; besides, I was being sent farther away than any and to the nastiest town.

"You are going to Perm," said Prince Golitsyn.

I said nothing. He was disconcerted and, for the sake of saying something, he added,

"I have an estate there."

"Would you care to send some commission through me to your steward?" I asked with a smile.

"I do not give commissions to people like you—*Carbonari*," added the resourceful old man.

"Then what do you wish of me?"

"Nothing."

"I thought you called me."

"You may go," Shubinsky interposed.

"Allow me," I replied, "since I am here, to remind you that you told me, Colonel, last time I was before the commission . . ."

All this melodramatic formality—the standing row of folded arms; the debating tactics of "Allow me, Colonel"—is the assertion of revolutionary virtue over these captors who persist in trying to palliate their sins by small acts of kindness. The sentence has already been passed, and nothing will be altered except history's impression of the scene: what a row of prigs! Young Herzen is enjoying his virtue and impudence, he values the old Prince's quick thinking; it is an amusing and complex scene, especially the atmosphere as of a not very stern and somewhat perplexed father trying to discipline his frisky sons without alienating them. But the compulsory priggishness—nothing for character and meaning, everything for effect—is a vulgar touch, out of Poe or socialist realism.

To the degree to which Herzen is a politician posing for campaign photos, this sort of vulgarity is acceptable to him, and it can spoil some of his most moving recollections. When his beloved wife was seduced by a family friend (a poet and fellow socialist) and died soon after, Herzen almost went mad with humiliation and grief: in his memoirs he tells the story with force and pathos and only a little self-protective sanctimony. But the effort is too much for him to keep up, politics breaks in, and, replying to a letter from Richard Wagner (who was a friend of the friend; Herzen's personal correspondence was carried on with terrifyingly public figures), he can't resist appealing to the verdict of history:

> I have come to know you through your fine work on the *chef d'oeuvre* of the future. You have excellently understood the bond uniting all the arts, which ought to be combined in harmonious, concrete creation. . . .
>
> A duel between him and me? Never! . . . As a socialist and a revolutionary, I appealed to the only authority I recognise. I had the manliness, the daring to submit the affair to the judgment of my friends the democrats. I showed the letters, I told the facts. My appeal raised a general outburst of condemnation. Herwegh's moral death was decreed. Despised by all decent men, excluded from the body of democrats, he will be forced to hide his ignominious existence in some remote corner of the world. For he will find no peace in France, Italy or Switzerland.
>
> I swear, and my friends swear it also—every day brings us a proof of it—that we are supported by all representatives of the militant revolution.

Meanwhile his wife was dead. Politics, preparing to take over from religion for these unillusioned nineteenth-century infidels, was becoming another manufacturer of wide-screen all-purpose prosthetic consolations.

For the exiled and bereaved the personal isn't enough, or it's too much to bear, and Herzen yearns for an assembly of secular saints, icons of suprapersonal nobility, touchstones of grace, like his friend the astonishing hero Garibaldi, during whose triumphal visit to England Herzen observes a characteristic scene:

> Various persons had gathered in the corridor; suddenly an old Italian, an emigrant from days long past, a poor fellow who made ice-cream, burst through, caught Garibaldi by the skirt of his coat and stopped him, burst into tears and said: "Well, now I can die. I have seen him, I have seen him!" Garibaldi embraced and kissed the old man. Then in broken and confused phrases, with the fearful rapidity of a peasant's Italian, the old man began telling Garibaldi his adventures, and wound up his speech with a wonderful flower of Southern eloquence:
>
> "Now I shall die at peace, but you—God bless you—live long, live for our country, live for us, live till I rise again from the dead!"
>
> He clutched his hand, covered it with kisses and went out sobbing.

Italian opera, no doubt; but opera by Verdi, in which the most grandiose public gestures can become shapely, humane, and passionate; and it is this sort of theater into which Herzen would like to transform the world. Herzen's stainless heroes are Garibaldi and Robert Owen, each a simple and generous man committed to realizing a grandiose public vision: to free Italy and inaugurate a republic; to found, in the midst of bourgeois society, model communities of unoppressed children and coöperative working adults. With these gentle large-scale pragmatists Herzen contrasts bloodthirsty large-scale theorists like Gracchus Babeuf, "the first French socialist" at the time of the Revolution:

> The time had come to restore . . . [the proletarian's] ancient, *inalienable* rights. . . . Where were they? Why is the proletarian the sovereign? Why is it to him that all the property plundered by others belongs? Ah! you doubt—you are a suspect fellow: the nearest sovereign takes you off to the citizen judge,

and he sends you to the citizen executioner, and you will not be doubting any more! . . .

Owen, seeing that people of the educated countries were growing up towards a transition to a new epoch, had no thought of violence and simply wished to help this development. Just as consistently from his side as Babeuf from his, he set about the study of the embryo, the development of the cell. He began, like all natural scientists, with a particular instance: his microscope, his laboratory, was New Lanark; his study grew and came to puberty along with the cell and led him to the conclusion that the high road to the installation of a new order was *upbringing.*

Herzen tells an anecdote about an early associate of Marx's, the German revolutionary Karl Peter Heinzen, a spiritual brother of Babeuf's, who wrote that "it would be sufficient to massacre *two millions* of the inhabitants of the globe and the cause of the revolution would go swimmingly":

> I cannot refrain from relating an extremely funny incident which happened to me in connection with this cannibalistic project. There was, and indeed still is, living in Geneva a Dr R., one of the most good-natured men in the world and one of the most constant and Platonic lovers of the revolution, the friend of all the refugees; he doctored them gratis as well as giving them food and drink. . . .
>
> . . . it was to him as a friend of Heinzen's that I appealed . . . when the latter published his philanthropic programme.
>
> "Why," I said to him, "does your friend write such pernicious nonsense? The reaction is making an outcry, and indeed it has every reason to: he's a regular Marat in a German setting! And how can one ask for two million heads?"
>
> R. was confused, but did not like to give up his friend.
>
> "Listen," he said at last: "you have lost sight of one fact, perhaps: Heinzen is speaking of the whole human race; in that number there would be at least *two hundred thousand Chinese.*"
>
> "Oh, well, that's a different matter; why spare them?" I answered and for a long time afterwards I could never think of this mitigating consideration without bursting into insane laughter.

Herzen did not favor the numerical type of revolutionary rhetoric, and he grew less and less convinced of the usefulness

of violence. Orwell, measuring Dickens the novelist and believer in education against Marx the advocate of violent revolution, comments: "If you hate violence and don't believe in politics, the only major remedy remaining is education." In other
words, reduce your scale (forget the two hundred thousand
Chinese) and extend your interests (think about individuals).
Only, as Herzen gloomily concludes, education doesn't work
any better than revolution or politics or model communities,
because the mob is quite content to remain as it is:

> Babeuf wished to *enjoin prosperity* and a communist republic
> on people.
> Owen wished to educate them in a different economic way of
> living, incomparably more profitable for them.
> Napoleon wanted neither the one nor the other; he understood
> that Frenchmen did not in fact desire to feed on Spartan broth
> and to return to the morality of Brutus the Elder, that they were
> not very well satisfied that on feast-days "citizens will assemble
> to discuss the laws and instruct their children in the civic vir-
> tues." But—and this is a different thing—fighting and boasting
> of their own bravery they do like.
> . . . [Napoleon] was not a reproach to the mob, for he did
> not offend it by either his purity or his virtues . . . *he belonged
> himself to the mob* and he showed it its very self . . . elevated
> into a genius and covered with rags of glory.

Herzen, the man whose conversation charmed Tolstoy,
would not settle for the modest human scale of novelists; and
the world is unwilling to sustain itself on the scale of grand
opera. Between Garibaldi on the heights and Napoleon among
the benighted masses were all the diverse unhistorical persons
(including Heinzen's two million) who customarily escaped
Herzen's attention, and who persisted in fascinating Tolstoy
even after he had decided that for the sake of its soul he must
narrow the range of the world's consciousness. Tolstoy is a
Roman by late conviction, not by feeling and practice; whereas
Herzen and Orwell are, after all, as Roman as Babeuf, propos-
ing for Falstaff and Stiva Oblonsky purity and law and civic
virtue, the same old web of "civilized" contracts and restraints
that didn't prevent Herzen's grief and humiliation or his wife's

stupidly premature death. Even civic virtue isn't immune to the private and personal.

Perhaps, like others who live for causes and the future, Herzen and Orwell had an affinity with deaths and endings. While they were still in their thirties, they reported the death of Europe: Herzen, from the dismantled barricades of Paris in 1848; Orwell, from Spain in 1937, when every revolutionary in sight was being jailed on the orders of the Communist Party. Each man lived the rest of his life in a mood of deepening skepticism about political action, yet each continued to be preoccupied with politics and public affairs, and neither seems to have imagined any satisfactory alternative to this preoccupation. As skeptics and spectators (Herzen began writing his memoirs at the age of forty), they were remote from the self-generating momentum of both the fanatical theorist and the practical leader. History had betrayed them, but, in "tumultuous, revolutionary ages like our own" (Orwell's dead phrase), they had nothing else; they remained faithful to causes and ideals that were unlikely to get another serious chance during their lifetimes, and, especially Orwell, they sounded more and more like incorruptible morticians:

> The Spanish war and other events in 1936–37 turned the scale and thereafter I knew where I stood. Every line of serious work that I have written since 1936 has been written, directly or indirectly, *against* totalitarianism and *for* democratic Socialism, as I understand it. It seems to me nonsense, in a period like our own, to think that one can avoid writing of such subjects. Everyone writes of them in one guise or another. It is simply a question of which side one takes and what approach one follows. And the more one is conscious of one's political bias, the more chance one has of acting politically without sacrificing one's aesthetic and intellectual integrity.

The worst one can say of Orwell is that he doesn't seem a hypocrite when he mentions his (or "one's") "aesthetic and intellectual integrity." What a burden to take to an early grave! Herzen, at least, had a childhood, a disastrous marriage, some shining heroes, and pyrotechnical talk for a visiting young Russian novelist, before he gave up the ghost.

1969

WOOLDRIDGE, KOESTLER, AND WATSON:
PROMETHEUS AT WORK AND PLAY

Dean E. Wooldridge is a computer scientist and a spoilsport. "Free will," he says,* "poses no problem—it simply doesn't exist." Life can be fully accounted for by the laws of physics ("the prevailing line of research and theory provides for the origin as well as for the chemistry of life an explanation based entirely on the inexorable workings of the ordinary laws of physical science in the inert ingredients of the earth"); the brain is a sequence of complex switching operations, and therefore functionally identical with the electronic computer; all biological processes, including intelligence and personality, are or soon will be exactly reproducible in and by machines; all behavior is reflex behavior, except perhaps for the occasional "random firing" of a few unruly neurons:

Another kind of complicating factor that impeded early understanding of reflex behavior is demonstrated by the sea urchin. Its spines usually display a certain random motion even when no stimulus is present, and their orientation toward an approaching enemy may also include some continuing restlessness. The disturbing control signal involved here is closely analogous to the

---

* *Mechanical Man*, McGraw-Hill.

29

noise on the circuits of the communications engineer. For the nerve cells of these lower animals, like many of those in the human body, do not always wait to receive a specific stimulus before "closing the switch" and sending voltage pulses out over the axon. Instead, there is a certain amount of random firing of the neurons. In the complex nervous systems of the larger animals, so many neurons must act cooperatively to produce significant movement of principal organs that the random firing of a few neurons cannot produce a conspicuous result (although an occasional flicker of an eyelid or twitch of a muscle may be due to this cause). In the small and primitive animals that we are now dealing with, however, there may be only a few interconnected neurons in the circuit that controls a major element of the body. Under such circumstances, the random firing of one or two neurons can produce observable restless movement of the affected part.

(If somebody's jaw twitches whenever he talks about the "inexorable laws" of something or other, don't call the psychiatrist, it's only a random firing.)

Man, then, is "no more than a complex machine": a view for which Dr. Wooldridge doesn't claim the patent, noting that it "has been discussed since the time of the ancient Greeks. Indeed it has long since been accepted as valid by many modern philosophers and scientists" (whom he doesn't name, leaving us to wonder when they will surface with a full-page ad in *The New York Times*). "But this book is not primarily addressed to that small and sophisticated group. And the content of most oral and written public pronouncements makes it clear that the large majority (including even some scientists and philosophers) have not yet accepted the conclusion to which our considerations have led us." One obstacle to be overcome is morality: "the disappearance of the mystical concept of Right and Wrong . . . may result in significant increase in the logical content of human thought," and thus facilitate acceptance of the "inexorable" conclusion ("Given the laws and the particles, all else follows inexorably") that thought and behavior are totally determined. Nor, when at last even the masses have come to understand that religion and morality are eyewash, will society change very much:

Ultimate recognition of the machinelike nature of man will certainly discredit the religious imperative that now helps hold . . . believers in line, and it may also weaken the institution of the church enough to eliminate most of its exhortative influence on . . . [social conformists]. But there is no reason to expect society to allow such weaknesses to remain uncompensated. For recent world history suggests that governments will not find it beyond their capability to fill the one need by investing their own institutions with a semireligious aura that the unanalytic can worship, and to fill the other by intensification of propaganda emphasizing the popular approval to be expected from behavior acceptable to the state. Whether this will make the citizen's life more or less pleasant is not our concern here. At issue is only the question of the continued moral behavior of individuals after they have learned that men are machines.

Maybe one should entertain the possibility that machines, let in on the secret of what they are, will behave as badly as if they were human: smash the furniture, challenge the doctrine of inexorability, disrupt the brain's electronic switching operations with methedrine and LSD, cheat on exams, misrepresent evidence. Already it appears that some machines—steamrollers like Dr. Wooldridge—aren't above suppressing such aspects of the evidence as suggest that man may be a specially adaptive creature. For example, an experiment that *Mechanical Man* makes much of is one purportedly demonstrating that "visual capability" is chiefly a matter of permanent neural circuitry:

> . . . the nervous systems of some animals possess a regenerative capacity: if nerves are cut, they grow back and ultimately function once again. Sperry was therefore able to establish, in an adult toad, a special kind of "newly formed" visual system. He performed an operation wherein the optic nerves were cut and reconnected inversely—that is, the right eye was connected to the nerve from the brain that previously had gone to the left eye, and vice versa. . . .
>
> Yet, after a few weeks, Sperry's toad was able to see again, apparently as well as ever! . . . That this had nothing to do with learning was proved by an interesting anomaly in the toad's new behavior: if a fly appeared opposite the toad's right eye, it darted its tongue out to the left to attempt to capture it; if the food appeared to the left, the toad would always strike to the

right. . . . No amount of experience ever caused the toad to correct its mistake. It was obvious that the leftness and rightness of the vision were wired-in, and not learned, concepts.

It seems odd that Dr. Wooldridge would not have been acquainted with a comparable experiment on man which proves that, though the toad doesn't adjust, man does:

> . . . we find in man the faculty of physical regeneration reduced to a minimum, but compensated by his unique powers to remould his patterns of behaviour—to meet critical challenges by creative responses.
>
> Even on the level of elementary perception, learning to see through spectacles which turn the world upside down . . . testifies to these powers. Experiments which create the same effect have been carried out on animals—reptiles and monkeys—by cutting the optic nerve and letting it grow together after twisting the severed end of the bundle half round the clock. As a result, the animals see the world upside-down, reach leftward when food is shown on the right, and downward if it is offered from above. They never get over the maladjustment. Human subjects, however, fitted with inverting glasses, do get over it. The effect at first is thoroughly upsetting: you see your body upside-down, your feet planted on a floor which has become the ceiling of the room. Or, with left-right inverters, you try to move away from a wall, and bump into it. Yet after a certain time, which may mean several days, the subject becomes adjusted to living in an inverted world, which then appears to him more or less normal again. The retinal image and its projection in the visual cortex are still upside-down; but, thanks to the intervention of some higher echelons in the hierarchy, the mental image has become reorganised. At the present stage of knowledge physiology has no satisfactory explanation for this phenomenon. All one can say is that if our orientation, our postural and motor reactions to the visual field depend on wiring circuits in the brain, living in an inverted world must entail a lot of undoing and re-doing in the wiring diagram.

This is from Arthur Koestler's latest big book synthesizing all knowledge.* The first two-thirds of the book is a voluminously argued and documented and, for the layman at any rate, persuasive account of a great variety of biological experiments

* *The Ghost in the Machine*, Macmillan.

and hypotheses leading to the general hypothesis that organic evolution is anti-entropic, hierarchical, and voluntaristic:

> The living organism is not a mosaic aggregate of elementary physico-chemical processes, but a hierarchy of parts within parts, . . . [each of which], from the sub-cellular organelles upward, is a closely integrated structure, equipped with self-regulatory devices, and enjoys a degree of self-government.

"In contrast to machines," the living organism is "primarily *active* instead of being merely *reactive*":

> Instead of "running down" like a mechanical clock that dissipates its energies through friction, . . . it is constantly "building up" more complex substances from the substances it feeds on, more complex forms of energies from the energies it absorbs, and more complex patterns of information—perceptions, feelings, thoughts —from the input of its receptor organs. . . . The same irrepressible "building-up" tendency is manifested in phylogenesis, in the phenomena of evolution by initiative, the slow progress towards more complex forms and functions, the emergence of new levels in the organismic hierarchy and of new methods of co-ordination, resulting in greater independence from, and mastery of, the environment.

So it comes as quite a shock, after all this optimistic evolutionism, when Koestler proposes that evolution at its very apex has gone wrong: that "the human mind is basically schizophrenic," that "the delusional streak which runs through our history may be an endemic form of paranoia, built into the wiring circuits of the human brain"; that "reason" is reliable and good whereas "passion" is unreliable and bad, but that "reason" has been doomed by an evolutionary split within the human brain itself. Koestler begins to sound more and more unambiguously like a retired political hack and second-rate novelist as he adduces Hitler, Stalin, "the ubiquitous rituals of human sacrifice," and the doctrine of the damnation of unbaptized infants in evidence of man's unregenerate nature:

> I can speak of this with some first-hand experience, based on seven years (1931–8) of membership in the Communist Party during Stalin's terror regime. In writing about that period, I have described the operations of the deluded mind in terms of

elaborate manoeuvrings to defend the citadel of faith against the
hostile incursions of doubt. There are several concentric rings
of defences protecting the fortress. The outer defences are de-
signed to ward off unpalatable facts. For the simple-minded this
is made easy by official censorship, the banning of all literature
liable to poison the mind; and by implanting a fear of contamina-
tion, or of guilt by association, through contact with suspected
heretics. Crude as these methods are, they quickly produce a
blinkered, sectarian outlook on the world. . . .

Koestler, to be sure, wasn't among the simple-minded; it took
"an eminently rationalist credo" to trap *this* "progressive intellectual";

> The Leninist theory of Scientific Socialism . . . was an offspring,
> in the line of direct descent, of the Age of Enlightenment. It was
> an eminently rationalist credo, based on a materialist conception
> of history, which derided all emotionalism [notice Koestler's
> pejorative word] as "petit-bourgeois sentimentality." How is it
> to be explained that millions of adherents of this rationalist doc-
> trine—including progressive intellectuals all over the world—
> accepted the logical absurdities of the "Stalin personality cult,"
> the show trials, purges, the alliance with the Nazis; and that those
> who lived outside Russia accepted them voluntarily, in self-im-
> posed discipline, without pressure from Big Brother? . . .

Well, one way of explaining it is to point out that even progressive intellectuals and ex-Communists like Koestler can still
write thick tomes glorifying the reductivist, Gradgrindian rationalism which got them into trouble in the first place. As a
member of the Party, Koestler visited the Soviet Union during
the famine of the years of collectivization; "saw entire villages
deserted, railway stations blocked by crowds of begging families, and the proverbial starving infants . . . with stick-like
arms, puffed-up bellies and cadaverous heads"; and "learnt to
classify automatically everything that shocked me as 'the heritage of the past' and everything I liked as 'the seeds of the future.' " The attitude which led the faithful to deny the evidence of their senses in favor of the Platonic utopias described
in the Party guidebooks is the same sort of rationalism which
leads Koestler, thirty-five years later, to define emotions as

"overheated drives," and which demands the triumph of reason over passion, "the breakthrough from maniac to man"; which calls itself empirical by mistaking its commitment to debate for a commitment to experience; which is instrumentalist and manipulative; which is (like Koestler's) patronizingly anxious, or (like Dr. Wooldridge's) merely cynical, about the unteachable rabble.

One would of course rather not believe that Koestler's past is to be explained in less agreeable terms; in the terms, for example, with which Harold Rosenberg responded to Leslie Fiedler's indictment of liberals for complicity in Communist crimes:

Whatever its weakness in understanding Communism and its techniques, liberalism was in no sense responsible for Communist vileness. It is false to say that a belief in freedom, equality, individuality induced adherence to the Red band, with its underband of party bosses, spies and masterminds. The liberal sentiment for radical equality and freedom was, in fact, the single intellectual mooring that held against the powerful drag of the totalitarian "we," supported by the offer of a heroic part and material reward through social scheming. . . .

The intellectuals and fellow travelers who followed the Communists through the execution of the Old Bolsheviks, the extermination of POUMists and anarchists in Spain, the Stalin-Hitler Pact, the sabotage of French and British resistance to the Nazis, the partition of Poland, all of which took place in public and behind no curtain of any kind, were not "innocent," to say nothing of "generous and open-minded." These scoundrels were, as a type, middle-class careerists, closed both to arguments and evidence, impatient with thought, psychopaths of "radical" conformity. The "idealism" of this sodden group of Philistines, distinguished from the rest of their species by their more up-to-date smugness and systematic malice, can be respected only by those who ignore its function in hiding from them the cynicism which hardened their minds against any human plea or any evidence embarrassing to the Party. Delirious at finding themselves on The Stage of History, they eagerly carried out the intellectual atrocities assigned to them, while keeping one eye on a post in the future International Power, the other on the present good spot in the government, the university, Hollywood or publishing. In concocting arguments and social boycotts to cover up acts of the Party they complemented the terrorism of GPU assassins. . . .*

In any case it is the prestige of science, not of any other rationalist system, that attracts Koestler now. The pathos of his laborious book is that, by the light of science, the prognosis he arrives at is either Armageddon or, in the nick of time, the invention of a drug that will paper over the cracks in man's unreasonable schizoid brain. "Nature," says Koestler, finding a scapegoat, "has let us down, God seems to have left the receiver off the hook, and time is running out."

Engineers and journalists! you haven't been talking about scientists at all, somebody will complain. Well, then, consider James D. Watson, who shared a Nobel Prize for participating in a "complex of discoveries" about DNA that another scientist has called "the greatest achievement of science in the twentieth century." † Dr. Watson's book‡ has been enthusiastically received everywhere, and not merely as a scientific document: "Perfectly fascinating and delightful . . . his engaging directness and awesome candor give an unusual insight into the creative processes of science," says Carl Kaysen, Director of the Institute for Advanced Studies at Princeton; "Like all good memoirs it has not been emasculated by considerations of good taste," says Dr. Medawar.

For those who are beginning to anticipate a Boswellian journal on sex among the giant-molecule models, here is the hottest item in the book:

> But regardless of what went through Chargaff's sarcastic mind, someone had to explain his results. Thus the next afternoon Francis buzzed over to Griffith's rooms in Trinity to set himself straight about the base-pair data. Hearing "Come in," he opened the door to see Griffith and a girl. Realizing that this was not the moment for science, he slowly retreated, asking Griffith to tell him again the pairs produced by his calculations. After scribbling them down on the back of an envelope, he left. Since I had departed that morning for the continent, his next stop was the

* *The Tradition of the New*, Horizon Press, pp. 236–7.
† P. B. Medawar, in *The New York Review of Books*, March 28, 1968, p. 3.
‡ *The Double Helix*, Atheneum.

Philosophical Library, where he could remove his lingering doubts about Chargaff's data. Then with both sets of information firmly in hand, he considered returning the next day to Griffith's rooms. But on second thought he realized that Griffith's interests were elsewhere. It was all too clear that the presence of popsies does not inevitably lead to a scientific future.

True, it is comforting that Dr. Watson and his co-prizewinner appear to be, by a scattering of evidence through their conversations, unimpeachably heterosexual:

Only by the most special pleading could I imagine the polynucleotide backbone bending enough to accommodate irregular base sequences. Even this possibility vanished when Francis came in. He immediately realized that a like-with-like structure would give a 34 Å crystallographic repeat only if each chain had a complete rotation every 68 Å. But this would mean that the rotation angle between successive bases would be only 18 degrees, a value Francis believed was absolutely ruled out by his recent fiddling with the models. Also Francis did not like the fact that the structure gave no explanation for the Chargaff rules (adenine equals thymine, guanine equals cytosine). I, however, maintained my lukewarm response to Chargaff's data. So I welcomed the arrival of lunchtime, when Francis' cheerful prattle temporarily shifted my thoughts to why undergraduates could not satisfy *au pair* girls.

Unfortunately, Dr. Watson's speculations about popsies are liable to be diluted by his rather obsessional scientific interests. He keeps his eyes open from time to time, though, on other nonscientific issues: observes, for instance, that the English serve lousy food, lack central heating, and have some impressive buildings:

. . . he altered our course to take me through King's along the backs, and through to the Great Court of Trinity. I had never seen such beautiful buildings in all my life, and any hesitation I might have had about leaving my safe life as a biologist vanished. Thus I was only nominally ["in name only"? or does he intend "minimally"?] depressed when I peered inside several damp houses known to contain student rooms. . . .

In everything but its science it is a breezy, complacent, superficial, somewhat vulgar book, about on the level of *Lucky*

Jim (as Dr. Medawar entitled his very favorable review of it). There are a few nice touches of ill will; and the representation of Linus Pauling oscillates amusingly between respectfulness and youthful malice. But no non-scientist would guess that a great, or even an interesting, mind was back of *The Double Helix*. (When Dr. Watson is on the verge of the discovery, he turns solemn and literary: "I felt marvelously alive when I awoke. On my way to the Whim I slowly walked toward the Clare Bridge, staring up at the gothic pinnacles of the King's College Chapel that stood out sharply against the spring sky. I briefly stopped and looked over at the perfect Georgian features of the recently cleaned Gibbs building," *etc.*)

The chasm between the two cultures persists; and the humanists on the far side brood over the fact that Dr. Watson was a 24-year-old graduate student, by his own admission not a very good chemist, when he shared in the most important chemical discovery of the century, and nine years older when he shared the Nobel Prize for it. Even John Steinbeck worked a lot harder, and certainly longer, for the Nobel Prize he was awarded in the same year. But science is cumulative, progressive, collaborative; wherever the scientist starts he has already gone most of the way. Scientific talent seems to be a very particular, anonymous resourcefulness, more a matter of picking the right problem at the right time and keeping at it till it cracks; so that freshness and luck can outwit knowledge and long practice (as Crick and Watson outwitted Pauling).

Scientific discoveries are such wonderful instruments for change that maybe it isn't surprising that some who make them are much like instruments themselves. Prometheus may have been pretty dull company, once he handed over the wood and matches and the set of camping instructions.

1968

OSCAR LEWIS:
FIVE CHARACTERS IN
SEARCH OF AN AUTHOR

Oscar Lewis is an anthropologist who has devoted himself, for two decades, to studying the rural and urban poor of Mexico. In 1959 he published *Five Families* (subtitled "Mexican Case Studies in the Culture of Poverty"), in which he superimposed the techniques of fiction upon the techniques of the social scientist: the book presents five Mexican families by reporting, from the lives of each of them, a complete actual day, its conversation stenographically recorded, its events narrated by an author who reserves and exercises the right to "some selection of data," who freely uses description and flashback "to give more depth and meaning" to what he retains, and whose point of view allows him, he would have us believe, unimpeded access to the minds of his characters. Mr. Lewis called his method "ethnographic realism" ("in contrast to literary realism"). To anthropologists (Oliver La Farge, for instance, who wrote the Foreword), the method, abandoning as it does the statistical paraphernalia of the scholarly monograph, may well have looked revolutionary; to a layman and a literary critic, *Five Families* reads like mildly interesting, rather old-fashioned naturalistic fiction written by a novelist who has a good many unassorted facts, a pedestrian style, and an unwarranted confidence in his capacity to imagine or to penetrate minds categorically different from, though not necessarily simpler than, his own.

Now, in *The Children of Sánchez*, Mr. Lewis has concocted a sort of fictitious, non-fictional stream-of-consciousness for his somewhat fictionalized characters, presenting the members of a single family (one of the five in the previous book) through their tape-recorded ruminations and recollections, which he has "selected, arranged, and organized" (in unspecified ways) "into coherent life stories," but which he keeps clear of the mediocre omniscient voice of *Five Families*. This voice does, however, speak in the Introduction, and the hash of social-scientistic and quasi-literary jargon it affects helps to expose some of the drawbacks in Mr. Lewis's newest and most boldly unmonographic method:

> This approach gives us a cumulative, multifaceted, panoramic view of each individual, of the family as a whole, and of many aspects of lower-class Mexican life. The independent versions of the same incidents given by the various family members provide a built-in check upon the reliability and validity of much of the data and thereby partially offset the subjectivity inherent in a single autobiography. At the same time it reveals the discrepancies in the way events are recalled by each member of the family.
>
> This method of multiple autobiographies also tends to reduce the element of investigator bias because the accounts are not put through the sieve of a middle-class North American mind but are given in the words of the subjects themselves. In this way, I believe, I have avoided the two most common hazards in the study of the poor, namely, oversentimentalization and brutalization. . . .
>
> The tape recorder . . . has made possible the beginning of a new kind of literature of social realism. With the aid of the tape recorder, unskilled, uneducated, and even illiterate persons can talk about themselves and relate their observations and experiences in an uninhibited, spontaneous, and natural manner. The stories of Manuel, Roberto, Consuelo, and Marta have a simplicity, sincerity, and directness which is characteristic of the spoken word, of oral literature in contrast to written literature. Despite their lack of formal training, these young people express them-

selves remarkably well, particularly Consuelo, who sometimes reaches poetic heights.

To catalogue and describe the inaccuracy and wooly-mindedness of the assumptions behind these unruffled sentences would itself require a scholarly monograph. A reviewer can begin by isolating the long-lived romantic assumption, which seems to have been appropriated as Article One by the modern breed of other-directed, people-liking social scientist, that everyone's experience is equivalent to the words in which he describes it; that a "spontaneous" autobiographical statement (solicited, it is true, over many days by many questions, and painstakingly edited afterward) is "life," not "art," functions in a special, extra-literary medium, and is necessarily both authentic and uniquely expressive. But of course everyone finds his words where he can. Under continuous assault by the contemporary popular literary genres—comic books, true-romance magazines, advertising, movies, radio, TV—besides such national and class sentimentalities as the cult of *machismo* (manliness) and the rote formulas of a residual piety, Mr. Lewis' five characters (Sánchez himself, as well as his four children) have as much trouble as the rest of us in finding, or inventing, a vocabulary by which they can reveal not just the general, mass-cultural preconceptions of their class and country but deeply themselves. Language, for them too, is an aesthetic medium, which can be used well or badly. It may be that in a genuinely primitive society, secure in its traditions and unsubjected to bogus art, language is a less difficult (as well as less random and less multitudinous) medium than it is for us. The Mexican urban poor, however, are not noble savages who react with pure intensity to the sun and the moon, life and death; they are like the rest of us, reacting in terms or in despite of all the bad art which is, like the ceaseless insidious Muzak in restaurants and supermarkets, the very sound of our lives. When Roberto says, "Life is a comedy and the world is a theatre and we are all actors," he could be quoting from a soap-opera variant on Italian *verismo;* when Manuel says, "Life around here is raw, it is more real, than among people with money," he is reciting one of the consolations of poverty invented by some second-rate nineteenth-century middle-class novelist; when Consuelo, the one who rises to "poetic heights," watches her father, "his short form, unmoving, standing in the kitchen, as though rooted to the cement floor . . . and the red tip of the cigarette burned in the dark," she is parroting the words of a debased literary manner traceable to Conrad and by now the atmospheric staple of every TV melodrama.

Mr. Lewis is moved, and wishes us to be equally moved, by an awareness of "their potentialities and wasted talents." What chiefly comes across in these accounts, however, is not a sense of potentialities and talents (no mute inglorious Miltons) but a quantity of more or less enlightening bits of information about the life of the poor (normally a half-dozen, and at times as many as twenty, persons of both sexes and all ages sleep in a single room eight feet square; delousing a child's hair before combing it is routine procedure; the rarest feeling is affection; there is much prejudice against persons with dark complexions; as the poor know them, the Mexican police are lawless, venal, and pathologically brutal), which accumulate into an impression of the terrible anarchic tedium of their days, punctuated only by animal sex or by outbursts of homicidal violence. Actually, Mr. Lewis' favorite, Consuelo, is the least engaging of the group because she is the artiest and most self-indulgent in her language; she rather resembles her endlessly self-vindicating brother Manuel. Roberto and Marta, whose talk (at least in translation) most nearly approximates a sort of alley-cat lingo, manifest an occasional bleak vitality; and Roberto's adventures as a runaway, a convict, and a street tough are the only consistently interesting episodes in the book. Finally and most impressively, the father emerges as the irreducible central fact of the consciousness of each of his children; and if his position seems in part inherited from his rural, patriarchal, Indian past, it is obviously in larger part determined by the tireless, stoical tenacity with which he provides food and shelter for them and their families, comes to them in their times of trouble, manages somehow to get them money in their times of need, stands always for them as the tower of strength without which they would find it impossible to imagine any stability at all.

Yet what is Mr. Lewis getting at? His conviction that he has produced "a new kind of literature of social realism" is naïve and unfounded. His assumption that "sincerity" is all—as if the truth of personality were measurable by polygraph—will not survive scrutiny: these people, confronted by the tape recorder and the guileless face of the North American professor, will give him as much of themselves as they can bear in the terms in which they can bear to contemplate it; and they will falsify and rationalize as crudely and unknowingly as the rest of us. How can we judge whether they are telling the truth about even the least self-incriminating data of family experience—a quarrel, a minor failure of responsibility, an untactful word, an irritable lapse of decorum? Mr. Lewis mentions the "built-in check" of his multiple autobiographies—as if five different kinds of lies about the same event will necessarily add up to the truth of it. This *Rashomon* device, if it is ever justified at all, is justified only as a deliberate effort to suggest the protean quality of experience, the wax on which each personality imposes the shape of its momentary need; and Mr. Lewis is quite innocent of such an intention. No, he thinks that what he is presenting is truth. It never occurs to him that if we ever know what to think of characters in a book, it is because they are created by an author without whose judgment and direction we should be left to flounder in guesses, enigmas, and boredom; there would not even be raw fact; for there is no such thing as raw fact about human experience.

How, notwithstanding, does Jesús Sánchez persuade us of his existence and his strength? Not, indeed, by what he himself says of himself, but by what his children say of him; because then, talking of him, they achieve the eloquence and authority of art, because only then do their mean cautions, their self-pity, their mawkish or casual appropriation of others for their own purposes, their attentive playing up to the scientific prying of the good-natured professor—only then do these screens fall away and leave them with the awed awareness of somebody not themselves, a separate, strange, unmanageable, providential person:

My father didn't speak to me for a month, and treated me badly. I felt terrible and was ashamed to look him in the face. I had been his favorite and I couldn't take any punishment. I was so upset that one night I began to cry very hard. I couldn't stop crying, until my *papá* spoke to me. I asked him to forgive me and he said, "Don't be a fool. I am your father and will never abandon you." After that I felt better.

But nothing else in their experiences provokes and sustains a comparable authority of awareness; and Mr. Lewis' method prevents him from taking on, however ineptly, the rôle of author, guide, and judge himself. One might in fact argue that whatever is good in the book is good because it somehow evades Mr. Lewis' apparatus.

The sense of frustration, of deadlock and stalemate, that pervades the book derives at least as much from its method as from the desolation of its characters. The method is a betrayal of the science from which it springs and the art to which it aspires. The social scientist, humane and quietly self-righteous, having exhausted his interest in the manipulation of questionnaires and statistics, has stepped in to take over the job abandoned by the artist: David Riesman, as Mark Schorer has pointed out, replaces Sinclair Lewis, not altogether to our advantage, as the chronicler of bourgeois America; and Oscar Lewis confidently regards his method as in the natural course of events succeeding the method of, say, Dickens in the continuing obligation to amplify and dramatize the short and simple annals of the poor:

> In the nineteenth century, when the social sciences were still in their infancy, the job of recording the effects of the process of industrialization and urbanization was left to novelists, playwrights, journalists, and social reformers. Today, a similar process of culture change is going on among the peoples of the less-developed countries but we find no comparable outpouring of a universal literature which would help us to improve our understanding of the process and the people. And yet the need for such an understanding has never been more urgent, now that the less-developed countries have become a major force on the world scene. . . .
> This situation presents a unique opportunity to the social

sciences and particularly to anthropology to step into the gap and develop a literature of its own.

And, concluding his Introduction, Mr. Lewis makes it explicit that his purpose is, ultimately, neither scientific nor literary, but ringingly political:

> It seems to me that the material in this book has important implications for our thinking and our policy in regard to the underdeveloped countries of the world and particularly Latin America. It highlights the social, economic, and psychological complexities which have to be faced in any effort to transform and eliminate the culture of poverty from the world. It suggests that basic changes in the attitudes and value systems of the poor must go hand in hand with improvements in the material conditions of living.

But "the material in this book" does nothing of the sort. Though the Sánchez family is a fact of the new politics that Mr. Lewis pretends to have defined, the politics of *The Children of Sánchez* is only the packaged left-liberal piety of its Introduction, and the rest of the book a pompous and muddled clue to the consciousness it presumes to reflect. As long as social scientists remain so insensitive to the shape of experience, so deaf to the medium of language, so editorially magnanimous in their political aims, and so unperturbed in the midst of all unmastered disciplines, we may yet decline to celebrate these self-proclaimed successors to the poets and novelists, who instructed us and gave us delight.

1961

II. Classics

LADY MURASAKI:
THE TALE OF GENJI

The Tale of Genji has been made accessible to English-speaking readers by Mr. Waley's immense and heroic labor of translation; and the translator, taking advantage of his semi-proprietary rights, treats the novel and its author, from time to time, with an embarrassing petulance. In his introduction, for example, he spends pages attempting to justify his own peevish impression of Lady Murasaki (while her diaries, from which he quotes for evidence, give only the impression of an extraordinarily observant and contemplative woman); and, struggling with the thousands of poems in the text (poetry being in eleventh-century Japan, on the evidence of the text, an art and a discipline practiced in all human relations by cultivated men and women), he registers his impatient objection to charged poetic speech by noting that it would be "tedious" to explain the "puns" and "ambiguities"—one assumes, from the few instances he allows us, that he means the elaborate ceremonial complexities of image and word-play—in which the poems apparently abound.

Mr. Waley convicts himself of something worse than peevishness and impatience, however, when he remarks of the opening chapter of the novel that it "should be read with indulgence" because "in it [Lady] Murasaki, still under the influence of her somewhat childish predecessors, writes in a manner which is a blend of the Court chronicle with the conventional fairy-tale." The non-Orientalist literary critic, armed only with what Mr. Waley has made of the text, must no doubt move with caution in the vicinity of watchful scholars and historians; but scholarship itself is never more liable to an unwary complacency than when it is infringing on the proper ground of criticism.

Lady Murasaki begins, it may be critically remarked, "in a manner which is a blend of the Court chronicle with the conventional fairy-tale" because she is beginning with a fairy-tale hero whose breeding, talent, virtue, and beauty are certified by his royal lineage, itself certified by the unfolding of genealogies in the first chapter. Genji is already, as a child, so beautiful that he is called *Hikaru*, "The Shining One." Half a century and hundreds of episodes later, years after his death, he is still remembered, by people who knew him only remotely or not at all, as a sunlike presence whose withdrawal darkened the world and made plain the instability of created things. In the superb first chapter alone, the contraries are proposed at once, in powerful fairy-tale isolation: the image of the lovely child growing up, and the bleak, insistently simple elegiac image of the Emperor's grief for Genji's dead mother.

No fairy godmother ever presided over a more fortunate childhood than Genji's. The young prince is "of unrivalled beauty" (15),* and the favorite of his father, the Emperor. Fearing that the child will be insecure at Court because his mother was a commoner, the Emperor "set seriously to work upon his education, and saw to it that he should be made perfect in every branch of art and knowledge" (16). He is by the time of his youth a master of the civilized accomplishments: the writing of poetry, the use and recognition of apt illusion, calligraphy, painting, singing, the playing of musical instruments, ritual dancing. During the first of the Imperial festivals described in the novel,

---

* Throughout this essay, numbers in parenthesis designate pages in the text, locating cited passages for the benefit of the reader wishing to check evidence in a very long novel. The edition is Mr. Waley's complete version: *The Tale of Genji*, by Lady Murasaki, translated by Arthur Waley, Houghton Mifflin, 2 vols.

Prince Genji danced the "Waves of the Blue Sea." To no Chujo
was his partner; but though both in skill and beauty he far sur-
passed the common run of performers, yet beside Genji he
seemed like a mountain fir growing beside a cherry-tree in
bloom. There was a wonderful moment when the rays of the
setting sun fell upon him and the music grew suddenly louder.
Never had the onlookers seen feet tread so delicately nor head
so exquisitely poised; and in the song which follows the first
movement of the dance his voice was sweet as that of Kalavinka
whose music is Buddha's law. So moving and beautiful was this
dance that at the end of it the Emperor's eyes were wet, and all
the princes and great gentlemen wept aloud. When the song was
over and, straightening his long dancer's sleeves, he stood waiting
for the music to begin again and at last the more lively tune of
the second movement struck up—then indeed, with his flushed
and eager face, he merited more than ever his name of Genji the
Shining One. (129)

Such beauty will do more than move to tears, it will seek and
attract; and Genji, electrically impressionable from his earliest
youth, is always in love, usually with several women at once, all
of whom oblige their lover (the exceptions are so rare as to war-
rant the almost incredulous scrutiny they receive) in spite of the
rigors of a moral code by which women of rank live sequestered
within the family and are properly visible, to strange men, only
as silhouettes whose words are brought by menials from behind
a screen. Genji's marriages, by the world's standards, are most
fortunate: his first wife is Princess Aoi, his royal cousin; after
her death, he marries the daughter of his half-brother the Emperor Suzaku. Attuned to Genji's facile and sentimental amorousness, the polygynous privilege of his rank permits him to
maintain two other recognized consorts, one aristocratic mistress, and an amazing variety of incidental affairs of the heart
(the phrase is exact, for Genji requires to be loved).

Though his career at Court is blighted for a time by his father's death and he is eventually forced into exile, he returns,
after a few years of peaceful rusticity among friends and re-
tainers, more powerful than ever; and his power increases
steadily until in the last decade or more of his life he is the
unchallenged political leader of his country, Chief Councillor
of the reigning Emperor and granted the unprecedented honor

of elevation to a rank equivalent to that of former Emperors, in a society in which Emperors not infrequently resign without sacrifice of great influence and respect. Ryozen, one of his sons, becomes Emperor; and the other, Yugiri, Chief Councillor after his father's death. Through Genji's influence, the daughter of his mistress becomes Empress to Ryozen; and his own daughter, the Empress of a succeeding Emperor. Genji dies at the height of his power and Apollonian reputation, full of honors and worldly accomplishments, mourned universally as the symbol of vigor and grace and splendor, the beautiful hero-prince to the end.

But the image, in the first chapter, of the mourning Emperor is an introduction and a portent of other consequences of vitality and beauty. After Genji's mother dies, even the constant Emperor turns for solace, finally, to another consort, a young princess who resembles the lady mourned. The spoiled young prince, petted and indulged by the ladies of the Court, learns to "set his heart upon possessing, even at the cost of endless difficulties, whatever custom and circumstance seemed to have placed beyond his utmost reach" (196): when he falls in love for the first time, it is with his father's new consort; and the son Fujitsubo bears, to become Emperor without ancestral right years later, is Genji's. This is the guilty secret—consequence of "this love that was a perpetual disaster" (133)—known only to Genji and Fujitsubo and, at last, to their son after he has become Emperor, which Genji carries with him through all his involvements and uneasy philanderings, which shadows his most transient liaisons (though it never has the power to prevent them) and makes him often yearn with a luxurious self-pity for the renunciatory simplicities of a monastic life he can never quite bring himself to accept.

Princess Aoi, "the very perfection of . . . [whose] beauty . . . seemed only to make all intimacy with her the more impossible" (37), is hardly permitted to be a wife to her roving husband at all, except, ironically, in presenting him with the only son he knows and can acknowledge as his own. The marriage disintegrates in a scene that Genji, filled with guilt, anger, and awakening desire, precipitates in her "supremely well-ordered house" (92):

". . . Why are you so cold and distant and proud? Year after year we fail to reach an understanding and you cut yourself off from me more completely than before. Can we not manage for a little while to be on ordinary terms? It seems rather strange, considering how ill I have been, that you should not attempt to enquire after my health. Or rather, it is exactly what I should expect; but nevertheless I find it extremely painful." "Yes," said Aoi, "it is extremely painful when people do not care what becomes of one." She glanced back over her shoulder as she spoke, her face full of scorn and pride, looking uncommonly handsome as she did so. "You hardly ever speak," said Genji, "and when you do, it is only to say unkind things and twist one's harmless words so that they seem to be insults. And when I try to find some way of helping you for a while at least to be a little less disagreeable, you become more hopelessly unapproachable than ever. Shall I one day succeed in making you understand. . . ?" and so saying he went into their bedroom. She did not follow him. He lay for a while in a state of great annoyance and distress. But, probably because he did not really care about her very much one way or the other, he soon became drowsy and all sorts of quite different matters drifted through his head. (93)

And he begins to think about the little girl he is planning, with a kind of perverse paternal sensuality, to take from her home and raise for purposes he will not yet define for himself.

Genji's second wife, Princess Nyosan, is forced on him in his middle age by his sense of obligation to her father, the former Emperor; and Genji, for the sake of his own voluntary attachments leaving her as lonely and unloved as he had left Aoi, discovers that the son she will bear is not his:

"It does not in the least surprise me that you should feel as you do. For one thing, novelties are inevitably more interesting, and you have known me since you were a child. But the real trouble is that I am too old for you. It is true. I am hideously old. Indeed, what in the world could be more natural than that an infant like you should desire to escape from me? . . ."

But as he said the words he caught in his own voice a familiar intonation. How often, years ago, those responsible for his up-bringing had adopted just this tone, and how dreary, how contemptible he had thought their self-righteous homilies! "Boring old man!" That was what she must be thinking, and in sudden shame he relapsed into a complete silence. . . . (674)

For Genji—lying, self-deceiving, self-excusing, pointlessly and ineffectually remorseful—has moments of self-revelation also; and he never consciously wishes to hurt. He cannot bear, in fact, to fail in acts of kindness toward any woman who has taken him, however briefly, as a lover; and though this kindness feeds on daydreams of sybaritic domesticity—

> "If only I had some large convenient building . . . where I could house these friends of mine and be able to keep an eye not only on them, but on any babies that might chance to get born, how much simpler life would be!" (294)

—it is nevertheless a kindness (and remorse) that embraces even women whom he has loved with embarrassment and no pleasure, homely neglected ladies pitifully coquetting him into affairs, and whom—like the shy Princess Suyetsumu with the long, red-tipped nose, "uniquely depressing and wearisome creature [that] she was" (473)—he feels obliged to maintain, if they allow him, in comfort and dignity "since it was certain that no one else intended to take the business off his hands" (473). The author is not, then, altogether ironical when she remarks on Genji's "constancy" toward the women of his more casual affairs:

> Being women of character and position they had no false pride and saw that it was worth while to take what they could get. Thus without any ill will on either side concerning the future or the past they would enjoy the pleasure of each other's company, and so part. However, if by chance anyone resented this kind of treatment and cooled towards him, Genji was never in the least surprised; for though, as far as feelings went, perfectly constant himself, he had long ago learnt that such constancy was very unusual. (228)

Life is never simple for Genji, capable as he is, at disconcerting moments, of a wry self-recognition, as when he overhears his own tiresome middle-aged voice upbraiding Nyosan or finds himself mirrored in the tranquil spirit of the Lady from the Village of Falling Flowers:

> "We are both singularly fortunate . . . I, in my capacity for self-delusion; she in hers for good-tempered acceptance of whatever comes her way." (469)

—capable, besides, of recognizing the horror of casual aging and of the irretrievable past:

> "It's very rusty," said the old porter dolefully, fumbling all the while with the lock that grated with an unpleasant sound but would not turn. "There's nothing else wrong with it, but it's terribly rusty. No one uses this gate now."
> The words, ordinary enough in themselves, filled Genji with an unaccountable depression. How swiftly the locks rust, the hinges grow stiff on doors that close behind us! "I am more than thirty," he thought; and it seemed to him impossible to go on doing things just as though they would last . . . as though people would remember . . . "And yet," he said to himself, "I know that even at this moment the sight of something very beautiful, were it only some common flower or tree, might in an instant make life again seem full of meaning and reality." (390)

Beauty, though customarily not the beauty of flowers or trees, is in fact enough to divert Genji from any "unaccountable" mood of depression, penitence, or futility: he is never free of the itch of amorousness, which has the power to keep him busy, scheming, unthoughtful, and entertained until its consequences drive him back into gloom or the aridity of self-contemplation. As a kind of ingratiating, perennially adolescent Don Juan, either titillated or remorseful, Genji has, unluckily, more persevering reasons for remorse. His affections are sincere and extensive, as well as superficial and temporary; and the cross-currents of these qualities are always imperiling whatever tentative equilibrium of spirit he has managed to achieve. " 'How it grieves me,' " he writes in a mood of bewildered repentance to Murasaki,* " 'to remember the many occasions when I have spoilt our friendship for the sake of some passing whim or fancy in which (though you could not believe it) my deeper feelings were not at all engaged. . . .' " (273)

From the union of his gifts of beauty and unspecific amorousness comes one of his numerous recurring predicaments: to have plural affections and (at least a few) constant, jealous women. One of these women who "misunderstand" him is

---

* "Murasaki" is not only the name of the author but the name she gives to her heroine. To avoid confusion I give the author her title of "Lady Murasaki" whenever it seems necessary to name her at all.

Princess Aoi. Another is his high-born mistress, the proud and demanding Lady Rokujo—"he had the greatest possible sympathy for her; but he was feeling rather tired of coping with injured susceptibilities" (159)—and she is able to revenge herself by causing the deaths, through the unconscious possessing spirit of her hatred, of Genji's plebeian mistress, Yugao; of Aoi; and, at last, of his favorite consort, Murasaki. Even Murasaki, who gives Genji his only experience of ordered, intimate domestic life and talk, and who loves him in spite of her clear-sighted appraisal of his moods and impulses, is tormented by his infidelities, which she can understand without being able to shield herself against them.

Genji drifts always in the current of his alert, nostalgic, hospitable sensuality. It overcomes him, typically, when he undertakes, after Rokujo's death, the guardianship of her daughter:

> One day when the autumn rain was falling steadily and the dripping flowers in the garden seemed to be washed to one dull tinge of grey, memories of long-forgotten things came crowding one after another to Genji's mind, and with eyes full of tears he betook himself to Lady Akikonomu's rooms. . . . He leant upon the pillar of her seat, the evening light falling upon him as he turned towards her. They had many memories in common; did she still recall, he asked, that terrible morning when he came to visit her mother at the Palace-in-the-Fields? "Too much my thoughts frequent those vanished days," she quoted, and her eyes filled with tears. Already he was thinking her handsome and interesting, when for some reason she rose and shifted her position, using her limbs with a subtle grace that made him long to see her show them to better advantage. . . ." (378f.)

But Genji's attempt to make his usual conquest, using the life-is-sad-and-gather-ye-rosebuds theme (which he has the gift to believe in), does not work, and leaves him this time as remorseful and provoked as he is usually remorseful and sated. His campaign against another unresponsive protégée, Tamakatsura, has a more permanent disagreeable consequence: to drive her into an unhappy marriage as the quickest escape from his importunities.

His sensuality has even political consequences. Having allowed himself to drift into an affair with one of the Emperor's concubines, he continues it incautiously at the home of her father, an influential court adviser, until accidentally discovered by the discourteous old man:

> Yes, there was Genji's paper lying conspicuously upon the floor. Were there no means of heading her father away from it? She could think of none and did not attempt to answer his question. It was evident that she was acutely embarrassed, and even though she was his own child he ought to have remembered that she was now a lady of some consequence, whose feelings, however reprehensible might be her conduct, he was bound in some measure to respect. Unfortunately there was not in his nature a particle either of moderation or restraint. He stooped to pick up the paper, and as he did so, without the slightest hesitation or compunction he opened the bed-curtains and peered right in. There full length upon the bed and apparently quite at his ease lolled a charming young man, who when the curtain stirred merely rolled quietly over and hid his face in the pillows. Enraged, astonished as the Minister was, even he had not quite the courage to press the discovery home. Blind with fury he thrust the paper into his pocket and rushed out of the room.
> Genji was indeed extremely concerned about the consequences of this incident, coming as it did in the wake of so many other indiscretions. But his first care was to comfort his companion, which he did as best he could. (223)

The immediate result is that Genji, fearing the use his enemies at court will make of the scandal, confirms his decision to go into exile. Yet wherever he goes, at whatever degree he finds himself on the political wheel of fortune, his present is full of emotional intrigues and anxieties; and even this abundant present is too limited, it overflows with his jealously minute retention of past feelings:

> Suddenly, as he drove away, there came into his mind a picture of this lady dancing with four others at the Palace. Yes, that was who she was. She had been one of the Gosechi dancers one winter long ago. How much he had admired her! And for a moment he felt about her exactly as he had felt before. It was this strange capacity of his for re-creating in its full intensity an emotion suspended for months or even years and overlaid by a thousand intervening distractions, that gained for him, faithless though he was, so large a number of persistent admirers. (277)

If this fairy-tale prince, rescued from his void and subjected to the pressing, entangling actualness of human relationships, has so little luck and so much vexation with his women, the reader may be tempted to shift the analogy to more sophisticated mythical constructions and imagine him a great amoral progenitor, Zeus-like in the immediacy, range, and transience of his liaisons as well as in divinely careless fertility, scattering heroic offspring over all the earth. But again, the facts are unaccommodating. Having expended decades of energy upon scores of women, Genji is able to produce three children. One of these, Ryozen, must remain unacknowledged, and becomes Emperor as the heir of his presumed father, the old Emperor (for Genji has, with one variety of divine carelessness, cuckolded his own father). Genji's daughter, the Princess Akashi, becomes through his influence Empress in a succeeding reign and the mother of his royal grandson. Yugiri, the only son that Genji acknowledges, becomes the most influential non-royal personage at court after his father's death. Yet there are no heroes, sexual or otherwise, among them; and even their worldly success is qualified by a sort of personal meagerness never characteristic, whatever his defects, of Genji. The Princess Akashi turns placidly from inconspicuous girlhood to contented royal motherhood, and appears at last only as a mild worrier about her son. Ryozen, a correct and uninspired ruler until he discovers the secret of his birth, lapses into a prevailing mood of guilt and melancholy, and eventually resigns the office he knows it has been sacrilegious (according to the cult of ancestors) for him ever to have held. Yugiri is the most interesting of the three, not only because—unlike the others—he is given the space and detail of a major character, but because, as well as being Genji's son, he is plainly the consequence and proof of Genji's sins and errors.

Yugiri grows up in the shadow of his illustrious father; but the pressures of public scrutiny and public expectation seem at first not to disconcert him: he is a "sensible, good-natured boy, who took life rather seriously" (405). Genji, fearful that Yugiri will be unpopular at court if his honors come too easily, has him appointed, on his coming of age, to a relatively humble grade of imperial preferment. Policy overrules affection, or rather in this instance readily supplants it; for the temperamental differences between the casual father and the solemn son have always been clear to both, and there is never anything more than a perfunctory, formal affection between them. The differences are ultimately too considerable to be borne by Yugiri. His feelings, waiting for a pretext, find a useful one in the difficulties of his first love affair. He falls in love with his childhood playmate, Kumoi; but her father has court ambitions for her, and breaks off the relationship. One reason Yugiri can find, in his smothered fury, for this misfortune is the low rank to which Genji has, as he feels, condemned him: Kumoi and her father would respect him more, he would indeed be acceptable as her husband, if Genji had not humiliated him. From the time of this event and for the rest of his life Yugiri is the more or less deliberate, always resentful opponent and competitor of his own sardonic image of Genji.

Nothing helps change Yugiri's mind, not even his eventual reconciliation with Kumoi after her father has lost hope of establishing her at court. Yugiri sets himself up—against the trivial philanderer Genji—as a model of fidelity and the domestic virtues; he is taken by the world at his own ostentatiously modest valuation, and by his good-natured father also: " 'Yugiri is a faithful fellow,' " (619) says Genji with rueful admiration, rejecting the possibility that Yugiri would think of marrying, for excellent political reasons, the daughter of a former Emperor and so bringing a rival to Kumoi into his household.

Yet the faithful fellow assuages his grief at having (apparently) lost Kumoi by becoming almost at once infatuated with a dancer, who in the course of their liaison bears him several children. After he has regained Kumoi and lived as an exclusively domestic husband for some years, he is moved by a sudden and violent passion for the Princess Ochiba, another daughter of the same former Emperor, and eventually brings her into his household as his preferred consort. But his great love is elsewhere and unacknowledged. Having caught an unobserved glimpse of Murasaki (she is, of course, strictly sequestered, and it takes a typhoon to level the screens that keep her invisible to her husband's son), he falls in love with her.

Yugiri's love for Murasaki, which he never mentions or acts upon, is perhaps the only fact that prevents him from being fixed as a decisively unsympathetic character. The author's irony, especially on call at moments when somebody seems about to act uncharacteristically, is at its most exquisite when she describes the compulsive discreetness of Yugiri's day-dreams:

> It was characteristic of Yugiri's high sense of propriety that when in his imaginings he became better acquainted with this lovely creature, it was not with Murasaki herself but with some-one in every respect exactly like her that he pictured himself spending hours of enchanted bliss. (531)

Yet Murasaki must also serve him as evidence against his father:

> It was heart-rending that the most beautiful woman of her gener-ation should fall to the lot of one whose other intimacies proved him so completely lacking in discrimination. (531)

In the great tragic scene of Murasaki's death, the last sight of her beauty is enough, for at least the period of bereavement, to bring Yugiri as close to his father as he ever will be:

> The daylight was still feeble, and he could see very little. But at that moment Genji himself held up the great lamp, bringing it so close to the couch that Yugiri suddenly saw her in all her loveliness. "And why should he not see her?" thought Genji, who knew that Yugiri was peeping. But in a moment he covered his eyes with his sleeve. "It is almost worse to see her now, while she is still unchanged," he said. "One thinks that she will speak, move. . . ." Yugiri brushed away the tears that kept on dim-ming his eyes. Her hair lay spread across the pillows, loose, but not tangled or disorderly, in a great mass, against which in the strong lamplight her face shone with a dazzling whiteness. Never, thought Genji, had her beauty seemed so flawless as now, when the eye could rest upon it undistracted by any ripple of sound or motion. Yugiri gazed astounded. His spirit seemed to leave him, to float through space and hover near her, as though it were he that was the ghost, and this the lovely body he had chosen for his habitation. (732)

For many days afterwards he remained in close attendance upon his father, trying by every means he could think of to distract and console him. The equinoctial gales had begun to blow, and tonight it came back vividly to Yugiri's mind how he had caught sight of her on the morning of the great typhoon. And then again on the day she died. That Genji should mourn was well enough; but what right had Yugiri to this grievous pain? And to hide his sorrow he drew a rosary towards him, and clicking the beads loudly he muttered, "Amida, Amida, Amida Buddha," so swiftly that the falling of his tears could not be heard. (733)

It is too late, however; Genji is soon dead, and Yugiri is already what he is, regardless of momentary faltering under the weight of disaster. He grows old into a kind of severe and undecayed Polonius, full of schemes and moralistic admonitions: Niou, Genji's grandson, gives us the image of "His Excellency always fussing round to see whether I am behaving myself" (837). It is the fussy old man, having suppressed in himself as well as he could and piously disavowed the "looseness" he decried in his father, who inherits most of the honors and privileges, though none of the glory, of his father; it is Yugiri who lives on more and more confirmed in his impenetrable sanctimony, who inherits and in fact populates with his numerous progeny—as the sunlike hero Genji ought to have populated—the world.

Even Niou, the grandson who deceptively resembles Genji and who will inherit the throne, is only the contrary, within the same moral constriction, of his uncle Yugiri. For all his charm and beauty, Niou is the heedless and unremorseful, the essentially indelicate and undiscriminating sensualist that Yugiri has self-righteously imagined in his father. The credulous Kaoru, arguing in behalf of Niou before a lady his friend desires, succeeds mainly in substantiating our impression of Niou's unlovely qualities:

". . . He is . . . the sort of man who if a woman took things as they came, did not set herself and her reputation on a pinnacle, was broad-minded and willing to take the world as she found it, overlooking casual shortcomings here and there and accepting a certain number of unpleasantnesses as inevitable in any relation-

ship—to such a woman I believe Niou might show a most un-
common degree of fidelity. . . ." (833)

Niou has no objection to making half-serious overtures to his
sister—" 'How loath am I that alien hands should tear from
fresh and tender roots the plant I may not touch!' " (878)—
and rape is for him only the logical extreme of his philosophy
of action:

> . . . Niou was holding her fast in his arms before she could so
> much as utter a cry. The preliminaries, he considered, had already
> been got over at the Nijo-in; here he could let himself go. . . .
> She burst into tears. For a very different reason Niou too was
> weeping; she had proved even more desirable than he expected,
> and he was profoundly depressed at the thought that he might
> never have such an opportunity again. (1005f.)

The seed of Genji, so seldom fertile, seems to deteriorate in
taking root: scruples become calculation, energy is channeled
into mean appetite, generosity of spirit atrophies, and the
subtle and warm-hearted responsiveness of Genji—for Genji is
an ardent connoisseur of the beautiful things he desires—vanishes altogether with his death.

For Kaoru alone, among those whom Genji has sheltered and
who survive him—Kaoru, whom the world regards as his son
but who is born to prove that even Genji can be cuckold as well
as cuckolder—Genji's image survives as a uniqueness touched
with divinity. And it is for Kaoru, appropriately, that this past
and dead magnificence leaves to the present only shadows and
the terrible weight of futility, as if everything in the world has
been done and no purpose remains:

> Genji's death . . . happening when I was a mere child made—
> I now think in looking back upon it—a disastrous impression
> upon me. I grew up feeling that nothing was stable, nothing
> worth while. . . . (829f.)

Kaoru has Genji's gift of self-contemplation, but it is obsessed
by the sense of failure and the guilt—once he learns that Genji
is not his father—of holding an unearned station in the world.
When he falls in love, it is with someone very like himself; and

there is only a single love scene between the shy pair, who have
spent a virtuous night in eager conversation:

> "This is what I ask for, this and nothing more," he said. "For
> you and I have the same feelings about such things—moonlight,
> flowers, the sky, all the subtle changes that go on in the world
> about us—and should never be unhappy so long as we could
> watch them together." (847)

But she sends him off, and there is nothing more till he comes
to watch her die.

Kaoru survives her death, as he survives everything else to
the end of the story, yearning wistfully after worldliness and
demonstrating for himself its futility, envying Niou's impersonal flares of appetite and coming deliberately and impartially
to judge Niou for what he is. Even when he finds another girl
to match the one he has lost, he loses her also, first to the insati-
able Niou and at the very end to her vows as a Buddhist nun.
The ultimate irony is that, loving her still but despising her for
her surrender to Niou, Kaoru believes that her vows are false
and that she is being kept in plausible seclusion by a new, more
ingenious lover. And, at this moment of Kaoru's crowning
(and unjustified) disillusion—the disillusion that confirms his
view of the instability and pointlessness of things—the whole
great action of the story comes to rest.

Vitality—even so irresistible as Genji's—cannot propagate
itself: the novel runs down in a coarsening of impulses and a
narrowing of choice, as with Niou and Yugiri; at last in a paral-
ysis of moral bafflement, as with Kaoru; always a denial of the
variety and abundance that Genji finds, creates, and is. The
memory of Genji's vitality is stronger than the lives of his sur-
vivors: he has been dead for many years, but the momentum of
his vitality persists even in his failure to pass it on. It is often a
protective, negative vitality, defining by contrast the ungener-
ousness of Yugiri, exposing in their inconsequence the intrigues
of Niou and of Genji himself, overwhelming the glum, spe-
ciously vindicated inertia of Kaoru, sustaining without inflexi-
bility the steady pressures of a vigorous civilization upon the
responsible and representative man.

Still more attractively, it can be positive, almost absolute. The most characteristic unencumbered expression of Genji's vitality is—for this statesman, social lion, and incorrigible lover —not political, or social, or even sensual, but domestic: in his lives with the three women who can instruct him, in their various ways, to be at his ease, liberated for the moment from sensuality and remorse and the expectations of the world.

Yugao, the plebeian girl who first pleases Genji by introducing him to the romance and diversion of classlessness, is able to introduce him also, most imperceptibly, to the atmosphere of domesticity:

> Their room was in the front of the house. Genji got up and opened the long sliding shutters. They stood together looking out. In the courtyard near them was a clump of fine Chinese bamboos; dew lay thick on the borders, glittering here no less brightly than in the great gardens to which Genji was better accustomed. There was a confused buzzing of insects. Crickets were chirping in the wall. He had often listened to them, but always at a distance; now, singing so close to him, they made a music which was unfamiliar and indeed seemed far lovelier than that with which he was acquainted. . . . She was wearing a white bodice with a soft, grey cloak over it. It was a poor dress, but she looked charming and almost distinguished; even so, there was nothing very striking in her appearance—only a certain fragile grace and elegance. (63f.)

And it is especially after her death that Genji, coping again with tempestuous women, summons up regretfully this image of comfortable domesticity:

> He longed to escape once more from the claims of these passionate and exacting natures, and renew the life of tender intimacy which for a while had given him so great a happiness. (109)

Yugao's comfortableness is for Genji spiced with romantic mystery and consecrated by the brevity of their affair; but the Lady from the Village of Falling Flowers has no such advantages. She is brought into Genji's household early and lives there in a sort of voluntary retirement, helping with equable good sense to raise his children, offering him always the refuge of her mildness and tranquillity as they talk "for a long while, chiefly of old times" (469), till he finds he must be on his way to another wing of his palace and another of his ladies.

If the undemanding Lady from the Village of Falling Flowers—she remains, appropriately, without a name in the story—is for Genji the type of domesticity, Murasaki is its demanding apotheosis. Murasaki is a refuge and a comfort, she allows Genji to relax and talk himself out, to come to her for advice, to be freely himself; but she is also, in independence of spirit and acuteness of observation, the only woman he ever meets who is a match for him.

Their relationship grows into a genuine marriage almost in spite of Genji. It starts even less promisingly than usual, as Genji's familiar generalized itch of amorousness is excited, this time, by a little girl who does not understand his advances and who withdraws into a sulk when he takes early advantage of his position as her "guardian." But she is soon reconciled to her ingratiating lover, who in turn gradually comes to find her more than a charming, exploitable child. Murasaki becomes Genji's recognized consort (she can never, because she was born a commoner, become his legitimate wife); and, barely out of childhood, she is already interesting and attractive enough to hold his attention as Aoi, for example, never could. Even though Genji continues to let his attention wander, he comes to feel more and more explicitly that Murasaki is the center of his life: a feeling that begins to strengthen into conviction while he is separated from her in exile. By the time Genji has settled all his consorts into his new palace, the pattern of his permanent relationships is clear: Yugao is the enshrined memory; the Lady from the Village of Falling Flowers is the calm, almost impersonal refuge; and Murasaki is the affectionate, spirited, and justifiably ironical wife who can at last, by her charm and the force and complexity of her affection, induce the glorious philanderer to limit little by little, most reluctantly, his interest in other women.

Genji never altogether renounces the roving eye, as if with a residue of professional pride; he always retains the power to hurt Murasaki by his infidelities and his deceit, often a self-deceit, in disavowing them. It is not, in fact, till he has spent his honeymoon with Princess Nyosan that he comes to recognize how engaged his feelings really are:

> . . . he now felt how unique Murasaki was. Surely his adoption of her was the one step in his life that he would never have cause to regret. Such time as he spent with Nyosan (whether by day or night) he found himself grudging more and more, till he was frightened at his own increasing inability to live more than an hour or two on end in any but Murasaki's company. (632f.)

If Murasaki can never bring herself to rejoice in Genji's somewhat qualified candor regarding his affairs past and present, it is nevertheless their sustained intimacy that encourages him to be nostalgically candid, even about what has been one of his two burdensome secrets:

> . . . he told her the whole story of his dealings with Yugao. It was apparent to her that he was deeply moved, and at the same time that he took great pleasure in recalling every detail of their relationship. ". . . such love as Yugao's, such utter self-forgetfulness, so complete a surrender of the whole being to one single and and ever-present emotion—I have never seen or heard of, and were she alive she would certainly be occupying no less important a place in my palace than, for example, the Lady of Akashi is occupying today. . . ." "Were she as much in your good graces as the Lady of Akashi, she would have nothing to complain of . . ." broke in Murasaki suddenly; for the Akashi episode still rankled. . . . (458)

Genji is all-important to her, and she becomes indispensable to him; but the weight of his unacknowledgeable sin and of the wasted years is as heavy upon him as the weight of his deceptions and trivial lecheries and their childlessness upon her. They speak to each other, on her last birthday, with a bare alogical frankness, as if to themselves:

> . . . presently he said: "What a strange life mine has been! I suppose few careers have ever appeared outwardly more brilliant; but I have never been happy. Person after person that I cared for has in one way or another been taken from me. It is long since I lost all zest for life, and if I have been condemned to continue my existence, it is (I sometimes think) only as a

punishment for certain misdeeds that at all times still lie heavily
on my mind. You alone have always been here to console me, and
I am glad to think that, apart from the time when I was away at
Akashi, I have never behaved in such a way as to cause you a
moment's real unhappiness. . . . It is only with people such as
you, whom I have known all their lives, that I am really happy.
. . . About Princess Nyosan . . . since she came, I have grown
even fonder of you than before; a change you would have noticed quickly enough, if it had been my affection towards someone else that was on the increase! However, you are very observant, and I cannot believe you are not perfectly well aware. . . ."
"I cannot explain it," she said. "I know that to any outside person I must appear the happiest of women—fortunate indeed far
above my deserts. But inwardly I am wretched. . . . Every
day. . . ." She felt it would take a long time to explain, and had
not the courage. (651)

Murasaki dies, and Genji is as inconsolable as perhaps it is
possible for him to be. Yet he cannot quite make the decision
to withdraw from the world into a monastic life; the world has
held him too long and continues to tempt him still, even into
another trivial lechery:

It so happened that as Genji came along towards the eastern
wing he found Chujo no Kimi taking a hurried sleep. She rose
quickly when she heard his step, and in the moment that elapsed
before she hid her face in the wide sleeve of her gown he had
time to note the liveliness of her features, the fine poise of her
head. . . . (740)

Finally persuaded, as he thinks, to renounce the world, he
celebrates his last religious festival "with unusual solemnity,
for he knew that it was the last he would see in his Palace"
(742):

This was the first occasion since Murasaki's death upon which
Genji had mingled with his guests. They thought him more
beautiful than ever, and the aged priest could not refrain from
tears of joy.

Remembering that this was the end of the year, little Niou
went scampering about saying everyone must do something to
scare away the demons and asking what noise he might make.
In a few days Genji would see the child no more; and sadly he

recited the verse: "Whilst I in heedless grief have let the days go by, together now the year and my own life are ebbing to their close." He gave orders that the New Year ceremonies should be performed with more than usual splendour, and saw to it that the princes and Court officers who came to the Palace should receive such presents and bounties as never before. (743)

But nothing, ultimately, works out as Genji has planned it, not even his long postponed decision. Soon, having botched and qualified every grand gesture he has felt obliged to make, having spent his unexampled vitality too generously with everybody else and not quite generously enough with the one who alone could engage and renew it, the man of sensibility, the remorseful Don Juan, the great lover spoiled by an uneasy conscience and the sense of something lost, the gifted and dazzling fairy-tale prince " 'whose like' "—says the Emperor Suzaku—" 'has never been seen in the world before' " (617), is dead, and leaves the world to those who—like Niou and Yugiri —will narrow it down to the breadth of their appetites or who —like Kaoru—too honest to alter it, will drown in its multitudinousness. Genji and the age of marvels are gone.

1955

CHAUCER'S NIGHTINGALES

Sweeney's nightingales which

> . . . *sang within the bloody wood*
> *When Agamemnon cried aloud,*
> *And let their liquid siftings fall*
> *To stain the stiff dishonoured shroud . . .*

can prove their independent animal nature only by perform-
ing, at a tragic crisis of the human spirit, the least dignifiable of
animal acts: so Mr. Eliot succeeds, by this suavely sonorous
shock of juxtaposition, in reclaiming for poets what for Chaucer is as natural as seeing:

> *A nyghtyngale, upon a cedir grene,*
> *Under the chambre wal ther as she lay,*
> *Ful loude song ayein the moone shene,*
> *Peraunter, in his briddes wise, a lay*
> *Of love, that made hire herte fressh and gay.*

Chaucer's nightingale happens to be decoratively placed, as-
sisting with its song in Criseyde's first revery of love; but it is a
bird to begin with and by no means merely decorative, it sings
(we may matter-of-factly suppose: "Peraunter, in his briddes
wise") for itself or for a prospective mate, it is true to its own

nature and indifferent to man, it can never be absorbed by an anthropocentrism that obsequiously elevates animal nature in order to degrade the human—

> *Hail to thee, blithe Spirit!*
> *Bird thou never wert . . .*

or grants it a sardonic equality—

> *The coxcomb bird, so talkative and grave,*
> *That from his cage cries Cuckold, Whore, and Knave,*
> *Tho' many a passenger he rightly call,*
> *You hold him no philosopher at all . . .*

or dissolves it into a nostalgic symbol of the humanly unachievable—

> *Thou wast not born for death, immortal Bird!*

or regards it as another emblem and incarnation of man's idea of indivisible deity—

> *I caught this morning morning's minion, king-*
> *dom of daylight's dauphin, dapple-dawn-drawn Falcon . . .*

or even limits it to a lover's serviceable ornament—

> *Wilt thou be gone? it is not yet near day:*
> *It was the nightingale, and not the lark,*
> *That pierc'd the fearful hollow of thine ear;*
> *Nightly she sings on yon pomegranate tree:*
> *Believe me, love, it was the nightingale.*

These are all of them ways of dealing with the enigma of animal nature (and of the non-human generally). Chaucer's way, which may be more precisely identified as a way of *seeing*, is not, then, the only way; but at least it differs, and deserves special scrutiny.

Chaucer is likely to start with discrimination and outline, with what can be detached and observed. Criseyde's nightingale, for example, is one of a distinct and specifiable kind, like the singing birds in the spring scene that opens the *Canterbury Tales*:

> *And smale foweles maken melodye,*
> *That slepen al the nyght with open ye*
> *(So priketh hem nature in hir corages)* . . .

—three lines of description that set apart the kind, note its habits and impulses, and establish its remoteness from the purposes of man, while the weightless fluidity of the first line affirms without taking into custody the beauty (free, alien, uncoerced) of birdsong.

Not that a bird is ever merely a bird: like Mr. Eliot's nightingales, Chaucer's birds may have a history and a symbolic value, as when Criseyde, falling asleep to the song of the nightingale, dreams

> *How that an egle, feathered whit as bon,*
> *Under hire brest his longe clawes sette,*
> *And out hire brest he rente, and that anon,*
> *And dide his herte into hire brest to gon,*
> *Of which she nought agroos, ne nothyng smerte;*
> *And forth he fleigh, with herte left for herte.*

The Promethean eagle of course symbolizes, in Criseyde's dream, her complex attitude toward the impending aggressions of love, but what sharpens and steadies this symbolism is the poet's attention to the identity of the bird itself: the lordliness —*darkened* by the disquieting simile "whit as bon"—inherent (and unembellished except by the one simile) in its very name and appearance; its own characteristic abrupt predatory violence as Criseyde's dread and anticipation direct it. The eagle is an eagle still, drawn out of its natural setting and the old cruel myth by the force of Criseyde's egoistic passionate anxiety (which protects itself by symbol), but in all that clarity of image reserving its mystery and uncompromised separateness.

Criseyde, borrowing from its public myth the pitiless bird of prey, invents in her need an *ad hoc* private myth, and by the details tells us more about her motives than she herself knows. So myth—the ready-made variety too—may serve the character as a screen against his anxieties and the reader as an index to them. On a spring morning the myth of Philomela and Procne invades Pandarus's dream to protect him, while he prepares to

launch his energy on Troilus's business of love, with the generalization that love—not only for himself—is cruel and ruinous:

> . . . *Pandarus, for al his wise speche,*
> *Felt ek his part of loves shotes keene,*
> *That, koude he never so wel of lovyng preche,*
> *It made his hewe a-day ful ofte greene.*
> *So shop it that hym fil that day a teene*
> *In love, for which in wo to bedde he wente,*
> *And made, er it was day, ful many a wente.*
>
> *The swalowe Proigne, with a sorowful lay,*
> *When morwen com, gan make hire waymentynge,*
> *Whi she forshapen was; and ever lay*
> *Pandare abedde, half in a slomberynge,*
> *Til she so neigh hym made hire cheterynge*
> *How Tereus gan forth hire suster take,*
> *That with the noyse of hire he gan awake,*
>
> *And gan to calle, and dresse hym up to ryse,*
> *Remembryng hym his erand was to doone*
> *From Troilus, and ek his grete emprise. . . .*

Man universalizes the human and domesticates the non-
human: so that even a bird may be the victim of a tragic passion. In the myth, as Pandarus's dream recalls it, Procne is
metamorphosed in consequence of a terrible disloyalty and
failure of passion. The myth is necessary to Pandarus. In the
moment of his own despair, when this newly self-appointed
manager of lovers and pledged betrayer of a blood-relative is
faced by the solitary shape of failure (the recognized true
image of himself), he might, if there were no such myth, have
to invent one; for the myth allows Pandarus to escape, from his
private failure and his abandonment of honor, into familiarly
desperate emotions to whose persons and circumstances he is
committed only by the illusion of universal sympathy.

Criseyde, while she is accompanied in her first freely amo-
rous imaginings by the voice of the nightingale, needs no escape
or protection, she is only *lulled:* her particular bird, singing
with its customary loveliness impervious to human crises,
comes to her not out of the myth it shares with its sister the
swallow (where, in a less comfortable mood of Criseyde's, it

might belong) but out of the deferential orchestra that nature provides for lovers. Pandarus's bird is a different sort of accompanist. Since Pandarus—the resourceful but luckless lover, in an embattled city the presumptive guardian of his otherwise friendless niece—comes fresh from promising with brisk daylight confidence to win his niece to the uses of his unresourceful passionate friend, he has good reason to languish, in wakeful night, for want of the sympathy and aid he offers others and to seek the protection of myth and self-forgetfulness. The eventual half-sleep into which he drifts after many a turn in bed (as the poet reports with unsentimental precision) is troubled, then, not by the savage family-myth which the swallow's song evokes and from which it at length disengages itself, but by the lonely recognition of his own failure and of his looming treachery to Criseyde which, in a dream, the universal poignance of the myth dims somewhat and makes more endurable. When "hire cheterynge," too close to be taken for anything but the "noyse" of a bird, dissipates the myth's grandiose pattern (and Pandarus's personal incubus) of betrayal and doom, the swallow withdraws—only a bird—into the featureless background of Pandarus's morning; and Pandarus, his shattered self remagnetized into the legwork-and-stratagem persona by which he holds off the waking world, resumes his name and business. The briskly colloquial diction—interrupted only during Procne's lament—slips back into place as if nothing has happened. The nightingale and the swallow, cut off from Criseyde's yearning and from Pandarus's premonition of ruin and dishonor, go on singing somewhere nevertheless, intact and unheard.

To demonstrate that animal nature is at many points indifferent and inaccessible to man is not to ignore, but rather to lead us toward identifying more carefully, its areas of contact with human nature. When Troilus, ramping in complacent unattached maleness before the lovelorn knights and squires of his company, is suddenly struck down by love, Chaucer's comment takes the form of a condensed beast-fable:

> *As proude Bayard gynneth for to skippe*
> *Out of the weye, so pryketh hym his corn,*

Til he a lasshe have of the longe whippe;
Than thynketh he, "Though I praunce al byforn
First in the trays, ful fat and newe shorn,
Yet am I but an hors, and horses lawe
I moot endure, and with my feres drawe." . . .

The fable is apt not merely because Bayard (the knightly
horse), "feeling his oats" too, behaves very much as Troilus
does and so serves the ironist's purpose of diminishing Troilus
to his animal aspect, nor because here Troilus's awakened appetite is in fact far more "animal" than Bayard's urge "to skippe/
Out of the weye," but, perhaps chiefly, because in the comic
balance between Bayard as Troilus and Bayard as horse the
passing resemblance between man and animal becomes their
irrepressible common fate: to keep imagining (though not all
animals are so articulate as Bayard) freedom where there is
none, or very little ("Yet am I but an hors"); to act incorri-
gibly as if the energetic and the beautiful ("ful fat and newe
shorn") are curbless and exempt from any law (but "horses
lawe/ I moot endure, and with my feres drawe"). Chaucer's
respect for distinctions is also a respect for significant like-
nesses.

Criseyde, too, has her time of identification with the mystery of impulse and of animal nature. Having recalled to us
Criseyde's dream of the rending eagle by this image—as she
yields at last to Troilus—of another resistless predatory bird:

What myghte or may the sely larke seye,
Whan that the sperhauk hath it in his foot?

Chaucer shows us now another view of the bird whose music
casually presided over Criseyde's earliest acceptance of the
possibility of love:

And as the newe abaysed nyghtyngale,
That stynteth first when she bygynneth to synge,
Whan that she hereth any herde tale,
Or in the hegges any wyght stirynge,
And after siker doth hire vois out rynge,
Right so Criseyde, whan hire drede stente,
Opned hire herte, and tolde hym hire entente.

From her briefly revived fear of surrender and outrage (like the lark's "fear" of the sparrowhawk), so that

> *Right as an aspes leef she gan to quake,*
> *Whan she hym felte hire in his arms folde . . .*

Criseyde moves into the diminished placid reassuring world of a country night: the timid nightingale, needlessly "abashed" by the harmless usual sounds of the night but recovering its confidence to sing out, is in this aspect and at this moment Criseyde herself, throwing off at last her fear of love and opening her heart to her lover. If this imagery is more than shimmering and Shelleyan, it is because we have learned, during the preceding four thousand lines of the poem, just how different Criseyde has always been—in the prudence, calculatedness, sophistication, vanity, cynicism, and appealing naïveté of her temperament—from any ascertainable animal nature, and by just how distressful, tortuous, steady, and Pandarus-plotted a route she has arrived at a moment when she recedes from all she is in order to become, for the moment, another sister of the nightingale and the instinctive simple celebrant of love.

In the tenderness and immediate pathos of this comparison (as everywhere else), Chaucer will not blur an outline, sacrifice anything marginal or past to the reader's vicarious absorption in the human center and present of the poem. The reader, like Criseyde, is not catapulted into an exaltation, he arrives at it; and what does the guiding is Chaucer's concern with the history as well as the local commotion of things, his acceptance of irreducible plurality, his acknowledgment of separate orders of existence each of them at some points contiguous and analogous to the others but each reserving an uninvadable self-sufficiency, his respect for a diversity of appearances: that perpetual grace of judgment which will not take a likeness or one aspect for the thing itself, or ignore the final isolation—even from its most reasonable linkages with the non-human world—of the human spirit.

There is ultimately a pathos beyond the reach of metaphor, a pathos attainable only when the human spirit has penetrated and lost all illusion of support outside itself, even the support of metaphor. Lear, exhausted after a lifetime of imperial rhetoric, says to his daughter:

> *I know you do not love me, for your sisters*
> *Have (as I do remember) done me wrong.*
> *You have some cause, they have not. . . .*

and Cordelia replies, "No cause, no cause." This earned simplicity of pathos is very rare in Shakespeare: his heroes and heroines live and die, characteristically, within Lear's lost illusion regarding the magical powers of rhetoric.

In Chaucer's world, however, whose disparate phenomena rhetoric can set in some order but has no power to alter or commingle, such nakedness of spirit is commoner and more likely. Rhetoric persists, of course (though with characteristic Chaucerian fineness of distinction), as long as there are illusions. At a moment when Troilus glories and can still take comfort in his princeliness and Criseyde's love, the poet himself suggests that we see Criseyde as, returning from the hunt, Troilus may see her:

> *. . . whan that he com ridyng into town,*
> *Ful ofte his lady from hire wyndow down,*
> *As fressh as faukoun comen out of muwe,*
> *Ful redy was hym goodly to saluwe.*

Thus Criseyde appears as the noble and beautiful hunting-bird of her worshipful falconer (while the poet may be implying, in this metaphor which not only identifies an instant of the lovers' relationship but catches up its history, that Criseyde has been and remains dangerous, possibly inconstant, not quite subduable). On the other hand, the Troilus who has accepted at last the fact of Criseyde's betrayal is beyond the self-indulgences, however reasonable, of rhetoric:

> *"And certeynly, withouten moore speche,*
> *From hennesforth, as ferforth as I may,*
> *Myn owen deth in armes wol I seche.*
> *I recche nat how soone be the day!*
> *But trewely, Criseyde, swete may,*
> *Whom I have ay with al my myght yserved,*
> *That ye thus doon, I have it nat deserved."*

Troilus has reached a summit of awareness from which he shares at last with his author a view of the futility, at such levels, of rhetoric. If Troilus's statement seems understatement, it is because the lover has lost his illusions regarding the efficacy, and perhaps the truth, of those partially enlightening lovers' metaphors that may seem, in retrospect, lovers' lies: Criseyde as lark, as nightingale, as falcon, as saint and love-goddess, as almost anything except the intolerably perplexed, timorous, untrustworthy, endearing woman she is.

Lear arrives at his clarity of awareness only through the most terrible wrenchings of spirit and language (as if the poet too must work his way through these). Troilus's ordeal may not be so terrible as Lear's; but Chaucer, scrupulously defining every counter of rhetoric his characters use or are used by, keeps us clear enough of the ordeal to leave it Troilus's only, and to grant to himself and the reader an inviolable and uninterrupted design. What Lear discovers after catastrophe and madness, Chaucer has been continuously instructing us in by an unillusioned examination of image and metaphor from the beginning: that nothing—no power or vanity of language or of temporary human comfort—can save man from the recognition of his own solitude and eventual powerlessness. Tragedy is beyond sulphurous and thought-executing fires, as it is also beyond larks and nightingales.

1957

Casanova's dazzled readers search for comparisons as if for antidotes. Surely he isn't such a nonpareil, surely there are other books like his.* Montaigne too was curious about everything on earth and skeptical about everything beyond it. Stendhal too was a brilliant and discriminating psychologist who dedicated himself to the subject of women, courtship, and love. Lorenzo da Ponte, Mozart's librettist and Casanova's friend (whom Casanova, providentially, assisted with the libretto of *Don Giovanni*), was another talented and energetic Italian adventurer who left us a record of his adventures. Benvenuto Cellini had ego and audacity to match Casanova's, as well as the luck to have been born a Renaissance Italian.

But they are all planets to Casanova's sun. Cellini is hobbled by the responsibility of his reputation as a genius, he justifies, he apologizes; he isn't free—as the private and disreputable Casanova is—to be witty even at the expense of duty, responsibility, ambition, those first infirmities of public minds: "If anyone calls me a sensualist," remarks Casanova genially, "he will

---

* *History of My Life*, by Giacomo Casanova. First translated into English in accordance with the original French manuscript by Willard R. Trask. Harcourt, Brace & World. Vols. I, II, III, and IV. (The translation will be complete in twelve volumes.)

be wrong, for the power of my senses never drew me from my duty when I had one." Da Ponte's memoirs are patchy and disappointing, he has forgotten much (including everything interesting about the two unique personages he knew well, Casanova and Mozart) and he recollects with an old man's dim querulousness: he could not, for instance, have paid his respects, as Casanova does at seventy-two, to

> Happy youth! I do not regret it, for it was always giving me something new; for the same reason I loathe my old age, in which I find nothing new except what I read in the gazette. . . .

Stendhal's irony has often the effect of depreciating the enthusiasms it is meant to invoke and define; Stendhal could not have affirmed his life, as Casanova does, by recalling without finickiness the very skin and smell of its pleasures:

> I have always liked highly seasoned dishes: macaroni prepared by a good Neapolitan cook, *olla podrida*, good sticky salt cod from Newfoundland, high game at the very edge, and cheese whose perfection is reached when the little creatures which inhabit them become visible. As for women, I have always found that the one I was in love with smelled good, and the more copious her sweat the sweeter I found it.
>
> What a depraved taste! How disgraceful to admit it and not blush for it! This sort of criticism makes me laugh. It is precisely by virtue of my coarse tastes, I have the temerity to believe, that I am happier than other men, since I am convinced that my tastes make me capable of more pleasure. Happy they who know how to obtain pleasure without harming anyone; they are madmen who imagine that the Great Being can enjoy the griefs, the sufferings, the abstinences which they offer him in sacrifice, and that he loves none but fanatics who inflict them on themselves. God can demand of his creatures only that they practice the virtues whose seed he has sown in their souls, and he has given us nothing which is not meant to make us happy: self-esteem, desire for praise, emulation, vigor, courage, and a power which no tyranny can take from us: the power to kill ourselves if, after calculating, be it rightly or wrongly, we are unfortunate enough to find it our best recourse.

Even Montaigne, by the light of Casanova, comes to seem a dilettante and philosophizer, he digests experience without having tasted it; he is too cautious or abstract to leave the field to persons and passions; he doesn't blaze up continually, as Casanova does, with the living images of a versatile and unrepudiated past:

The object of my desires arrived at midnight. Dismayed to see that it took great agility on her part to climb up on the new bale, I lift my plank, set it aside, and, lying down, offer her the whole length of my arm; she takes hold of it, climbs, and, straightening up, is astonished to find that she is in my balcony down to her waist. She brought the whole length of her bare arms into it without any difficulty. We wasted only three or four minutes congratulating each other on having independently worked for the same end. If on the previous night I had been more her master than she had been mine, on this night she commanded my entire body. Alas! stretch my arms as I would, I could not possess more than half of hers. I was in despair; but she, though she had me entirely in her hands, was ready to weep because she could satisfy only her mouth. She heaped a thousand Greek curses on the wretch who had not made the bale at least half a foot bigger. Even then we should not have been satisfied; but my hand could have soothed her ardor somewhat. Though our pleasures were sterile, they occupied us till dawn. She departed without making a sound; I put back the plank, and went to bed in great need of regaining my strength.

. . . The next night . . . was the last night. . . . Surrendering to her senses, no longer able to resist the fire which was burning her soul, the charming Greek told me to stand up, bend over, take her under the armpits, and pull her up onto the balcony. What lover could resist such an invitation? Naked as a gladiator, I stand up, I bend over, I take her under the armpits and, without needing the strength of Milo of Crotona, I was pulling her up when I felt my shoulders grasped and heard the guard's voice saying, "What are you doing?" I let go, she flees, and I fall on my stomach. I have no wish to get up, and I let the guard shake me. He thought the effort I had made had killed me, but I was worse than dead. I did not get up, because I wanted to strangle him. Finally I went to bed without addressing a word to him, and even without putting back the plank.

For Casanova has his failures, and he describes them as candidly as his successes. "I think you are very amusing," says a

lady he has been importuning; "I advise you to calm yourself."
At the foot of a staircase he learns "a lesson in physiology"
from the daughter of a washerwoman:

> . . . I sprang on her and, partly by persuasion, partly by swift
> action, I subjugated her on the last steps; but at the first thrust of
> our union a most extraordinary sound, proceeding from the place
> next to the one I was occupying, stayed my fury for a moment,
> and the more so because I saw the victim put her hand over her
> face to hide the shame she felt at her indiscretion.
>
> I reassure her by a kiss and make to continue, but lo! a second
> sound, louder than the first; I proceed, and now comes the third,
> then the fourth, and so regularly that it was like the bass of an
> orchestra giving the time for a piece of music. This aural phe-
> nomenon, together with the embarrassment and confusion which
> I saw in my victim, suddenly took possession of my soul; all to-
> gether they presented so comical an idea to my mind that, laugh-
> ter having overpowered all my faculties, I had to let go. . . .

There are, of course, the accidents of war, which he accepts—
especially in the retrospect of his ungrudging old age—with
suitable gallantry: "It was the seventh infection, and I got rid
of it, as always, by dieting for six weeks. I have never done
anything in my life except try to make myself ill when I had
my health and try to make myself well when I had lost it. I
have been equally and thoroughly successful in both, and today
in that particular I enjoy perfect health, which I wish I could
ruin again; but age prevents me."

He is usually, though, the great lover; not the great seducer
(like the demonic imaginary nobleman whose story he helped
his friend da Ponte to write), but the humane and generous
lover, admirer, idolater, husband, companion, poet and painter,
servant and teacher of every woman he loves: "Alas for those,"
he exclaims, and proves his sincerity over and over again, "who
think that the pleasure of Venus is worth anything unless it
comes from two hearts which love each other and which are in
perfect concord!" A French Casanovist—who else?—has
counted one hundred and twenty-two women to whom Casanova makes love in the pages of his *Life*, from 1735 (when he

was ten!) to 1774 (when the *Life* abruptly breaks off).*
Among these encounters most no doubt are casual ones (as with
the Greek slave girl or the washerwoman's daughter); but many
of them are intense and involving, recollected with passionate
vivacity and a fullness of detail that challenges the greatest fiction (not to mention anybody else's memoirs).

Casanova is no Platonist of love, he has no general idea of
women. He loves the hot-blooded lady Donna Lucrezia and
her haughty sister; the credulous, pathetic Duchess of Char-
tres; the downright country girl in pursuit of a husband,
Cristina; the trusting and affectionate sisters Nanetta and Marta
("This love, which was my first, taught me almost nothing
about the way of the world, for it was perfectly happy, un-
broken by trouble of any kind, and untarnished by any interested motives"); the freethinking nun, M. M., who is his most
adorable and most proficient pupil:

> About the first hour of the night I went to the temple of my
> love and, waiting for my idol to arrive, I amused myself by look-
> ing at the books which made up a small library in the boudoir.
> They were few but choice. They included all that the wisest
> philosophers have written against religion and all that the most
> voluptuous pens have written on the subject which is the sole
> aim of love. Seductive books, whose incendiary style drives the
> reader to seek the reality, which alone can quench the fire he
> feels running through his veins. Besides the books there were
> folios containing only lascivious engravings. Their great merit
> lay in the beauty of the drawing far more than in the lubricity
> of the poses. I saw engravings for the *Portier des Chartreux*, made
> in England, and others for Meursius, or Aloisia Sigea Toletana,
> than which I had never seen anything finer. In addition the
> small pictures which decorated the room were so well painted
> that the figures seemed to be alive. An hour went by in an in-
> stant.
>
> The appearance of M. M. in her nun's habit wrung a cry from
> me. I told her, springing to embrace her, that she could not have
> come in better time to prevent a schoolboy masturbation to

---

* Gérard Bauër, Préface to *Mémoires de Casanova*, Librairie Gallimard,
Vol. I, p. xxxiv. M. Bauër points out that one hundred and twenty-two
women over thirty-nine years averages out to only three a year.

which all that I had seen during the past hour would have driven
me.

"But in that saintly dress you surprise me. Let me adore you
here and now, my angel."

"I will put on secular clothes at once. It will take me only a
quarter of an hour. I do not like myself in these woolens."

"No, no. You shall receive the homage of love dressed as you
were when you brought it to birth."

She answered only with a *Fiat voluntas tua* ("Thy will be
done") delivered with the most devout expression as she let
herself fall on the commodious sofa, where I treated her with
caution despite herself. After the act I helped her take off her
habit and put on a plain robe of Pekin muslin which was the
height of elegance. I then played the role of chambermaid while
she dressed her hair and put on a nightcap.

Delighting as he always does in the rituals of domesticity,
Casanova is at his most domestic with the gracious and subtle
Henriette, with whom he shares the most idyllic episode in the
Life, a marriage of true minds that concludes when she must
leave him to return to her husband and family. So she writes
him:

"It is I, my only love, who had to forsake you. Do not add to
your grief by thinking of mine. Let us imagine that we have had
a pleasant dream, and let us not complain of our destiny, for
never was an agreeable dream so long. Let us boast of having
succeeded in being happy for three months on end; there are
few mortals who can say as much. So let us never forget each
other, and let us often recall our love to renew it in our souls,
which, though parted, will enjoy it even more intensely. . . . I
do not know who you are; but I know that no one in the world
knows you better than I do. I will have no more lovers in all
my life to come; but I hope that you will not think of doing
likewise. I wish you to love again, and even to find another
Henriette. Farewell."

Casanova recovers eventually, as Henriette bids him to and
knows he will, as he does from all his setbacks. "Happy or unhappy, life is the only treasure which man possesses, and they
who do not love it do not deserve it." His fidelity to life persists through everything, it not only saves Henriette's letter but

treasures her wonderful story of the Abbess who objected to
her playing the 'cello because one "could not hold the instru-
ment except by assuming an indecent posture." But grief is real
too, and Casanova remembers what it too was like:

> It stupefies; it does not make its victim want to kill himself for
> it stops thought; but it does not leave him the slightest ability to
> do anything toward living. I found myself in a like state six years
> later—but not on account of love—when I was put under the
> Leads [the State Inquisitors' prison in Venice], and again twenty
> years later, in 1786 at Madrid, when I was imprisoned at Buen
> Retiro.

Six years later, locked away by the State Inquisitors for over
a year in a cell too low to stand up in, furnacelike under the
leaden roof, he is given pious books to read, one a Spanish nun's
Life of Mary, which leads him to speculate on the precarious-
ness of sanity:

> A reader with a mind more susceptible to the miraculous and
> fonder of it than mine is in danger, when he reads it, of be-
> coming a visionary and a maniacal scribbler like the virgin her-
> self. The need to occupy myself with something led me to spend
> a week over this masterpiece of hyperexalted invention; I said
> nothing about it to the stupid jailer; but I could bear no more.
> As soon as I fell asleep I was aware of the plague with which
> Sister d'Agreda had infected my mind, weakened by melancholy
> and bad food. My extravagant dreams made me laugh when I re-
> called them in my waking hours, for I wanted to write them
> down, and if I had had writing materials I should perhaps have
> produced a work up there even madder than the one Signor
> Cavalli had sent me. From that time on I saw how mistaken they
> are who attribute a certain strength to the human mind; its
> strength is only relative, and a man who studied himself thor-
> oughly would find nothing in himself but weakness. I saw that
> though men do not often go mad, it is nevertheless true that the
> thing is easy. Our reason is like gunpowder, which, though very
> easy to ignite, nevertheless never catches fire unless fire is ap-
> plied to it; or like a drinking glass, which never breaks unless
> it is broken. The Spanish woman's book is just what is needed to
> drive a man mad; but for the poison to take effect, he must be
> confined under the Leads alone and deprived of any other occu-
> pation.

The book does not, however, drive him mad, this intrepid and impenitent rationalist. Soon he is planning his escape (nobody has ever escaped from the Leads), and after months of labor is on the point of succeeding when he is moved to another cell; plans another escape that requires moment-by-moment collaboration with one prisoner and systematic mumbo-jumbo terrorizing of another, succeeds at last after every harrowing apprehension, and plunges off to freedom and the prospect of new adventures. We have reached the end of the fourth volume (and failed to note that Casanova is a gambler as compulsive as Dostoevsky, a Freemason, a cabalist, a magician; that, having in youth entered on a very promising career in the Church, he might with a little luck and prudence have become a Cardinal like M. M.'s other lover, or even Pope). In this handsome, authoritative edition there are eight volumes and scores of women yet to come, and eighteen more years of an unparalleled and exemplary life.

1967

Tolstoy survived to become, at the focus of world publicity as the most famous living man, his own implacable judge: this complete artist of civilized society who came to anathematize social pleasures and the art that celebrates them; enthusiast of the flesh and of every traditional male preoccupation, *l'homme moyen sensuel* to the highest power, who became the latter-day apostle of celibacy, non-violence, and spiritual love. Yet, though he had renounced the body, it had not—even toward the disastrous end of the most public unhappy marriage since Socrates'—altogether renounced Tolstoy. Not till he was eighty-one could he inform his English biographer that he was no longer susceptible to sexual desire; at eighty-two, two weeks before his death, he recorded in his "secret" diary (his "regular" diary was of course read and copied daily by friends, family, disciples) a final vignette of the unregenerate flesh:

> Yesterday I began doing exercises—the old fool wanted to get younger—and I pulled a cupboard over on myself and hurt myself for nothing. There's an eighty-two-year-old fool for you!

It is impossible to know too much about Tolstoy. Everything fits, surprises, and magnifies. He could not have helped, even in front of a movie camera, living all our lives; and his corresponding prescience of death must have required the desperate measures he took:

> When Thomas Mann patronises Tolstoy's moralising and his attempts to disown the flesh, and praises Goethe's majestic and self-justifying development, the soft impeachment is exasperating; and not only because Mann—"the ironic German"—was himself so evidently preoccupied with the Goethean national succession and with himself as the incumbent of Goethean poise. For surely the collapse of the sense of existence in Tolstoy is the surest proof both of how superb and how universal it had been? All of us are subject to such a temporary collapse: Tolstoy experienced it on an overwhelming scale. Tolstoy's embodiment of a kind of universal physical existence would be nothing if it had not been so continually haunted and obsessed by the question of what there was, what there might be, outside himself. A Tolstoy who continued to write novels of the same kind would be an intolerable phenomenon, for his egotism seems to encompass all physical existence. But what grows with it, haunts it, and finally dominates it, is the admission of its limitations, the confrontation of self with what is not self, of life with death. Tolstoy is not ill, not perverse; he plays out in himself, and on his scale, the most universal and inevitable of human dramas. He *is* the state of our existence: he does not, like Goethe, attempt to conquer it and to put himself above it. Ultimately, as Thomas Mann comes near to admitting, Goethe cared for nothing but himself. Tolstoy *was* nothing but himself, and his sense of what awaited him, and what was outside him, is correspondingly more intimate to us all, and more moving.

The author of this paragraph is John Bayley, in a book* which at once takes its place as the best in English on any Russian novelist. As Mr. Bayley says, "a Tolstoy who continued to write novels" like *War and Peace* and *Anna Karenina*, a Tolstoy whose gigantic appetite for physical experience persisted to the edge of the grave, would be "an intolerable phenomenon." Ernest Simmons has an anecdote about an admirer of Tolstoy's on his last visit to the great man:

> "We must prepare ourselves. A pleasant end soon awaits us," Tolstoy remarked to the eighty-one-year-old Stasov when he was

---

* *Tolstoy and the Novel*, Viking.

visiting him at Yasnaya Polyana in 1904. "What end?" Stasov
queried, still full of the joy of life in spite of his age.

"Death, of course. I'm sure that even you expect it."

"To hell with it!" Stasov exclaimed. "An abomination, a filthy
thing to prepare oneself for! I often sleep badly and toss about
in bed when I think that death will come."

"But don't you feel your old age and that the end is near?"
asked Tolstoy.

"I feel nothing of the kind, nor do I deny myself anything as
formerly, and I hope that you, Leo Nikolayevich, don't give up
anything. You still ride horseback and play lawn tennis." †

Stasov is heroic and touching; but Tolstoy has been through all
that a thousand times, he has arrived without smugness or un-
breakable calm at a "sense of what awaited him," "what was
outside him," mysteries which Goethe or Mann can only
convert into literature.

A Mann or a James works by keeping his judicious distance
from everything; he belongs nowhere; because none of his subject is in his bones, he need never consider its ultimate irrelevance to matters of life and death, or doubt its perpetual fascination. Thus Mr. Bayley observes that "Neither Balzac nor
Henry James could possibly have said, as Tolstoy did, that
they were 'not interested' in many of the pursuits and classes of
Society. Because they remain in their lives *outside* the world,
they take possession of it in their books, they must necessarily
be interested in everything *inside* it. Those who are inside anyway—like Tolstoy and, in her different way, Jane Austen—
have no need to feel this compulsive interest."

> . . . it is one of . . . [Tolstoy's] most mesmeric characteristics
> that he writes about Moscow and Petersburg social and family
> life as if it were a universal thing, and as if his readers would
> understand what he understood in it. Possibly Homer made the
> same assumptions. Certainly Balzac and Proust did not. They
> are showing us over their acquired territories: Tolstoy belongs
> to his. If Balzac had been a banker he would not have wanted to
> explain to us all the processes of banking; if Proust had been a
> duke it would not have occurred to him to conduct us with such
> relish through all the tones and nuances of the French aristocracy.

† Ernest J. Simmons, *Leo Tolstoy*, Vintage, Vol. II, p. 354.

In Tolstoy's hands Moscow and Petersburg family life becomes a universal thing. Irrespective of social level some families are like this, some like that: and the conventions of collective existence in each powerfully affect the fates and fortunes of individual members, when these go on to lead their own lives. Jane Austen, like Tolstoy, took this for granted. In *Mansfield Park* she shows us nothing of the Crawfords' upbringing, but she makes quite clear what effect its shortcomings had on the crucial decisions of their adult lives.

Tolstoy, so Mr. Bayley demonstrates, belongs to his world as he belongs to his body. His confidence is the confidence of the self in its own indispensable reliability, and his genius is to sense and define this confidence in others. "The prisoners who are shot just before we meet Karataev . . . are unable to understand or believe what is going to happen to them—'they could not believe it because they alone knew what their life meant to them, and so they neither understood nor believed that it could be taken from them.' 'They alone knew what their life meant to them'—that is the point, and that is the secret of how Tolstoy gives them their freedom." Tolstoy's unimpeded solipsism is like God's (and quite unlike vanity), he makes his creatures after his own image:

> We shall find this *samodovolnost*, this self-sufficiency, everywhere in his novels, but particularly in *War and Peace*. Everywhere we shall find references to his characters being pleased with themselves. It is the condition of their vitality—deprived of it, they cease to exist. It is neither formulated nor approved; it is simply an attribute of life, of the fully sentient being. Yet to say it is not approved is to stretch the facts: of course Tolstoy is wholly on its side; he cannot help endorsing it; it is an aspect of his own huge confidence in himself and his own being. This confidence is deeply aristocratic, not so much in the class sense —though that of course comes into it—but in the sense in which complete self-sufficiency is the most aristocratic of feelings. . . . Most of Tolstoy's women—and especially Natasha—possess this *samodovolnost* in its most potent form. No one is more aware than Tolstoy that young girls, however seemingly innocent and unaware, have an intense physical selfconsciousness. . . . I suspect that much of the resentment that some readers feel for Tolstoy's heroic characters—and particularly Natasha—is due

to their calm invincible aristocratic conceit. She does not con-
descend to be intelligent, says Pierre admiringly of Natasha.

For such a paragon of Tolstoyan self-sufficiency, even love is
close to pure impulse and appetite, a trap that springs itself:
"Natasha's love is generalised, founded on her own sense of
herself and—less consciously—on her almost explosive expec-
tancy, her need not to be *wasted*." The world is merely what
the ego cannot do without.

Mr. Bayley's argument is, then, straightforward and clear.
Tolstoy's "almost disconcerting simplicity," he says, "comes
from . . . [his] massive and casual assumption that the world
is as he sees it, and as he says it is. He needs no theory about
how to see the world and how to convey its reality." *War and
Peace* is the great moment of confidence, of "equivocal har-
mony," in which everything moves freely and everything is in
its place, in which the world is at the service of every intense
consciousness. *Tolstoy and the Novel* is a triumphant brief not
so much for Tolstoy as for the celebrant of personal exuberance and family happiness, the creator of Natasha and her spacious social milieu, the philosopher-historian for whom freedom means not to be "wasted," means "discovering how life
intends to imprison one, and going gladly and whole-heartedly
into that imprisonment": the author of *War and Peace*. Mr.
Bayley is never less than brilliant and ebulliently analytic (his
discriminations are so minute and so unremitting that, now and
then, they fatigue the reader into the suspicion that they may
be more subtle than their texts); but he has his thesis, and he
intends to clear the decks of everything else. So the pretenders
—Balzac, James, Conrad, and the like—are briskly disposed of,
with a show of respect. The grand challenger—Dostoevsky—is
allowed far more room and scrutiny, but comes off not much
better than Balzac. What Tolstoy writes before *War and Peace*
is, for all its excellences, an imperfect foreshadowing. What he
writes after is a falling away from that benign and unthreat-
ened equilibrium: for Mr. Bayley regards even *Anna Karenina*
as flawed by Tolstoy's "growing sense of personal crisis,"
which prescribes not a "subject that interests and appeals to

him, but . . . one that obsesses him"; and *The Kreutzer Sonata* and *The Death of Ivan Ilyich*, "terrible and powerful," are nevertheless "failures, because their heroes do not seem at home in the world into which Tolstoy has forced them."

Not that Mr. Bayley is unaware of what the Russian critic Shestov calls the *mensonge* of *War and Peace:* its prudery, for instance; its not quite ingenuous satisfaction with the most commonplace conjugal and familial virtues, especially in the Epilogue; its magician's pretense of comprehensiveness (if Dostoevsky didn't exist, the scrupulous reader of Tolstoy would have to invent him). The conclusion of *War and Peace*, says Mr. Bayley, "is moving and unique, because we feel as if the problems that Tolstoy was to wrestle with for the rest of his life are just about to break in. Tolstoy and ourselves are like conductor and orchestra at a sublime concert, for whom urgent messages and queries are being held over until the final movement reaches its close."

Just so; and, if so, *War and Peace* is a stupendous idyll, a *tour de force* on the scale of Mt. Everest. The messages and queries may be held over, but even in the face of sublimity we can remember the unsettled internal weather of our lives. *War and Peace* attracts and awes us; it is, as Mr. Bayley finely says, "the solid kingdom of the flesh," which we would do well to claim and inhabit; it is a promise, like Blake's "lineaments of satisfied desire." On the other hand, *The Idiot*—or *The Kreutzer Sonata*, or *The Death of Ivan Ilyich*—is a succession of urgent messages and questions, it reminds us of what we must cope with, put up with, shore our sanity against.

Mr. Bayley argues, however, that Ivan Ilyich is unconvincing not because of what he does but because in his given identity he would not do it: as Tolstoy says, "when characters do what from their spiritual nature they are unable to do, it is a terrible thing." Ivan Ilyich, if he were faithful to the nature with which Tolstoy has endowed him, would never be awakened by the imminence of death; he

. . . would disappear among such scraps of recollection from his childhood as Tolstoy gives him ("the taste of French plums and how they wrinkle the mouth up")—disappear without other dignity than the right and proper one of being himself. That dignity requires that his death should take place on the same level as "the visitings, the curtains, the sturgeon for dinner," because these were the materials of his life. He is not Prince Andrew. We feel for him as we might for an animal compelled by its master to perform some unnatural trick.

But one need not be Prince Hamlet or Andrew to begin to doubt one's life as it approaches its end. If Ivan Ilyich is Everyman, and if Everyman evades thought by attaching himself to routine, then the sudden amputation of routine may be a strong enough shock to provoke thought; and, once the mind begins to move, it might well drift into self-consciousness and self-doubt. Mr. Bayley does not admire the parabolic Tolstoy; and *The Death of Ivan Ilyich* looks like a ferociously unrelieved parable, in which characters seem to be just what they stand for, feelings are "unnaturally" sustained, revelations are "unnaturally" abrupt and uncompromising. Mr. Bayley regrets the absence of Tolstoy's geniality, which vanished with the Epilogue of *War and Peace;* he refuses to accept in its place Tolstoy's furious urgency, which besets the ordinary man with extraordinary trials, knocks him down for what he is and lifts him up for what he is coming to be, makes him a consistent and terrifying representative of human solitude but never forces him to do tricks (neither is Pierre, talking cheerful domestic nonsense with Natasha, doing tricks in that other story with a very different, and not necessarily more accurate, view of individual and social and family life).

For Mr. Bayley, the Tolstoy of *War and Peace* is the nonsectarian Lord of Creation, whereas the later Tolstoy takes on the likeness of the schizophrenic Deity of the two Testaments, half Thunderer and half creeping Jesus. Gorky's comment, however, is more helpful: that God and Tolstoy were "like two bears in one den." The old man never lost his divine cunning; but, in the years after his physical prime, he grew more and more alert to the other presence, the silent and undefeatable rival.

1967

CONRAD

Joseph Conrad is a puzzle for both the critic and the biographer. His reputation, forty years after his death, remains as protean and unfixable as many of the incidents of his unprecedented life. Criticism, which agrees on the importance of his example and influence, has not yet managed the approximation of a consensus regarding the relative merits of his individual novels: one could, for instance, compile collections of essays by intelligent critics on *Chance* and *Victory*, proving with equal vigor that these books are either masterpieces or fluent botches. The biographer of Conrad finds himself still turning over and reconsidering the enigmatic and self-contradictory personal records that Conrad seems to have taken some trouble to rearrange, alter, or suppress in his letters and under the guise of candid reminiscence.

Conrad is at the same time one of the most and one of the least autobiographical of writers. His experiences—especially his nautical experiences—were admittedly, and often with astonishing directness, the material of his novels; whereas his memoirs, when they are not inaccurate and misleading, are as reticent as those of any writer who has undertaken the confidential mode at all. Certainly, his life appears to be the material of art—of bad art however: summarized, it gives the impres-

sion of a meretricious novel. He was born of patriotic Polish
gentry in their landlocked captive fatherland; at the age of
four, companion of his parents into political exile in Russia;
orphaned at eleven; in his 'teens, abruptly self-exiled to western
Europe, a sailor and Carlist gun-runner off the coasts of France
and Spain; at twenty, beneficiary and (almost fatal) casualty of
a grand passion; master mariner in the British merchant marine
before he was thirty; voyager to the heart of black Africa;
ultimately, the most celebrated living novelist in a language he
did not begin to speak till he had reached manhood. Thus reca-
pitulated, it is less a life than a romance; and Conrad was not
above touching it up here and there with mysteries and misrepresentations. Like his friend and occasional collaborator, Ford
Madox Ford (one of his collaborations with whom was a novel
named *Romance*), he was a romancer and a rhetorician. As
with Ford, so with Conrad it is sometimes hard to make out, or
even to guess at, the resistant, independent contours of his material, the substance of his life and of a world at large. The
actual is swallowed up by his insistence on dispensing with it; it
may not even survive as the smile on the face of the tiger. Joce-
lyn Baines, having tried to ascertain and sort out the facts
about an adventure of Conrad's youth, tactfully discusses Conrad's habit of reticence and evasion, and offers the requisite
cautions:

> . . . there are aspects of Conrad's version which are hard to rec-
> oncile with the known facts or are directly contradicted by them;
> and, if this were not sufficient warning, it is always dangerous
> unreservedly to accept a person's own account of his past. Few
> people relate events with any semblance of accuracy, even if
> they try to do so immediately after they have occurred; whereas
> Conrad's inaccuracy of memory was notorious among those who
> knew him and he was writing about his life in Marseilles several
> decades later. Moreover, in his autobiographical writings it was
> Conrad's aim to recreate a true impression of events rather than
> accurately to reproduce the facts, while in his fiction his inten-
> tion was, obviously enough, artistic and not autobiographical.

Plainly, Conrad is an extreme case, whether he conceals his
youthful attempt at suicide under the more acceptable crisis of
a duel, or, the author of Part First of *Under Western Eyes*,

angrily disclaims any indebtedness to Dostoevsky; whether he supplies his docile French friend and biographer with hopelessly jumbled and mistaken personal chronologies, or constructs the intricate enclosures of method within whose innermost circle the "events" of *Chance* or *Victory*, *Lord Jim* or *Nostromo* may more or less confidently be presumed to occur. E. M. Forster's judgment of Conrad, that "the secret casket of his genius contains a vapour rather than a jewel," testifies to the aura of unseizability that much of Conrad diffuses, an aura of indifference or hostility to the refractory and specifiable actual. "Illusion" is one of Conrad's favorite words. The writer for whom reality appears, characteristically, as a trick of the imagination does not scruple to modify it for his own artistic and private purposes.

Conrad is the nearly perfect skeptic who happens also to be a novelist. His rhetoric is the act of will that intends to certify what is not otherwise certifiable, perhaps not even intelligible, possibly not even there; and the continuous problem for the critic of Conrad is to determine just when this powerful unity of intention unexpectedly encounters a set of external conditions as vexatious and intransigent as itself. The effect of Conrad's very best work is obstruction and deadlock, an opposition of matched and mutually paralyzed energies; the effect of his worst is manner without matter; and both effects are liable to be found (as in *Heart of Darkness*) side by side in the same novel. Against those who wish to ascertain and sort out the facts of his life or the qualities of his fiction, Conrad the man defends himself with the ingenuity of the pyrrhonist for whom both life and art are not—as they are for Conrad the novelist—contests between will and the stubborn actual, but pure invention, the autonomous and unreflected will.

The set of external conditions that Conrad could least successfully wish away was the mariner's life that he lived for two decades of his youth and manhood. Conrad never tired of denying indignantly that he was a writer of sea-tales, nor was he so special and local a writer. Yet those of his works which most successfully challenge the nullifying blast of his temperament are tales of the sea, or of distant coasts and places—tales of adventure that a thoughtful man might pick up and mull over,

or put together and develop, while on the job as a merchant
seaman or off duty in some remote port or other. The obvious
instance is *Typhoon*, a short novel which is, straightforwardly
enough, an account of a typhoon and of a ship that weathers it.
The language is as densely referential as a logbook's, except
that no ship's captain (except Conrad) could ever have sustained its precision and sardonic humor, or—as when the boat-
swain looks in on the tumbled coolies in the hold—could have
roused it to the pitch of descriptive passages matching the per-
turbation and wonder of the mighty storm itself:

> He pulled back the bolt: the heavy iron plate turned on its
> hinges; and it was as though he had opened the door to the
> sounds of the tempest. A gust of hoarse yelling met him: the air
> was still; and the rushing of water overhead was covered by a
> tumult of strangled, throaty shrieks that produced an effect of
> desperate confusion. He straddled his legs the whole width of the
> doorway and stretched his neck. And at first he perceived only
> what he had come to seek: six small yellow flames swinging
> violently on the great body of the dusk.
>
> It was stayed like the gallery of a mine, with a row of stan-
> chions in the middle, and cross-beams overhead, penetrating into
> the gloom ahead—indefinitely. And to port there loomed, like
> the caving in of one of the sides, a bulky mass with a slanting
> outline. The whole place, with the shadows and the shapes,
> moved all the time. The boatswain glared: the ship lurched to
> starboard, and a great howl came from that mass that had the
> slant of fallen earth.
>
> Pieces of wood whizzed past. Planks, he thought, inexpressibly
> startled, and flinging back his head. At his feet a man went slid-
> ing over, open-eyed, on his back, straining with uplifted arms
> for nothing: and another came bounding like a detached stone
> with his head between his legs and his hands clenched. His pig-
> tail whipped in the air; he made a grab at the boatswain's legs,
> and from his opened hand a bright white disc rolled against the
> boatswain's foot. He recognized a silver dollar, and yelled at it
> with astonishment. With a precipitated sound of trampling and
> shuffling of bare feet, and with guttural cries, the mound of
> writhing bodies piled up to port detached itself from the ship's
> side and sliding, inert and struggling, shifted to starboard, with
> a dull, brutal thump. The cries ceased. The boatswain heard a

long moan through the roar and whistling of the wind; he saw
an inextricable confusion of heads and shoulders, naked soles
kicking upwards, fists raised, tumbling backs, legs, pigtails, faces.
"Good Lord!" he cried, horrified, and banged-to the iron door
upon this vision.

Conrad never quite overcame his tendency—as of an
occasionally faulty foreigner's ear for English—toward
platitude and clumsy repetitiveness ("effect of desperate confusion," "inextricable confusion"; "overhead" used twice in
some half-dozen lines for jarringly different purposes; "ahead"
closely following the second "overhead"); but the passage,
taken as a whole, is as bizarre and energetic as it is uninterruptedly in touch with external conditions. It has the momentum of an almost absolute coincidence between manner and
matter; it confirms the breadth of man's ambition by certifying
the existence and magnitude of his adversary; it defines the
gusto and terror of total engagement. Another, and still more
impressive, example of what might be called Conrad's power of
conjuration is the storm episode in *The Nigger of the "Narcissus."* And Conrad's greatest, his subtlest, his most extended and
most richly detailed example—perhaps the greatest descriptive
passage in English fiction—is the episode of the voyage upriver
in *Heart of Darkness.*
 In recent years it has become the critical fashion to depreci-
ate such "set-pieces" ("descriptions of sunsets, exotic seas and
the last plunge of flaming wrecks": so F. R. Leavis pigeonholes
them in his impatience to bring to light the plain virtues of
Conrad's psychological realism). Critics devote themselves to
Conrad's political acumen (*Nostromo, The Secret Agent,
Under Western Eyes*) or to his pre-Jungian intuitions (*Lord
Jim,* "The Secret Sharer," "Amy Foster," the "unspeakable"
and "inscrutable" aspects of *Heart of Darkness, The Shadow
Line*). The political critic discovers that Conrad has uncannily
prophesied the forms and impulses of modern totalitarianism
(as Shakespeare was once praised for having anticipated
modern psychotherapy). The Jungian critic, on the other
hand, is likely to eschew public issues for coterie hallucina-

tions: alert to register the interminable significances in the
night journeys of Conrad's gloomier protagonists (Jim, the
captain in "The Secret Sharer," Marlow in *Heart of Darkness*); or pondering, as in one notorious essay, the mystic
phoneme that not only occupies the front of the secret sharer's
name but names the shape of his room. Mr. Baines, forthright
Englishman, dismisses the more absurd among these lay ana-
lysts under the term "alchemical critics": they "appear to have
assumed the mantle of the alchemists or dabblers in the occult;
to them literary texts are arcana offering knowledge to those
who can find the key." * Not that some of the political and
depth-psychology critics aren't, some of the time, capable of
helpful commentary on Conrad. Morton Zabel's introduction to
Under Western Eyes is informative about the political origins
of that novel, and their assimilation into recurrent Conradian
themes. Thomas Moser has written authoritatively on Conrad's
misogyny and its part in the feeblenesses and oversimplifica-
tions of his later work. Even Albert Guerard, self-consecrated
to the boldest literary-Jungian banalities, now and again breaks
free for a persuasive examination of Conrad's text.

Whatever one's doubts about the strenuous political and
symbolic stresses of much Conrad criticism, it would not do to
imply that Conrad's choice of a maritime or exotic subject out
of the solidities of his seafarer's life guarantees the attentiveness
to fact, the unobstructed intensity of observation, that one
finds in *Typhoon*. Both *Youth* and *The Shadow Line* are similar to *Typhoon* in the sailor's routine they are grounded in and
the kinds of suspense they are intended to generate. But *Youth*
is undermined by the yeasty apostrophizing that Conrad,
through the voice of Marlow, is liable to offer as moral
illumination:

> Oh, the glamour of youth! Oh, the fire of it, more dazzling than
> the flames of the burning ship, throwing a magic light on the
> wide earth, leaping audaciously to the sky, presently to be

* Conrad's friend and confidant, Richard Curle, has noted that "Conrad
was a realist, who disapproved altogether of the type of symbolism represented by such a work as Herman Melville's *Moby Dick*, a book which
he detested." Richard Curle, *Joseph Conrad and His Characters*, Fair
Lawn: Essential Books, Inc., p. 171.

quenched by time, more cruel, more pitiless, more bitter than
the sea—and like the flames of the burning ship surrounded by
an impenetrable night.

The Shadow Line suffers from comparable leakages of facile
skepticism ("an immensity that receives no impress, preserves
no memories, and keeps no reckoning of lives"); and it takes an
awkward, disingenuous fling at the quasi-supernatural. Its principal shortcoming, though, is what certain critics have regarded as its triumph—an unreserved endorsement of the idea
of duty, whether through the stiff upper lip of the all too
quietly noble Ransome (" 'You think I ought to be on deck?'
. . . 'I do, sir.' ") or expressly by the narrator himself as he
condemns the dead captain:

> . . . the end of . . . [the captain's] life was a complete act of
> treason, the betrayal of a tradition which seemed to me as im-
> perative as any guide on earth could be.

The author of *Heart of Darkness* knows that life is not so readily reducible to this idea of peremptory routine honorably carried out, this simple prop for the complex man whose strongest
memory from twenty years of sea-life was a harrowing boredom, and who in *Typhoon* understood that Captain MacWhirr
could serenely ride out the storm—could indeed be heroic—
because he lacked the treacherous gift of imagination: "skim-
ming over the years of existence . . . , ignorant of life to the
last."

As for the exotic Conrad, like Swinburne he is his own paro-
dist. "The Lagoon" is as ludicrous as Max Beerbohm's parody
of it; it pours out cataracts of the silliest and most narcissistic
prose by any major writer in English:

> The ever-ready suspicion of evil, the gnawing suspicion that
> lurks in our hearts, flowed out into the stillness round him—into
> the stillness profound and dumb, and made it appear untrust-
> worthy and infamous, like the placid and impenetrable mask of
> an unjustifiable violence. In that fleeting and powerful distur-
> bance of his being the earth enfolded in the starlight peace be-
> came a shadowy country of inhuman strife, a battle-field of
> phantoms terrible and charming, august or ignoble, struggling

ardently for the possession of our helpless hearts. An unquiet
and mysterious country of inextinguishable desires and fears.

Conrad's two earliest novels have exotic settings also; but in
fact for the most part—barring the incontinent last hundred
pages of *An Outcast of the Islands*—they are interestingly
plotted and soberly written books that initiate into English fiction, and treat with some penetration, the theme of moral
decay in an alien setting. The early Conrad does have stories to
tell that survive his annihilating temperament; the drawback is
that he has not yet learned or worked out adequate techniques
for giving them room to move and grow in. Both *Almayer's
Folly* and *An Outcast of the Islands* are disfigured not so
much by self-admiring exoticisms as by a crippled and dragging
pace, a reliance on endlessly summarizing flashbacks. Those
moments which ought to be their most vivid are buried in
pages of spasmodic and breathless catching up.

The point, at any rate, is not that *Typhoon* succeeds because
it is about the sea, or *Heart of Darkness* because its setting is
exotic, or either of them because it has numerous passages of
magnificent descriptive prose. Conrad's descriptive power, in
these persistently scenic tales as in *The Nigger of the "Narcissus,"* is striking in itself, it produces set-pieces for anthologies
and excitement for those readers who enjoy scraps of charged
prose, it reveals and vindicates Conrad's attachment to the
places and occupations of his young manhood, it profits by the
picaresque resonances of ships at sea and sojourns in strange,
far places. Crucially, however, what it does is to mediate and
dramatize the extreme and therefore isolating actions—a typhoon, a reversion to savagery, a mortal illness—that determine
and disclose character. Conrad's solipsistic temperament solves
the problem of morality by the doctrine of extremity; his descriptive power provides the exploratory and illustrative scenes
of trial and definition.* Man proves his moral nature not so-
cially, not by talk or love or daily living, but by solitary ordeal,

---

* The language of "the earlier Conrad" is "important to us" because it
is "struggling to digest and express new objects, new groups of objects,
new feelings, new aspects." T. S. Eliot, *Selected Essays*, Harcourt, Brace
& World, p. 285.

by passing through circumstances catastrophic and lonely enough to wring out of him all possible insincerities, not least the insincerity of a consoling rhetoric. Failing such disciplinary circumstances and the power to dramatize them, Conrad's fiction is likely to dilate with conspicuous ease into politics or symbology or the pneumatic ironies of the "Cosmic Joke," Conrad's term for the spectacle of the inexhaustibly contemtible human condition.

To discuss Conrad as if he were a unique and self-created phenomenon is, of course, to ignore the thoroughly literary ambiences of his Polish childhood and of his English writing career, his acknowledgments of obligation to various masters, his adaptation of modes of fictional statement inaugurated by others. Sometimes the influence is comical in its unaccommodated identifiability, as in the opening sentences of *An Outcast of the Islands:*

> When he stepped off the straight and narrow path of his peculiar honesty, it was with an inward assertion of unflinching resolve to fall back again into the monotonous but safe stride of virtue as soon as his little excursion into the wayside quagmires had produced the desired effect. It was going to be a short episode—a sentence in brackets, so to speak—in the flowing tale of his life: a thing of no moment, to be done unwillingly, yet neatly, and to be quickly forgotten. . . .

Usually, however, the influence, whether of James's magisterial obliquities or of the remote exactitudes of Flaubert and Maupassant, is absorbed into Conrad's own manner and preoccupations. An outstanding instance is the early story, "An Outpost of Progress," Conrad's first working of his Congo recollections. It is as Flaubertian as *L'Éducation Sentimentale,* and its two principal figures are transferred alive from *Bouvard et Pécuchet.* The wholly Conradian result is a comedy of squalid hubris which concludes in murder and self-crucifixion, and which by the unrelieved blackness of its humor makes Flaubert seem sunnily genial. Incidentally, Conrad takes this early occasion to make explicit, in an assertion that weakens the otherwise diabolic objectivity of the story, his doctrine of extremity:

Few men realize that their life, the very essence of their character, their capabilities and their audacities, are only the expression of their belief in the safety of their surroundings. The courage, the composure, the confidence; the emotions and principles; every great and every insignificant thought belongs not to the individual but to the crowd: to the crowd that believes blindly in the irresistible force of its institutions and of its morals, in the power of its police and of its opinion. But the contact with pure unmitigated savagery, with primitive nature and primitive man, brings sudden and profound trouble into the heart. To the sentiment of being alone of one's kind, to the clear perception of the loneliness of one's thoughts, of one's sensations—to the negation of the habitual, which is safe, there is added the affirmation of the unusual, which is dangerous; a suggestion of things vague, uncontrollable, and repulsive, whose discomposing intrusion excites the imagination and tries the civilized nerves of the foolish and the wise alike.

The haranguing note is untypical. Mostly, Conrad's tone in this story is sardonically casual, flexible, almost colloquial; and it allows him to modulate into remarkable effects that he can only portentously attempt in later, more self-conscious works; for instance, Kayerts' hallucination after he has murdered Carlier:

. . . he reflected that the fellow dead there had been a noxious beast anyway; that men died every day in thousands; perhaps in hundreds of thousands—who could tell?—and that in the number, that one death could not possibly make any difference; couldn't have any importance, at least to a thinking creature. He, Kayerts, was a thinking creature. He had been all his life, till that moment, a believer in a lot of nonsense like the rest of mankind—who are fools; but now he thought! He knew! He was at peace; he was familiar with the highest wisdom! Then he tried to imagine himself dead, and Carlier sitting in his chair watching him; and his attempt met with such unexpected success, that in a very few moments he became not at all sure who was dead and who was alive. This extraordinary achievement of his fancy startled him, however, and by a clever and timely effort of mind he saved himself just in time from becoming Carlier. His heart thumped, and he felt hot all over at the thought of that danger. Carlier. What a beastly thing! To compose his now disturbed nerves—and no wonder!—he tried to whistle a little.

Then, suddenly, he fell asleep, or thought he had slept; but at any rate there was a fog, and somebody had whistled in the fog.

He stood up. The day had come, and a heavy mist had descended upon the land: the mist penetrating, enveloping, and silent; the morning mist of tropical lands; the mist that clings and kills; the mist white and deadly, immaculate and poisonous. He stood up, saw the body, and threw his arms above his head with a cry like that of a man who, waking from a trance, finds himself immured forever in a tomb. "*Help! . . . My God!*"

Comparing this passage (even the stigmatic clusters of post-nominal adjectives in the last paragraph are not altogether un-functional) with the heavy-handed and repetitive business, in *Under Western Eyes*, of Razumov's delusion that he is walking over Haldin's body, one can better judge when Conrad is simply a rationalistic copyist of Dostoevskian mysteries, and when he composes a scene that, in its ambiguous tremor between sleep and waking, is fit to stand with the Doestoevskian mysteries: with, say, the hallucinatory episode in *Crime and Punishment* that culminates in Svidrigaïlov's suicide.

If *Under Western Eyes* is an accomplished and labored imitation of Dostoevsky by a novelist who has stopped believing in ghosts, *The Secret Agent* and *Nostromo* are Conrad's Flaubertian novels. *The Secret Agent* has been "rediscovered" in recent years, along with the other political novels of Conrad, by critics who marvel at Conrad's insight into the psychology of revolution and the psychology of despotism. However clairvoyant Conrad may have been in these matters, *The Secret Agent* is a masterly, if somewhat fatigued, Flaubertian exercise in the form of a thriller. The fact that the criminals are spies and bomb-carrying anarchists, rather than routine murderers, is not so noteworthy as it purports to be; the spies, anarchists, policemen, and Russians could come out of any clever melo-drama; Stevie is a maladroitly obvious, and undeveloped, cousin of Dostoevsky's saintly idiots. Only the Verlocs achieve a degree of pathos, though never with the inwardness that would make their plight the animating center of the novel.

Nostromo is something else again, a novel of large intentions and on a heroic scale. It is the rock on which most Conrad critics founder, shouting "Masterpiece!" while their misgivings

gleam like eyes through the unexamined defects of their convictions. Mr. Baines interrupts his very sympathetic consideration to remark on "the weakness of Conrad's characterisa-
tion":

> It is evident that most of the characters, in particular the leading
> ones, exist for what they represent rather than for what they are.
> Although they play important roles in the development of the
> themes and are in that respect vivid and real, their psychology
> is on the whole crude, blurred, or even unconvincing.

Dr. Leavis calls *Nostromo* Conrad's "most considerable work"
and "one of the great novels of the language," continues to
praise it without qualification, and unexpectedly ends with
what appears to be about as severe a qualification as one could
make:

> At any rate, for all the rich variety of the interest and the tight-
> ness of the pattern, the reverberation of *Nostromo* has something
> hollow about it; with the colour and life there is a suggestion of
> a certain emptiness. And for explanation it is perhaps enough to
> point to this reflection of Mrs. Gould's:
>
>> It had come into her mind that for life to be large and
>> full, it must contain the care of the past and of the fu-
>> ture in every passing moment of the present.
>
> That kind of self-sufficient day-to-dayness of living Conrad can
> convey, when writing from within the Merchant Service, where
> clearly he has known it. We are made aware of hostile natural
> forces threatening his seamen with extinction, but not of meta-
> physical gulfs opening under life and consciousness: reality on
> board ship is domestic, assured and substantial. "That feeling of
> life-emptiness which had made me so restless for the last few
> months," says the young captain of *The Shadow Line*, entering
> on his new command, "lost its bitter plausibility, its evil influ-
> ence." For life in the Merchant Service there is no equivalent in
> *Nostromo*—no intimate sense conveyed of the day-by-day con-
> tinuities of social living. And though we are given a confidential
> account of what lies behind Dr. Monygham's sardonic face, yet
> on the whole we see the characters from the outside, and only
> as they belong to the ironic pattern—figures in the futilities of a
> public drama, against a dwarfing background of mountain and
> gulf.

Dr. Leavis overestimates the tidiness and metaphysical comfort of Conrad's representations of life at sea; but the case he belatedly makes against *Nostromo* is just. *Nostromo* is a novel full of astute, even aphoristic observations; its subject is a related group of serious issues seriously scrutinized and elaborated; it is brilliantly put together with the mature skill of an extraordinary craftsman; and it is hollow. It is a prodigiously ingenious waxworks museum, which in certain lights and to certain innocent minds appears to be an assemblage of live human beings.

What has happened by the time of *Nostromo* is that Conrad's rhetoric has grown hard and polished, the painstakingly articulated exoskeleton of suppressed and no longer acknowledgeable nightmares; the monocle through which a formidable uncle surveys, from his languid position by the fireplace mantel, the places, colors, and theatrical tableaux of a safely emptied world:

> He laughed wildly and turned in the doorway towards the body of the late Senor Hirsch, an opaque long blotch in the semi-transparent obscurity of the room between the two tall parallelograms of the windows full of stars.
> "You man of fear!" he cried. "You shall be avenged by me—Nostromo. Out of my way, doctor! Stand aside—or, by the suffering soul of a woman dead without confession, I will strangle you with my two hands."

By the time of *Chance* and *Victory* (to say nothing of such fag-end adventure-stuff as *The Arrow of Gold*, *The Rescue*, and *The Rover*), even the rhetoric has lost its stately air, it is shabby and hurried; the familiar technical devices—the time-shift; the plurality of narrators, of whom Number One learns from Number Two what Number Two has learned from Number Three about Characters Five and Seven—are flung with a desperate hurly-burly into creaky plots which, if they lacked the name of Conrad and his increasingly mechanical prestidigitations, would plainly enough mark the abdication by the artist of any pretense to an adult interest in human issues.

In any case, Conrad is not a novelist but a writer of novellas. His impulse exhausts, or only artificially protracts, itself beyond their length: the length of a nightmare or of a moral test, not—as novels require—of history or biography. The enduring Conrad is the Conrad who had learned his scope and his method without having yet decided to evade the force of his obsessions. His great and unprecedented works were all written within a period of six years: "An Outpost of Progress" in 1896, *The Nigger of the "Narcissus"* in 1897, *Heart of Darkness* in 1899, *Typhoon* in 1902. *Lord Jim*, the only other considerable work during this period, is, as Conrad himself seems to have thought,* essentially a short story expanded far beyond its proper limits; expanded, besides, by Marlow's more than customarily confused and high-flown ruminations (so dear to the Jungian critics that *Lord Jim* is the pet of their idolatry): as Mr. Baines has commented, "one may be tempted to wonder whether even Conrad himself was always quite clear as to what he was trying to say or, in this case, whether there was not some unresolved ambiguity in his own attitude to the events described." Conrad was never, even during this period, quite insusceptible to the promptings of his self-indulgent skepticism, whether translated into the deliquescent jargon of Marlow (a much overrated personage, whose only necessary and luminous incarnation is in *Heart of Darkness*) or served out as a sauce without meat: "The Lagoon," it is disconcerting to recall, was written within a month of "An Outpost of Progress" and published in the same volume.

The primary fact about Conrad criticism is the insensitivity with which it has performed its task of discrimination among the tales and novels of the most uneven fiction-writer in English. Meanwhile, one may hazard one's own provisional formulation. Before 1896 Conrad was an exceptional novice, already an innovator with his own individual tone and theme; after 1902 he was a distinguished and, at last, deservedly famous professional writer writing novels; in his best fiction between those years he is doubtless the most original, and very likely

---

* In Richard Curle's copy of *Lord Jim* Conrad wrote: "When I began this story, which some people think my best . . . —personally I don't—I formed the resolve to cram as much character and episode into it as it could hold. This explains its great length which the story itself does not justify."

the greatest, writer of novellas in English (his only rival is Melville). His claim on our attention is profound and durable, but his reputation should not be permitted to base itself—as recent criticism has more and more aggressively encouraged it to do—on one combination or another of those of his books which most pretentiously repudiate the boundaries of his claim. His finest work is as irreplaceable as, after all, the present renown of some of his weakest books is a judgment on the more eccentric hobbies of modern criticism.

1965

SHAW

Almost the easiest thing to do with Shaw is to compile a list of his errors and inadequacies as playwright, pamphleteer, vegetarian, anti-vivisectionist, lover, husband, human being, self-confessed great man. Quite the easiest thing is to read him. Except his plays, that is, which (not to embarrass Sophocles and Shakespeare) are to *Volpone, The Country Wife, The Way of the World*, even *The Importance of Being Earnest*, as Paul Henry Lang's music criticism is to Shaw's: not the difference between tenth and first, but between nothing and something. The wrangle about Shaw's reputation dashes off on the track of this false scent; but Shaw is no more a dramatist than Voltaire. Intelligence having been banished from the English theater since 1700 (the sole anomaly is *The Importance of Being Earnest*, pastel fantasia on muffins and cucumber sandwiches), Shaw's mere rigid simulacra of intelligence on the stage dazed audiences into the hallucination that they were participating in a renaissance. The point is not that Shaw's plays are tracts, but that they are so much duller, clumsier, more banal than his undramatized tracts, prefaces, reminiscences, *feuilletons* on the arts, letters to newspapers and random correspondents. Any five consecutive pages of Shaw's four volumes of music criticism are superior in wit, humor, taste, discrimination, accuracy, robust-

ness, exuberance, and human understanding to *Saint Joan, Man
and Superman, Caesar and Cleopatra, Candida, Major Barbara,
Heartbreak House, The Devil's Disciple,* and *The Doctor's
Dilemma* singly, in combination, or quintessentially distilled.
Eight years after his centenary, Shaw continues to elude judicious criticism because the critics are either bemused or horrified
by the wooden Leviathan of his drama. Meanwhile the Shaw
bibliography proliferates. Of these five books,* three are the
most recent ones about him, the others belated gleanings from
his polemical output.

Unluckily, Shaw is sometimes not even a clever and engaging polemicist. He was always ready to be excited by just
about any topical and public issue, and had—perhaps still has—
the power to convince many readers that his excitement is a
portent and provocation of massive social changes; a politician's rather than a critic's power. It is characteristic of him
that a collection of essays, prefaces, letters which the editor
feels justified in titling *On Language,* and which Shaw took the
trouble to turn out regularly over a period of fifty years,
should be not on language but on the public symbols by which
we make it out: on our inefficient alphabet. Shaw was a lifelong
advocate of a phonetic—what nowadays would be more precisely called a phonemic—alphabet. In this volume he keeps
insisting, with the propagandist's memorized thin stock of arguments and examples, that its use would not only save oceans
of ink, paper, time, and energy, and so, among other consum-
mations, permit a writer to double or triple his productivity,
but fix a universal pronunciation of English and so eliminate
the most obvious and, according to Shaw, most stubborn of
class distinctions. No doubt there would be huge economies,
after some years of spectacular chaos; maybe the next Shakespeare, scribbling phonemically, would leave us seventy-four or
one hundred and eleven plays (though God forbid a phonemic
Lope de Vega). On the other hand, against Shaw's hope of

* *On Language,* by G. B. Shaw, edited by Abraham Tauber, Philosophical
Library; *The Religious Speeches of Bernard Shaw,* edited by Warren S.
Smith, Pennsylvania State University Press; *G. B. S. and the Lunatic,* by
Lawrence Langner, Atheneum; *The Loves of George Bernard Shaw,* by
C. G. L. DuCann, Funk & Wagnalls; *A Guide to the Plays of Bernard
Shaw,* by C. B. Purdom, Crowell.

abolishing class by imposing a uniform pronunciation, linguistic science assures us that the pronunciation of a language cannot be eternally fixed by its orthography: phonemic spelling will not confound Oxbridge and Cockney into egalitarian indivisibility. At any rate, Shaw worries the issue like a civic-minded terrier and declares, with his cross-grained Irish charm, that he will not "grudge . . . even . . . a world war" as a prerequisite to the establishment of a rational alphabet: "The waste of war is negligible in comparison to the daily waste of trying to communicate with one another in English through an alphabet with sixteen letters missing."

Nor is the other posthumous volume more attractive. There is nothing in *The Religious Speeches of Bernard Shaw* that isn't far more entertainingly explicit in a half-dozen of his prefaces, as well as flatfootedly declaimed in *Man and Superman* and *Back to Methuselah.* Shaw professed himself relieved and invigorated to accept, in place of the omnipotent Hebrew and Christian Jehovah, an evolving Deity to the perfecting of Whose identity every superior man must in pure altruism dedicate the strength of his conscious will. However comforting such a belief may have been to Shaw, it seems unlikely to comfort the generality of mankind, who tend to hold out for present guarantees. The speeches do disclose who Shaw's authorities are (not that he ever dissembles his reliance on them), and how grossly he can simplify their dicta: Ibsen, Tolstoy, Nietzsche, Bergson, Lamarck, Samuel Butler. Shaw conceives himself to be doing the job of the streetcorner orator, and he blends vulgarity, hearty condecension, toadying, and aggressive heterodoxy into the standard mixture. But he is also Shaw, and it is amusing to see him relapse into the more congenial role of temperance lecturer: "The world must consist of people who are happy and at the same time sober."

The new books by Shaw's chroniclers and commentators aren't very helpful either. The late Lawrence Langner, founder and director of the Theatre Guild, was responsible, beginning in 1920, for the first and numerous later productions of many of Shaw's plays in New York and at Westport. His memoir opens, unprepossessingly, in a shower of solecisms and clichés:

The shock created by Shaw on the modern world was that of an alert intelligent mind—armed with the weapons of rapierlike wit and bludgeoning horseplay, intent on destroying the shibboleths of Victorian morality—whose thrusts delighted the younger generations which followed him.

On the evidence of the book, however, Langner was genuinely if rather inarticulately devoted to the theater in general and to Shaw in particular; and it is touching to learn of his ineffectuality in commercial dealings with that paranoiacally adamant businessman, who "was so proud of his royalty scale that he was blind to the fact that throughout his lifetime, institutions such as the Theatre Guild were seldom able to pay their way by producing his plays. While G.B.S. had earned about $350,-000 in royalties from the Guild, the Guild in turn had lost about the same amount in the production of his plays." Which seems to prove—though Langner cannot have intended to prove—that if Shaw had gallantly forsworn all royalties the Theatre Guild would have broken even on his plays. Langner attempts, also, to comment tactfully on Shaw's "blind spot" regarding "love and sex," on his celibate marriage ("I sensed a relationship between them which I was to learn afterward was based upon the deepest respect for each other's qualities"), on the post-1918 development of Shaw's increasingly embittered, Armageddon's-eye view of world politics; but it is a tact without focus or penetration.

If there were a tactful term for Mr. DuCann's book, one would hasten to use it and be done. To publish a book entitled *The Loves of George Bernard Shaw* is not necessarily shameful; Mr. DuCann has taken considerable pains to gather information, some of it made public here for the first time, especially about Shaw's early amours; he prints lengthy excerpts from Mrs. Shaw's appalling letter to T. E. Lawrence (a letter about which Shaw himself knew nothing till after her death), to whom she confided—at seventy!—the terrors and revulsions of a life that might have ended in madness if it had not settled into an asexual marriage with a famous man; the book preserves a wonderful anecdote about the judgment that Charlotte Payne-Townshend's sister passed on the wealthy Charlotte's marriage to Shaw (already a well-known playwright, critic, and Socialist agitator):

> The bride's sister, Mrs. Cholmondeley, who was not at the ceremony, sent no felicitations. Quite the contrary; she wrote to the autumnal bride: "Don't ask me to meet this man. And as a last kindness to me and for my sake, I ask you to secure your money."

It is the tone, the very smell, of the book that baffles tact; a peculiarly English journalistic tone in the vicinity of which the New York *Daily News* appears as a pillar of taste, sobriety, and wide-eyed innocence. It is the tone of much of the English evening and Sunday press, headlines for which are likely to read as follows: HAMPSTEAD SHOCKED BY VICE-RING ORGIES; MADAM TELLS DISGUSTING STORY OF ABANDONED LIFE; NEIGHBOURS OUTRAGED BY STRANGE GOINGS-ON IN BAYSWATER. The trick is to sidle up with lip-licking orotundity for a near view of all the nasty acts and then to deplore with equally orotund English indignation the filthy swine who perform them. The New York *Daily News* says, People are swine and don't you just love to wallow! The English gutter press says, People are swine and isn't it too bad that we upright citizens have to read all about their wallowing. "Once G.B.S. went much further in dishonouring his parents," writes Mr. DuCann severely. "He asserted that he had been begotten after a brawl when his father was fuddled with drink. Whether that was true or untrue, a son should never have said that, for what good could this blackguarding of his parents do?" And another whiff:

> Shaw's candor (if you are disposed to praise him), his lack of delicacy (if you are not), is amazing. Admitting that he is fully entitled to tell the truth, and nothing but the truth about himself and about the affair, one still asks: Why was it necessary to make the name of Mrs. Jenny Patterson as notorious as the reputation of Potiphar's wife, when he, G.B.S., was no Joseph in the matter, especially when the poor woman was in her grave?

"Why did Shaw give her name?" snuffles Mr. DuCann in still another of the innumerable nose-drips of moralism in this reechy book. "It was the conduct of a cad." Mr. DuCann ought to know.

Very much on the other hand, Mr. Purdom (who observes that he saw his first Shaw play in 1904!) is a gentleman and a Shavian. His book seems intended as a manual for a senior course on his hero. It is divided, ingratiatingly, into three parts: The Man, The Dramatist, and The Plays, Mr. Purdom is confidently obsolete enough to sweep away, with one superb gesture of contempt, Picasso, Klee, Eliot, and Dylan Thomas, "to go no further," as practitioners and victims of those tendencies in "modern art" against which Shaw is the vigorous corrective: "Nearly all modern art . . . is little more than the very clever and technically expert effort of artists to work for or to speak to themselves." Treading softly in the vicinity of Shaw's aversion to sex, Mr. Purdom comes up with an unusual vindication:

> In his marriage, when he was approaching forty-two, a basis of sexual abstention was established to which Shaw remained faithful. This seems to have brought about an induced impotence in him, which may have been a defect from a natural point of view, but was certainly no defect in him as an artist, for it has a conscious origin. As a man in whom the emotional elements were controlled, Shaw provides an example of the lover presented in Plato's *Symposium,* who is not subject to carnal love. This is not something to deride, but to honour. To achieve that state does not lessen a man, either as man or artist, for it is a victory of the spirit, that is, of consciousness. . . . It is my contention that he made himself physiologically incapable in one direction for the sake of increased capacity in another [the writing of his plays].

Mr. Purdom will some day explain how an impotence "induced" by external conditions can be considered a triumph of will and consciousness. In any case, he seems prepared to agree that—on the principle, "If thine eye offend thee pluck it out" —the way to increase one's capacity as a Christian is to adopt the procedure of Origen.

Discussing the dramatist, Mr. Purdom makes the ritual associations between Shaw and Shakespeare, Dickens, Blake ("To Shaw, as to William Blake, religion and politics are one"; though one would rather not imagine the horror with which Blake would have regarded any page of Shaw).

Part Three is an awesomely industrious scrutiny of every one of Shaw's fifty-three plays (down to the feeblest squibs), for each of which Mr. Purdom provides a summary of the plot, descriptions of the characters, suggestions for performance (he often remarks—and he is right—that this or that play "can easily be made not very interesting" if it is not done with verve and intelligence by a perfect cast under ideal stage conditions), notes on dates and circumstances of professional productions, precise designations of "climaxes" and "anticlimaxes" (which he seems to think playwrights supply at appropriate refreshing intervals like cartons of hot buttered popcorn). Mr. Purdom suffers also from a complicated obsession concerning the nature of the dramatic protagonist. He believes that every satisfactory play must have a single principal character; and, far more eccentrically, that the events and other characters in a play are to be seen entirely from the standpoint of the protagonist, virtually as his dream: "the protagonist, i.e. the character from whose point of view the dramatic action takes place"; "There is no difficulty in seeing that the entire action is from Tanner's point of view"; "The play is . . . [Joan's] vision throughout, including the epilogue, which should be seen as her meditation"; "When we see Candida presented by Marchbanks as protagonist we accept her as the marvelous creature he sees her to be"; "The play is, of course, [Higgins's] . . . presentation of the comic situation . . ." So much for the dramatist's vaunted impersonality in allowing each of the characters to speak for himself; but Mr. Purdom is not disposing of this notion, he seems never to have heard of it.

It is not surprising that the man who wrote the plays solicits—as his champions and depreciators—this trio of naïf, newspaper moralist, and stage-struck entrepreneur. The prodigality of gab, the self-assertion, the affectation of strong-mindedness and impudence, the pretense of convention-shattering wit, the "serious" ideas, the *fin-de-siècle* claptrap—

> Ive been threatened and blackmailed and insulted and starved. But Ive played the game. Ive fought the good fight. And now it's all over, theres an indescribable peace. [*He feebly folds his hands and utters his creed*]: I believe in Michael Angelo, Velasquez, and Rembrandt; in the might of design, the mystery of color, the

redemption of all things by Beauty everlasting, and the message of Art that has made these hands blessed. Amen. Amen. [He closes his eyes and lies still].

(the artist's dying speech in *The Doctor's Dilemma*!), the clatter of ruthlessly inane paradoxes—all these qualities of the mountebank, taking his opportunity in a medium which had excluded even the semblance of intelligence for two centuries, are just the qualities to make a secular religion for those who, if somewhat otherwise disposed, would follow or deride Mme. Blavatsky or the latest swami instead.

The indictment is overstated, no doubt. *Pygmalion* is a pleasant and durable romantic comedy, flawed only by Shaw's preposterous insistence that his puppets not fall into each other's arms at the curtain. *The Devil's Disciple* has moments of blustery melodrama; the epilogue to *Saint Joan* almost achieves imagination. No doubt one could find salvageable phrases, perhaps speeches, in some of the other plays. *Heartbreak House,* which has been considered (by Shaw himself, among others) Shaw's "masterpiece," is Wilde without wit, Chekhov without pathos, Ibsen without iron—and Shaw without brains; Stark Young describes it as "garrulous, unfelt and tiresome" (epithets which will serve for almost any Shaw play). *Caesar and Cleopatra* and *Saint Joan* are Hollywood epics, with bubble-gum dialogue by Joseph L. Mankiewicz and low-budget casts. *Man and Superman* has the style and present utility of a unicycle.

Eric Bentley wrote an amiable and flattering book about Shaw, in the foreword to which he quoted a number of aspersions on his subject. Since he has missed or ignored some of the more pungent instances, here is a supplement. Wyndham Lewis on the language of *Saint Joan* and *Back to Methuselah:* "[The characters] . . . speak the jargon of the city tea-shop; as you read you fancy them in bathing drawers, a London bank clerk and his girl, great Wells readers . . ." Tolstoy on Shaw's mind: "I read Shaw [who had sent him *Man and Superman, John Bull's Other Island, Major Barbara,* and *The Impossibilities of Anarchism*]. His triviality is astounding. Not only is he devoid of a single thought of his own that elevates

him above the banality of the city mob, but he does not understand a single great thought of the thinkers of the past. His
whole attraction rests in the fact that he is able to express artis-
tically the most stale trivialities in a most perverted modern
way, as though he were saying something his own, something
novel. His chief characteristic is this—a tremendous self-
confidence equaled only by his complete philosophical ignorance." Yeats on Shaw as the incarnation of the anti-poetic: "I
had a nightmare that I was haunted by a sewing-machine, that
clicked and shone, but the incredible thing was that the machine
smiled, smiled perpetually." The great and prophetic music
critic Corno di Bassetto, writing in 1889 about his future alter
ego, G. B. S.: "Mr. Gilbert's paradoxical wit, astonishing to the
ordinary Englishman, is nothing to me. Nature has cursed me
with a facility for the same trick; and I could paradox Mr.
Gilbert's head off were I not convinced that such trifling is
morally unjustifiable."

The old joke is a statement of fact: Shaw's prefaces *are* better than his plays. His journalism—especially on music—is best
of all, the bright if somewhat metallic efflorescence of a mind
that was most genial and active when it wasn't persuaded that it
had a stage to conquer and immortal things to say. As the
world grew less and less likely to accept the advice he so abun-
dantly offered, Shaw—who had the asceticism of the painlessly
self-deprived, and really didn't understand why people ate
meat, drank alcoholic beverages, and fornicated at haphazard—
grew more and more vindictively certain of its damnation.
Shaw's latter years are disagreeable to contemplate not because
like Swift he "expired a driveller and a show," or feared death
like Voltaire, but because the spirit of Ruskin, William Morris,
Sidney Webb—the spirit of Shaw's youthful awakening and his
true faith—had turned out not to be capable of fulfilling itself;
not in fact, after 1918, to be capable of working at all. It was
the breath in the toy balloons of Shaw's plays; it was also the
wind in the sails of Shaw's polemical writing. When it died,
Shaw died with it, the millionaire socialist reduced to applaud-
ing the butcheries of a Stalin, the superannuated ghost making
faces at itself in the mirror of history.

1964

HEMINGWAY

A *Moveable Feast* is the legacy we could hardly have dared hoped for. Yet in the Preface, at the very outset, the dead author speaks with the voice to which, during the last three decades of his life, he coercively accustomed us:

> For reasons sufficient to the writer, many places, people, observations and impressions have been left out of this book. Some were secrets and some were known by everyone and everyone has written about them and will doubtless write more.

That stiff metronomic swagger, and the pretense of large, efficiently withheld implications, together make up Hemingway's public manner, the prose style and life style that dominate his last thirty years, the unsubtle virus of his literary influence, the old impostor's parody of the young writer whose Paris apprenticeship this book belatedly celebrates, and whose voice it so sadly recollects.

The distinction between the young man in Paris and Papa on safari must be made against some resistance, since even the most sensible of Hemingway's critics assume a qualitative continuity in his work. They will grant an occasional failure—*Across the River and into the Trees* seems to have appalled everybody except Carlos Baker—but they anticipate, and are rewarded by, triumphant recoveries. So *The Old Man and the Sea,* that reduction to mushy parable of the Hemingway fish-and-game know-how, is discussed by Philip Young as if it were one of Beethoven's last quartets; and Young is almost equally impressed by numerous other exercises in the musclebound public manner. Young's book is nevertheless the best on Hemingway, because its reading of the Nick Adams stories—of the first and vintage Hemingway—makes sense of the stories, and nonsense of the dumb-ox label affixed to their hero by critics from Wyndham Lewis to D. S. Savage: "His typical central character, his 'I,' " writes the latter, "may be described generally as a bare consciousness stripped to the human minimum, impassively recording the objective data of experience"; Hemingway's fiction constitutes "a special form of that which might be termed the *proletarianization* of literature: the adaptation of the technical artistic conscience to the subaverage human consciousness."

The thesis of Young's book proposes, on the other hand, that critics like Savage are describing, if anybody at all in Hemingway's fiction, not Nick Adams, "the Hemingway hero" (the author's own persona and very nearly his autobiographical self), but a possible standard for Nick to aim at, "the code hero," the bullfighter or prizefighter or big-game hunter, who teaches Nick (or Hemingway) "to try to live by a code," though "the lessons" are not always "of the sort the hero can immediately master." Nick himself, neither a dumb ox nor a deadpan reporter, nor a man so skilled in his vocation as to perform it with the unreflective ease that Nick envies and would like to emulate, is

> . . . sensitive, masculine, impressionable, humorless, honest, and out-of-doors—a boy then a man who had come up against violence and evil and been wounded by them. The manhood he had attained was thus complicated and insecure, but he was learning a code with which he might maneuver, though crippled, and he was practicing the rites which for him might exorcise the terrors born of the events that crippled him.

The stories about him must be read not separately but collectively, as a sort of mosaic-novel, an unexplained segment here and another very much elsewhere in time and place though always about the same life, scattered pieces only ultimately converging into the full picture; and their common subject is the traumatic event (or events) that Nick passes through, re-lives in sickness and nightmare, tries to forget or put out of mind, never quite escapes from or grows beyond: the stories are, in Young's phrase, "bound tight about a core of shock."

The old writer of *A Moveable Feast* might agree, as he re-calls an afternoon that the young writer spent with Gertrude Stein. The redoubtable lady, having just made a practical ob-jection to the *"inaccrochable"*—as of a painting too indecent to be hung—language of a story of his (she herself wished and expected to be published in the *Atlantic Monthly*), proceeded to a somewhat qualified defense of homosexuality:

> Miss Stein thought that I was too uneducated about sex and I must admit that I had certain prejudices against homosexuality since I knew its more primitive aspects. I knew it was why you carried a knife and would use it when you were in the company of tramps when you were a boy in the days when wolves was not a slang term for men obsessed by the pursuit of women. I knew many *inaccrochable* terms and phrases from Kansas City days and the mores of different parts of that city, Chicago and the lake boats. Under questioning I tried to tell Miss Stein that when you were a boy and moved in the company of men, you had to be prepared to kill a man, know how to do it and really know that you would do it in order not to be interfered with. That term was *accrochable*. If you knew you would kill, other people sensed it very quickly and you were let alone; but there were certain situations you could not allow yourself to be forced into or trapped into. I could have expressed myself more vividly by using an *inaccrochable* phrase that wolves used on the lake boats, "Oh gash may be fine but one eye for mine." But I was always careful of my language with Miss Stein even when true phrases might have clarified or better expressed a prejudice.

The old writer is at last trying to come at the truth of his experience directly, not, as the young one did, obliquely and implicitly, not evading it by bluster and tricks as Life Maga-zine's champion bull-thrower learned to do. For the pathos of Hemingway's reputation is that he got it years after his best work had been done, and that he felt obliged to sustain it by accepting and coarsening the public rôle of the true-born American writer: tough, terse, athletic, unliterary (this omnivorous man of letters who read every book he could lay his hands on), "a bare consciousness stripped to the human minimum, impassively recording the objective data of experience."

The reputation had its lethal effect on criticism, which either attacked the public image as if it were all there was of Hemingway, or praised virtually all of Hemingway as if the public image were quite unrelated to the work. Even Young's book, good as it is on the Nick stories, founders on the public image, since Young's thesis doesn't help him to distinguish between the early master and the old impostor. The real thing ("Big Two-Hearted River," for instance, Young's examination of which is a model of intelligent analysis in support of a critical position) gets confused with so brassy a counterfeit as "The Short Happy Life of Francis Macomber." It is bad enough that "Macomber" exhibits Hemingway's crudest sketches of his code hero and his bitch-heroine; but worse that the code has been simplified into imbecile bravado: if a man runs away from a charging lion he is a coward, and if he stands to face it he has confirmed his manhood. Nick Adams—the boy in "The Doctor and the Doctor's Wife," the youth in "The Battler," the man in "Big Two-Hearted River"—inhabits a world in which the problem of choice, unlike Macomber's, is unresolvable by any single action, and more difficult than lions.

The style of the Nick stories—however it may have launched itself with tips from newspaper reporting, Sherwood Anderson, Miss Stein—is as original and personal an invention as anything in literature; but it is also one of the narrowest in range, and among the least usefully imitable. Just as Lawrence speaks of "shedding one's sicknesses in books," so Hemingway speaks of writing as the writer's own therapy: "If he wrote it he could get rid of it. He had gotten rid of many things by writing them." Still, Lawrence's "sicknesses" have a breadth of curiosity, an impetus into the outer world, an intimate and hereditary connection with literary tradition, that ventilate and generalize the great resourceful style that bears them. The sickness that Hemingway tries to get rid of has no such outward impulse, it seeks only to withdraw from any further contact and damage; and the style it generates is an opaque thin membrane against which it obscurely presses and reluctantly defines itself without quite breaking through into a void of hysteria (except now and then, as in "A Way You'll Never Be" and, perhaps, "Homage to Switzerland"). Some of the most remarkable effects of this barely managed control occur in extended passages of dialogue:

"Come on back in the shade," he said. "You mustn't feel that way."

"I don't feel any way," the girl said. "I just know things."

"I don't want you to do anything that you don't want to do—"

"Nor that isn't good for me," she said. "I know. Could we have another beer?"

"All right. But you've got to realize—"

"I realize," the girl said. "Can't we maybe stop talking?"

They sat down at the table and the girl looked across at the hills on the dry side of the valley and the man looked at her and at the table.

"You've got to realize," he said, "that I don't want you to do it if you don't want to. I'm perfectly willing to go through with it if it means anything to you."

"Doesn't it mean anything to you? We could get along."

"Of course it does. But I don't want anybody but you. I don't want any one else. And I know it's perfectly simple."

"Yes, you know it's perfectly simple."

"It's all right for you to say that, but I do know it."

"Would you do something for me now?"

"I'd do anything for you."

"Would you please please please please please please please stop talking?"

He did not say anything but looked at the bags against the wall of the station. There were labels on them from all the hotels where they had spent nights.

"But I don't want you to," he said, "I don't care anything about it."

"I'll scream," the girl said.

The woman came out through the curtains with two glasses of beer and put them down on the damp felt pads. "The train comes in five minutes," she said.

"What did she say?" asked the girl.

"That the train is coming in five minutes."
The girl smiled brightly at the woman, to thank her.

Later writers, including Hemingway, radically mistook the vibrations of such dialogue (from "Hills Like White Elephants") and fabricated a whole subliterature of stylized detectives, criminals, deep-sea fishermen and smugglers, virtuous and easy-virtue ladies, all of whom lavishly and complacently protected the reader from polysyllables and complex sentences. But the Nick stories, and such related ones as "Hills Like White Elephants" (the unnamed young man is really Nick, and has Nick's troubles), are in fact waking nightmares: the early Hemingway style is the indispensable discipline that keeps them from erupting into psychosis; it could scarcely be more inappropriate, except as parody, to the expression of an assured and knowledgeable reticence.

Hemingway did not, at any rate, maintain the early style and its preoccupation. Soon he had less to say about Nick and more about the code hero, in such stories as "Fifty Grand" and "The Undefeated," more about the code itself in all the novels: if the Nick stories are classifiable as the nightmare stories, the second group might be designated the know-how stories. In even the best of these the style appears more mannered and sententious, less continuous with its material. The preoccupation with merely keeping sane gives way to a shallower and less convincing preoccupation with physical competences, especially when there is the flavor of death in them: expertness in a dangerous athletic vocation signifies moral delicacy or at least intense moral awareness, as if to court death in a ceremony of skill (like the bullfighter, or the big-game hunter) is finally to live well. In even the better novels—*The Sun Also Rises* and *For Whom the Bell Tolls*—the effort to refract the external world through the style which had so successfully subjectivized and rejected it produces the sense of strain and affectation that is, in the public mind, the Hemingway style, "impassively recording the objective data of experience." The irreducible sickness is still there, but the novels, when they consider it at all, grotesquely simplify it (as with Jake Barnes) or pretend that it will yield to vocational or political or erotic affirmations. Hemingway's novel-heroines are particularly offensive because they sound like the girl in "Hills Like White Elephants" compelled to read affectionate lines she doesn't believe to a man pretending he isn't Nick: the dialogue between the lovers in *A Farewell to Arms* is deprivation itself, displayed in the frozen attitudes of a period coyness; this novel in which Nick is to be saved by passion precipitates him into the most puerile of daydreams. The last step, which Hemingway takes in stories like "Macomber" and "The Snows of Kilimanjaro" as well as in the late novels (except *For Whom the Bell Tolls*), is self-parody: the old impostor betrays the youthful master by attaching their name to parodies of the code, parodies of the style, emetic effusions of self-pity (as in "Kilimanjaro"), parodies of masculinity and pride.

A Moveable Feast makes another beginning. Hemingway's unexorcised sense of hurt and injury continues to cramp and trouble the all too recognizable style but *A Moveable Feast* is an unexpected book by a not yet secure old master, it shoots for the moon and accomplishes moments of pride, amusement, melancholy, and—most unexpectedly—love. It has fine wry vignettes: the encounters with Miss Stein, and their terrible climax in the overheard conversation between her and her "friend"; the comic and catty description of Pound's efforts to raise money from penniless writers (like young Hemingway) so that Eliot could leave his job at the bank and devote all his time to writing; the evening with the painter Pascin and his girls:

"Chez Viking," the dark girl said.

"Me too," her sister urged.

"All right," Pascin agreed. "Good night, *jeune homme*. Sleep well."

"You too."

"They keep me awake," he said. "I never sleep."

"Sleep tonight."

"After Chez Les Vikings?" He grinned with his hat on the back of his head. He looked more like a Broadway character of the Nineties than the lovely painter that he was, and afterwards, when he had hanged himself, I liked to remember him as he was that night at the Dôme. They say the seeds of what we will do are in all of us, but it always seemed to me that in those who make jokes in life the seeds are covered with better soil and with a higher grade of manure.

The best episode is Hemingway's account of Scott Fitzgerald. Gleaming with malice no doubt as well with moment-by-moment revelations of its subject (the memorable scenes in literary history will certainly include the one in which Hemingway reassures Fitzgerald about the adequacy of his sexual equipment), it is much closer to an absolute statement of the case than what Fitzgerald himself tried to write in *Tender Is the Night*, the minor tragedy of the weak, gifted man destroyed by a ferociously competitive wife:

> Zelda had hawk's eyes and a thin mouth and deep-south manners and accent. Watching her face you could see her mind leave the table and go to the night's party and return with her eyes blank as a cat's and then pleased, and the pleasure would show along the thin line of her lips and then be gone. Scott was being the good cheerful host and Zelda looked at him and she smiled happily with her eyes and her mouth too as he drank the wine. I learned to know that smile very well. It meant she knew Scott would not be able to write.

—a wife whose irreversible victory over her husband is to go mad:

> That night there was a party to welcome us at the Casino, just a small party, the MacLeishes, the Murphys, the Fitzgeralds and we who were living at the villa. No one drank anything stronger than champagne and it was very gay and obviously a splendid place to write. There was going to be everything that a man needed to write except to be alone.
>
> Zelda was very beautiful and was tanned a lovely gold color and her hair was a beautiful dark gold and she was very friendly. Her hawk's eyes were clear and calm. I knew everything was all right and was going to turn out well in the end when she leaned forward and said to me, telling me her great secret, "Ernest, don't you think Al Jolson is greater than Jesus?"
>
> Nobody thought anything of it at the time. It was only Zelda's secret that she shared with me, as a hawk might share something with a man. But hawks do not share. Scott did not write anything any more that was good until after he knew that she was insane.

Much has been said about the cruelty of Hemingway's portrait of Ford Madox Ford. But Hemingway had perfected his hatreds too (his treatment of Wyndham Lewis makes his attitude toward Ford appear almost kindly); and the dialogue he records—though it may well have been that Ford was putting him on with a poker-faced travesty of the English gentleman—is a very funny epiphany of transatlantic relations:

"Was Henry James a gentleman?"
"Very nearly."
"Are you a gentleman?"
"Naturally. I have held His Majesty's commission."
"It's very complicated," I said. "Am I a gentleman?"
"Absolutely not," Ford said.
"Then why are you drinking with me?"
"I'm drinking with you as a promising young writer. As a fellow writer in fact."
"Good of you," I said.
"You might be considered a gentleman in Italy," Ford said magnanimously.

That concluding adverb, which none of the previous Hemingways would have indulged, is a sign of the fresh start, in which adverbs and metaphors are allowed to amplify and relax the texture of the prose:

"I think it would be wonderful, Tatie," my wife said. She had a gently modeled face and her eyes and her smile lighted up at decisions as though they were rich presents.

For Hemingway at the very end took the risk of attempting his authentic love story. We will never know just what Nick or Hemingway was suffering from, or whether it was many things, or whether all these sufficient things screen off the genuine unfaceable article: his puritanical home, his ambitious and disappointed mother, his war wounds, his father's suicide.

A Moveable Feast suggests something besides: a broken heart. The heroine—Hemingway's only live and persuasive heroine—of *A Moveable Feast* is the first Mrs. Hemingway. The book is in praise of her and of what he lost when he let her go, since losing her he gave up not only her love and his but his youth and his friends and Paris, everything that encouraged him to write the early stories and that he suppressed in order to emerge as the formidable and nerveless public figure:

> When you have two people who love each other, are happy and gay and really good work is being done by one or both of them, people are drawn to them as surely as migrating birds are drawn at night to a powerful beacon. If the two people were as solidly constructed as the beacon there would be little damage except to the birds. Those who attract people by their happiness and their performance are usually inexperienced. They do not know how not to be overrun and how to go away. They do not always learn about the good, the attractive, the charming, the soon-beloved, the generous, the understanding rich who have no bad qualities and who give each day the quality of a festival and who, when they have passed and taken the nourishment they needed, leave everything deader than the roots of any grass Attila's horses' hooves have ever scoured.

The vision of youth in an unspoiled spring is the vision that the old writer would give most, and heartbreakingly tries hardest, to evoke:

> When I saw my wife again standing by the tracks as the train came in by the piled logs at the station, I wished I had died before I loved anyone but her. She was smiling, the sun on her lovely face tanned by the snow and sun, beautifully built, her hair red gold in the sun, grown out all winter awkwardly and beautifully, and Mr. Bumby standing with her, blond and chunky and with winter cheeks looking like a good Vorarlberg boy.
>
> "Oh Tatie," she said, when I was holding her in my arms, "you're back and you made such a fine successful trip. I love you and we've missed you so."
>
> I loved her and I loved no one else and we had a lovely magic time while we were alone. I worked well and we made great trips, and I thought we were invulnerable again, and it wasn't until we were out of the mountains in late spring, and back in Paris that the other thing started again.

There are no charging lions or leaping marlin in *A Moveable Feast*, or wars or rumors of wars. That Hemingway could have resolved to risk such a candor of private regret and longing against the grain of his so carefully cultivated reputation, less then a year before his death, is the proof of the strength he could still muster, and the most touching reminder of the splendid young writer he was trying to recall. The book is new, and stands with the best of his early stories.

1964, 1970

III. Critical Theory

THE TWO VOICES OF MR. ELIOT

"These last thirty years have been, I think, a brilliant period in literary criticism in both England and America. It may even come to seem, in retrospect, too brilliant. Who knows?" So Mr. Eliot, characteristically giving with one hand what he takes back with the other, concludes his latest American lecture;* even though he won't tell us outright, *he* knows how brilliant is too brilliant; and we are invited to recall, wryly, that it was our sixty-year-old smiling public man who, forty years ago, began to provide the critical oeuvre and the poetic practice without which neither the brilliance nor the very fact of this efficient age of criticism is conceivable.

There is no use ignoring the confusion between Eliot the poet-critic—great and legitimate successor to Dryden, Johnson, and Coleridge—and Eliot the Dean of English Letters. The confusion exists; it was created by Eliot himself in his earliest published criticism; the portentous and slippery authority of what Eliot himself has called his *"Times-Literary-Supplement-leading-article manner"* † obscured, in 1919, the revolutionary

---

* "The Frontiers of Criticism," in *On Poetry and Poets*, Farrar, Straus and Cudahy.
† "A Note on *Monstre Gai*," *The Hudson Review*, VII, Winter 1955, p. 526.

originality of "Tradition and the Individual Talent" as, in 1956, it frock-coated the platform cuteness of "The Frontiers of Criticism," in which Grandfather Eliot takes his licks at the earnest academic critics who regard themselves, with some justice, as his only true heirs. Dylan Thomas once remarked to a *New York Times* book reviewer that when Eliot wrote prose it was good honest prose with no poetic nonsense about it. Pound, having more faith in the good sense of poetry, has less in the evasions of Eliot's diaconal prose, which finally provoked a Poundian snort: "Grapes in a barrel of sawdust!" The proportion of sawdust to grapes has always been a matter of concern for the serious reader of Eliot's criticism.

What, for instance, is one to make of the *conclusion* to "The Three Voices of Poetry"?

> For the work of a great poetic dramatist, like Shakespeare, constitutes a world. Each character speaks for himself, but no other poet could have found those words for him to speak. If you seek for Shakespeare, you will find him only in the characters he created; for the one thing in common between the characters is that no one but Shakespeare could have created any of them. The world of a great poetic dramatist is a world in which the creator is everywhere present, and everywhere hidden.

It is true that "The Three Voices of Poetry," and most of the other pieces in Eliot's new volume, were first delivered as lectures, and some allowance may be made for the diffuseness solicited by a public occasion; but the quality of hollowly amplified classroom platitude in this fluent peroration—Dr. Frank Baxter bringing Shakespeare to the TV audience on a rainy Sunday afternoon—can hardly be attributed to anything less grave than a total lapse of intelligent attention from the subject.

The subject may in fact provide some of the explanation. Until his own dramatic experiments, Eliot was never much interested in poetic drama. His series of essays on the Elizabethan and Jacobean dramatists apart from Shakespeare were superb closet studies by an essentially lyric sensibility, selections and appreciations of impressive verse extracts rather than attempts to elucidate the relations between verse and dramatic action.

This bias Yvor Winters has harshly characterized as "Mr. Eliot's sentimental and semi-critical interest" in the Elizabethan and Jacobean dramatists, and it plays a part in Eliot's over-rating of them as dramatists. In two essays in the new volume, however, two of the latest—"Poetry and Drama" and "The Three Voices of Poetry"—Eliot explicitly undertakes to vindicate, or at least to describe, his own plays according to a more comprehensive theory of poetic drama; only the theory is about as thin as the practice ("Lavinia, would you kindly pass the toast?"), and will scarcely strike anyone as making up what was lacking in his earlier essays on the drama. The theory would be interesting if it could be thought of as having issued in first-rate drama; but Eliot's account of his procedures in working out the action of *The Cocktail Party* does not help, reminding us as it does of the air of glacial contrivance in the play itself. The theory might also be interesting if it seemed to enlarge our understanding of poetic drama as a genre; but in its particulars—that the audience must cease to be conscious of the medium, that prose is as artificial as verse, that the drama-tist must sympathize with all of his characters in order to cre-ate them, that the two pitfalls of the "poetic dramatist" are the assignment of poetic lines to inappropriate characters and the failure to keep the plot moving, that as spectators of poetic drama we ought not to be "transported" into "an imaginary world totally unlike" our own, but "on the contrary, our own sordid, dreary daily world" ought to be "suddenly illuminated and transfigured"—in these particulars, the theory seems to be directed neither at the working playwright nor at the intel-ligent spectator, and therefore at nobody except the Dean of Letters' stadium-sized audiences eager for the illusion of easy understanding.

This level of self-protective tranquil banality is uncharacter-istic; but the Dean speaks out plainly enough in several of the other essays. "Virgil and the Christian World" is an official, rather perfunctory tribute to Virgil's *anima naturaliter Christi-ana;* "Goethe as Sage" occupies itself mainly with disavowing Eliot's earlier aspersions on Goethe by setting up an em-barrassingly unexamined quality called wisdom, which Goethe is thereupon presumed to possess and to exemplify; the

protracted blurb on Kipling stumbles from one astonishing
perversity of undocumented judgment to the next—Kipling's
work "comes to show a unity of a very complicated kind";
"the question whether Kipling was a poet is not unrelated to
the question whether Dryden was a poet"; "Kipling's position"
among "great verse writers" is "not only high, but unique."

"The Social Function of Poetry" differs in more than the
forlorn dignity of its intention. Eliot, in the middle of World
War II, is trying to establish, from his not yet consolidated
position as a latter-day Arnold, the social importance of the
poet in a society which has stopped listening ("When a civilization is healthy," Eliot sadly remarks, "a poet speaks to all").
The essay has a genuine patriotic ring, and makes perhaps the
best case that can be made for the intimate relations between the
poet as live sensibility and the language as, even in our time, he
can modify it for the people who use it daily and will never hear
of him; but the tone is justifiably elegiac. We have come a long
way since Arnold.

How much has reputation—or the responsibility of reputation—altered Eliot's attitude toward the critic's job? In the
'twenties, the great decade of his criticism (as well as of his
poetry), he wrote about the poets and the critical issues that
engaged him immediately in his job of practicing poet. In the
'thirties, he was beginning to write about figures and issues
whose interest for him was enjoined by the social responsibility
of his growing reputation, which Eliot may regard—with good
reason—as the last international reputation available to any
poet through the powerful representativeness of his poetry. In
the 'forties and 'fifties, the process is, with a few gratifying
exceptions, virtually complete: the poet is lost in the public
man, and that always disquieting carapace of the Eliotic prose
style has thickened into a means of shutting out fresh perception. The tone is opaquely official; disingenousness, special
pleading, waspish authoritativeness, elaborate confessions of
humility—all of them, in the earlier Eliot, rhetorical devices in
the strategy of maneuvering the reluctant reader into a closer
look at the object—have become themselves the chief visible
objects; almost nothing serious remains beyond what can be

assimilated into the social obligations of the public man on the platform.

The disingenuousness in "What Is a Classic?" is of special interest. Certainly, Eliot's particular aim of establishing Virgil as the classic of the Western world is unexceptionable, and successful on its own terms—though once the terms have been set, one may wonder whether one is arriving at a poet or at a convenient plug in the funnel of literary history. Virgil is "a classic in all senses": "that is not to assert," Eliot adds with uneasy asperity, "that he is the greatest poet who ever wrote—such an assertion about any poet seems to me meaningless" (though Eliot has made assertions about Shakespeare and Dante, on various occasions, that come very near this sort of meaninglessness). A classic poet appears at a time of maturity: maturity of civilization, of language, of literature, of manners; at a time when society has achieved a moment of order and stability. His literature has a history behind it, and his language has developed into a common style. He has a comprehensiveness of outlook and a breadth of appeal, he has an awareness of history; in him "the whole genius of the people is represented"; "when a great poet is also a great classic poet, he exhausts the language of his time." Since Virgil is the complete spokesman of the destiny of Rome, and since Rome is at the center of European civilization, Virgil is irremovably the European classic. So we are led to the bottom of the funnel, dimly perceiving that Eliot's criteria narrow us down, with an inevitability matched only by their aesthetic irrelevance, to the one poet for whom they are, it is almost fair to say, retroactively invented: the criteria are, in any case, primarily historical, and Eliot would have a better right to them if he did not seem to regard our dreary acquiescence in an historical fact as acceptance of an aesthetic fact.

By the time the millstones of Eliot's definition have ground down everything between them, we are not likely to be appeased by the one example of Virgil's "maturity" that Eliot allows us—the maturity of "manners" in the underworld encounter between Dido and Aeneas; the poet has come to appear such an impersonal and dogged mouthpiece of history and prophecy that we are ready to give up the classics, now we know what they are. But the disingenuousness goes deeper; or it may come to appear less as disingenuousness than as Eliot's indifference to sustained reasoning, an indifference that has tended to be disguised by the *look* of reasoning on the impassive surface of his style and by the insights that (less and less frequently) break the surface. Arguing hard for Virgil, Eliot must push aside Dante, at least to a less central position: "in the Divine Comedy, if anywhere, we find the classic in a *modern* [italics clearly implied] European language"; and he must dispose altogether of Chaucer, who, though he has many classic qualities, "cannot be regarded in my sense as a classic of English literature," because, though with him we come close to the common style of Virgil and Dante, "Chaucer is using a different, from our point of view a cruder, speech."

Perhaps from Eliot's momentarily very limited point of view cruder; the statement is so question-begging—is Dante's speech, from the twentieth-century Italian's point of view, comparatively crude?—that one almost prefers to dismiss it as Eliot's failure to remember anything of Chaucer beyond the summaries of the literary histories. Eliot's criteria may, after all, be pertinent: one might propose that Chaucer reflects as much maturity of civilization, of language, of literature, of manners as Virgil (compare Troilus and Criseyde with Dido and Aeneas and see how frigid and inflexible, in the comparison, Virgil is), that he has as much command of a common style, as comprehensive an outlook and as broad an appeal, as thorough an awareness of history as any other poet at all; that he is perhaps more representative of "the whole genius of the people" than any other poet in the world; that Chaucer is the culmination of the High Middle Ages in England as Dante is in Italy; that Dante as innovator made the choice of *his* vernacular over the formal and literary Latin as Chaucer made the choice of his over the courtly and literary French of the Plantagenets; that Chaucer as European traditionalist learned from his courtly French and Italian predecessors and contemporaries as Dante from the courtly Provençals; that Chaucer—like Dante, and like every other supreme poet in a language—has no successors, for the classic in a super-Eliotic sense is indeed the poet who has realized all the potentialities of the language, and the language must change—as it had changed by Shakespeare's time—before there can be another. Moreover, this Chaucer is alive, while the Virgil of Eliot's special plea is monumentally dead.

What remains, in the new volume, is much—five essays (though only two of these were written after 1940)—that belongs to the great successor to Dryden, Johnson, and Coleridge. Eliot's tribute to Yeats, "the poet of middle age," is brief and just, the model of a concise memorial statement (and particularly impressive in its rightness considering Eliot's lack of sympathy for the man Yeats). The piece of Byron not only selects and sets in order, with Johnsonian authoritativeness and conviction, the proper commonplaces about Byron, but offers that sort of casual insight which was once the personal stamp of an Eliot essay:

> I cannot think of any other poet of his distinction who might so easily have been an accomplished foreigner writing English. The ordinary person talks English, but only a few people in every generation can write it; and upon this undeliberate collaboration between a great many people talking a living language and a very few people writing it, the continuance and maintenance of a language depends. Just as an artisan who can talk English beautifully while about his work or in a public bar, may compose a letter painfully written in a dead language bearing some resemblance to a newspaper leader, and decorated with words like "maelstrom" and "pandemonium": so does Byron write a dead or dying language.

There are, finally, the essay on Dr. Johnson and the two great essays on Milton.

The essays on Milton have been so often discussed, and so often misrepresented, that it might be adequate merely to note the more patent misrepresentations. In the first place, "Milton I" is not a denigration of Milton but an appraisal of his influence ("although his work realizes superbly one important element in poetry, he may still be considered as having done damage to the English language from which it has not wholly recovered"), and an attempt to make as explicit as possible the distinction—which most readers have felt, and many have suppressed in the interest of temporary enthusiasm or of obeisance to the literary histories—between Milton on the one hand and, on the other, Homer and Dante and Shakespeare, in whose company he is often (as by Arnold) unhesitatingly placed.

In the second place, "Milton II" is not a recantation of "Milton I" but rather a very deliberate footnote. It takes, as Eliot concedes, two to make an influence, and Milton can hardly be held accountable for being an "injudicious choice of a model." This time, besides, Eliot is careful to document his sense of Milton's greatness: "it is his ability to give a perfect and unique pattern to every paragraph, such that the full beauty of the line is found in its context, and his ability to work in larger musical units than any other poet—that is to me the most conclusive evidence of Milton's supreme mastery"; and he notes "the peculiar feeling, almost a physical sensation of a breathless leap, communicated by Milton's long periods, and by his alone."

Nevertheless, Milton is "as a poet . . . the greatest of all eccentrics"; "his style is not a *classic* style, in that it is not the elevation of a *common* style, by the final touch of genius, to greatness. It is, from the foundation, and in every particular, a personal style, not based upon common speech, or common prose, or direct communication of meaning. . . . There is no cliché, no poetic diction in the derogatory sense, but a perpetual sequence of original acts of lawlessness." Not that Eliot is merely exalting the common style, with its implications of directness and maturity, at the expense of others, except as a necessary phase in one of the life-cycles of the language: "verse should have the virtues of prose, . . . diction should become assimilated to cultivated contemporary speech, before aspiring to the elevation of poetry." And he concludes that by the time of his second essay "poets are sufficiently liberated from Milton's reputation"—through the efforts, of course, of Pound, Leavis, and Eliot himself—"to approach the study of his work without danger, and with profit to their poetry and to the English language." The Milton scholars are still huffing at Eliot on Milton, but the points he makes remain uncontroverted.

In "Johnson as Critic and Poet" Eliot is not, for a change, concerned to defend or to rectify; he is assessing a major figure of the past in the spirit of Johnson himself, with the authority conferred upon him by his age's acknowledgment of his eminence. Eliot observes that if Johnson's satire, *London*, fails because Johnson is a moralist without compromise and lacks "a certain divine levity," *The Vanity of Human Wishes* succeeds because the meditative poet in Johnson had for once found a subject equal and appropriate to his energies, and the moralist had "found a perfect theme . . . an idea which the reader will not for a moment question"; and he goes on to consider what he denotes as the specialization, rather than the defect, of poetic sensibility that both enabled Johnson to write one of the last great Augustan poems and unfitted him to judge the verse of such un-Augustan sensibilities as Donne and Milton:

> What is lacking is an historical sense which was not yet due to appear. . . . If the eighteenth century had admired the poetry of earlier times in the way in which we can admire it . . . there would have been no eighteenth century as we know it. That age would not have had the conviction necessary for perfecting the kinds of poetry it did perfect.

The great accomplishment of Johnson's age was the common style: "When standards for a common style exist, the author who would achieve originality is compelled to attend to the finer shades of distinction," and only thus to "stir the emotions of the intelligent and judicious." Johnson's criticism—its limitations, but most particularly its weighty and instructive virtues—bases itself on Johnson's respect for the emotions of the intelligent and judicious, his respect, that is, for the aesthetic canons of an age whose most illustrious and representative critic and poet he himself was; ultimately, it bases itself on his accepted responsibility, in so measured and comprehensive a critical summation as *The Lives of the Poets*, for the preservation of the language and of the specific humane perceptions it embodies and sustains.

At his best, when he wishes or when the subject enforces the operation of his unique powers, Eliot too reminds us of this responsibility of the poet and the critic; and in the totality of his critical labors, despite his more and more frequent gratuitous complicities with an audience he has learned to entertain too well, he reminds us that the only work comparable to *The Lives of the Poets*, in scope, in discrimination, in the authority of deserved eminence, is that library of criticism of which he has now given us a second volume.

1957

CHARACTER AND EVENT IN FICTION

Here is a definition, from Webster's New Collegiate Dictionary, of the word "fiction": "1. A feigning or imagining; as, by a *fiction* of the mind. 2. That which is feigned or imagined; esp., a feigned or invented story. 3. Fictitious literature; specif., novels. 4. *Law.* An assumption of a possible thing as a fact irrespective of the question of its truth."

Or we may begin by considering what fiction is not. It is not, for instance, biography, which in its legitimate procedures we can safely say has nothing to do with feigning or imagining, or with the assumption of possible things as facts irrespective of the question of their truth. When somebody exclaims, looking up starry-eyed from a book on the life of somebody else, "It reads just like a novel!" his enthusiasm is the index of a hardened incapacity to take either mode seriously. The first criterion of biography is truth, and at the first sign of untruth —whether its cause seems to be the biographer's dishonesty, or his insistence upon fitting things in with Procrustean neatness ("just like a novel") or his plain ineptitude at recognizing and arranging facts—at that sign the document before us ceases to be biography.

Moreover, what a man actually said and did—so seldom verifiable by the reader, so perishable in the oblivions of history—

has a special preciousness that, ready as we are to concede everything to fiction, we tend to undervalue. The biographer or historian who lies, to the extent to which he lies casts doubt on the possibility of ever retrieving the sense of how it was to be alive—how life uniquely and quotidianly went—in any of the innumerable personal and communal pasts of mankind. Parson Weems invented an anecdote about a future General and President who said, "I cannot tell a lie"; and when the American boy discovered that the anecdote was itself a lie, he grew up to be the elder Henry Ford, who said, inventing modern America, "History is bunk."

What about the great biographies, however—those that we consider, in their scope and proportions and justness of illustrative detail, not only true annals of a life and time but works of art? How nearly is their greatness related to their truth? Suppose a scholar were to discover and demonstrate that Boswell's Dr. Johnson never existed, that his books were written by a committee consisting of Sir Joshua Reynolds, Edmund Burke, and Oliver Goldsmith, and that Boswell's biography is a stupendous hoax of the sort that a number of literary amateurs think they have exploded regarding the Stratford actor William Shakespeare. Or even that, though Dr. Johnson did live and was quite capable of such actions and assertions as Boswell attributed to him, Boswell's Dr. Johnson is in fact the ingenious and plausible hallucination of an uncannily imitative and spectacularly unscrupulous young coxcomb (as in any case Boswell was) who chose to lie his way to immortality. Certainly, *The Life of Johnson* would become a literary curiosity, neither truth nor fiction, rather like Macaulay's History; its interest for us would be inward toward the motives and aberrations of the author, not outward toward the actions and assertions that would—if the account were truthful—throw generous light upon the man and the time they pretend to represent.

Nor do we need to invent such a case. Ford Madox Ford was one of the most intelligent and gifted men of letters during the past century: he was a great editor, a sympathetic friend to most of the first-rate poets and novelists of his time, and a distinguished and prolific writer on a variety of subjects in a variety of genres. His numerous autobiographical pieces include fascinating and characteristic anecdotes about writers he did in point of fact know well: James, Conrad, Lawrence, Pound, and many others. Only, it is clear—from much other evidence and testimony—that probably most and possibly all of the anecdotes he tells are false, that at almost every moment he is arousing and baffling our expectation of truth, that not merely what he reports James or Lawrence to have said and done on particular occasions, but the alleged occasions themselves, are the product of his fertile and imaginative incapacity to recall and represent anything that actually happened. (Dr. Johnson—as recorded by Boswell!—has a definitive opinion on this sort of incapacity. "Talking of an acquaintance of ours, whose narratives, which abounded in curious and interesting topics, were unhappily found to be very fabulous; I mentioned Lord Mansfield's having said to me, 'Suppose we believe one *half* of what he tells.' JOHNSON. 'Ay; but we don't know *which* half to believe. By his lying we lose not only our reverence for him, but all comfort in his conversation.' BOSWELL. 'May we not take it as amusing fiction?' JOHNSON. 'Sir, the misfortune is, that you will insensibly believe as much of it as you incline to believe.' " Which is exactly what happens with fanciers of James or Conrad or Lawrence or Pound, who skim through Ford's pages looking for anecdotes they incline to believe.) Now it is noteworthy that, though Ford was also a novelist, this incapacity to tell the truth did not conversely amount to a talent for fiction; quite the contrary: the characters and events in his carefully constructed and beautifully written novels seem at length, not distinct substantial creations, but muffled cries for help, troubled prefigurings of some truth he is trying to tell only about himself. The compulsion to lie derives, obviously enough, from an obsession with unpalatable truth; and, though both phenomena may properly engage the student of literary pathology, neither is related to the talent for biography or the talent for fiction.

Fiction is not truth; nor is it falsehood; nor is the talent for fiction a talent, as Plato suggested, for lying. "It is not the function of the poet," says Aristotle (and the word "poet" we may replace for our purpose, as Aristotle's description warrants, by the cumbersome but more general term "writer of

fiction")—"It is not the function of the poet to relate what has
happened, but what may happen . . . according to the law of
probability or necessity. The poet and the historian differ not
by writing in verse or in prose. . . . The true difference is
that the latter relates what has happened, the former what may
happen. Poetry, therefore, is a more philosophical and a higher
thing than history: for poetry tends to express the universal,
history the particular." And Aristotle is plainly staking off the
province of what since his time has come to require a more
inclusive name than "poetry" when he remarks that "the poet
or 'maker' should be the maker of plots rather than of verses;
since he is a poet because he imitates, and what he imitates are
actions. And even if he chances to take an historical subject, he
is none the less a poet; for there is no reason why some events
that have actually happened should not conform to the law of
the probable and possible, and in virtue of that quality in them
he is their poet or maker."

So we may, on the authority of Aristotle, begin to supersede
our sketchy and cautious dictionary definition by a fuller and
more adventurous working definition. Fiction, for Aristotle, is
the representation in language of action which, whether or not
it has acually happened, achieves its meaning and magnitude
not (as an action in history or biography must do) by conforming to accomplished fact, by arousing and satisfying our
expectation of truth, but by conforming to the law of probability or necessity. Fiction may be in prose or in verse, it may be
comic or tragic, it may be narrative or dramatic or expository,
it may be long or short; but it does not represent character or
virtue or wisdom or any other quality directly—what it represents is any probable or necessary sequence of events that start
from and arrive at: what it represents is a complete and self-
sufficient action.

Now this definition, if we provisionally accept it, gives us
our theoretical base of operations. Not only does it establish as
generally, and perhaps as uncontroversially, as possible what
fiction is, but it offers autonomy to each of the modes of
fiction, and it does not exalt one mode above any other. As
soon as the critic assumes that fiction is a direct representation
of character, of qualities and virtues, then that mode of fiction

which seems to him to represent most directly and most economically truth and justice, goodness and wisdom, will tend to crowd out all the others. The naïve critic may prefer the drama or even the cinema, because in these modes he is confronted by "real persons," the very embodiments of qualities. And there are such exclusivist heresies as that of Yvor Winters, who has ended by refusing serious consideration to all modes of fiction except the short expository poem.

Perhaps the major difference between fiction in prose (short stories, novellas, novels) and fiction in verse (every genre of verse from the lyric to the epic) is that whereas in verse fiction the emphasis is strongly on the language that defines the action, in prose fiction the emphasis is quite as strongly on the action that defines the characters. In prose fiction the unit is not, as in poetry, the word, but the event—a fact that helps to explain why prose fiction so remarkably survives the sea-change of language even in bad translations (for evidence, look up some of the nineteenth-century English translations of Turgenev and Dostoevsky still embalmed in Everyman's Library), and why almost no poetry, even narrative poetry, survives translation at all (look up any English translation of Pushkin's narrative poem *Eugene Onegin,* and then any translation of his novel *The Captain's Daughter;* or glance at any English "modernization" of the most novelistic of supreme poets, Chaucer). Fiction—as, having reached the point of distinguishing it from poetry, and by right of common usage, we may abbreviate the term "prose fiction"—fiction, like poetry and Mr. Eliot's Sweeney, "gotta use words" to talk to us; the words are the only visible structure of the fictional event, the event comes to us only through the words that constitute it, and doubtless the more precise the language—other things being equal—the more fictionally effective the event. Yet great fiction can survive, not only translation, but a measurable proportion of bad and dull writing in the original. One of the reasons for this fact—an embarrassing fact for admirers of fiction—is, of course, mere length: short stories are longer than lyrics, most novels are longer than dramas or epics; and just as an epic can have dullnesses (even Homer nods) that would sink a lyric, so a work of fiction of the mere physical bulk of *The*

Brothers Karamazov has room for patches of bad writing that no epic could survive. A more fundamental reason, however, may be discoverable in the major difference—the difference in emphasis—between fiction and poetry.

In the beginning of poetry is the word; in the beginning of fiction is the event (and this hypothesis seems to be borne out empirically for working poets and novelists, as well as theoretically for critics). The word is particular and special; the event is less particular, at least to the degree to which it seems conceivable in different ways, susceptible to a variety of verbal formulations. Yet the formal and repetitive regularities of meter tend to generalize the event, as prose tends to fragment and particularize it. So that we may try to state the relation between language (a meaningful sequence of words) and action (a complete, causally linked sequence of events), in poetry and in fiction both, as a balance of opposing impulses. The action which metrical language defines is likely to be typical, general, thematically summarizable by aphorism and metaphor; the words of a poem must therefore be precise and special enough to establish, nevertheless, the individual force, the poignant singularity, of the action (as in two very dissimilar poems with very similar actions—Herrick's "To Corinna, Going A-Maying," and Marvell's "To His Coy Mistress"). On the other hand, the action which prose defines is likely to be a sequence of highly detailed and circumstantial events; the words of a work of fiction need, therefore, not be so precise and special (if indeed they give the impression of being *too* precise, too "poetic," they will overload and damage the particularity of the events); and the thematic quality of fiction, the sense of its general application to human affairs, comes, more indirectly, from the gradual accumulation of its particular events into a nexus of characters and human relationships—a "world." The poet moves, by way of meter, from the particularity of his words to the typicality and general applicability of his action. The writer of fiction moves, by way of prose, from words which must at least give the impression of not arrogating all right of precision to themselves, through the precise particularity of his events, to the typicality and general applicability of the world of characters and relationships into which his events ultimately cohere. One can make up lists of exceptions: Chaucer and Shakespeare, to mention only English poets; but this is only to say that the very greatest poets combine the virtues of poetry and fiction (nor do they manage to combine these virtues by writing short expository poems). It remains safe to say that the virtues of poetry are not necessarily the virtues of fiction.

Moreover, though both poetry and fiction "move," the fact that the unit of fiction is the event indicates that movement is a prime determinant in the nature of fiction. We may define a fictional event as the representation in language of any phenomenon which is observed as a process rather than as an entity. To start with event, as the writer of fiction does, is to accept the obligation to observe as processes even those phenomena we ordinarily observe as entities: *i. e.*, persons and things. It is in the nature of fiction, then, to emphasize change and development: not, as in philosophy, in terms of principle; nor, as in poetry, through the ideogrammic summations of aphorism and metaphor; but change and development caught continuously in the act. It follows that ideally, in fiction, characters and events are indistinguishable; that characters observed as entities or as principles or as ideograms impede the fictional action; that events do not illustrate character, they are the media in which processes are observed in the act of individuating those continuously changing phenomena we call persons and things. All of which is not to say that characters may not be abstractly considered, or that they may not in some special ways transcend the events that constitute them.

Yet fictional events are combinations of words; and the dependence of fiction on language remains so slippery and equivocal an issue as to exasperate poets and those critics who are committed to poetry. The lightning of fiction seems to strike between events and characters, and the fact that it must be conducted through an atmosphere of language will not soothe the partisans of poetry. Not that they do not have their favorite novelists. They do; and the novelists are those who are asserted to be capable of handling language with extraordinary precision, subtlety, economy, virtuosity, mastery—what you will by way of compliment. One name that turns up often is

Conrad (who also is capable of handling language, now and then, as a *bad* poet handles it). But the name that recurs like incense and prayer is Henry James.

The argument about James has been going on for a long time now. It is important to note that his most eminent and most nearly convincing admirers are those men of letters—critics and poets—who make clear that their first devotion is to poetry, and that they extend this devotion to James because they find him the novelist who writes almost as precisely, with almost as subtle a sense of the circumscriptive and evocative power of words and phrases, as the best poets. It is equally important to note that much of the depreciation of James speaks with the voice of offended philistinism: a voice which insists that James is a snob, that he writes only about rich and idle people, that he does not know what "real life" is like, that his style begins in effeteness and ends in obscurantism, that to take pleasure in James is to retreat into the hermitage of mere art.

Still, without settling the argument, a few additional remarks about his works may bear on the notions of fiction being advanced here. The partisans of poetry, it will be assumed, agree that subtlety of language is no end in itself; that language is significantly subtle in proportion as it makes persuasive and valuable connections and discriminations between human phenomena; that the action which the language purports to represent must in fact be adequately represented, and of sufficient magnitude to be worth representing.

The Portrait of a Lady is usually regarded as one of James's best novels; by those admirers of James who dislike his last phase (Dr. Leavis, for one), it is likely to be regarded as his masterpiece. The action of the novel is characteristically Jamesian, and in its outline certainly of sufficient dignity and magnitude: the awakening of a charming and ingenuous American girl to saddened self-knowledge, to a kind of unpracticeable wisdom, by her giving herself in marriage to that immemorial American dream of corruption, the worldly European (or Europeanized) fortune-hunter. The novel is written with all the affectionate evocation of locale, and of the varied details of cultivated human behavior, that James excels at; it savors its enormous length, proceeding with a majestic deliberateness of documentation in an intelligent and lucid prose that has none of the involutions and frequent archnesses of James's late manner; it is, as James himself declared, his first conscious and planned effort—and, it is fair to add, an heroic effort—to write a great novel.

Yet consider what James does at the very heart of his action, the awakening itself. One huge section of the novel concludes as the heroine, still all unknowing, marries the fortune-hunter. The next section opens several years later, and shortly we discover that the heroine now knows all. Do we wish to learn *how* she has come to know all, how her feelings of innocent idolatry were gradually worn away by evidence too compelling to ignore? Do we perhaps even believe that it is almost by definition the novelist's talent to show such events in the act of occurring? It is not that James has altogether forgotten his responsibility: soon after, he devotes a passage to the heroine's thoughts, in which we are offered some elaborately developed metaphors—a distant figure at an unreachable window, a serpent in a bank of flowers—to make up for the missing events. But the procedures of poetry will not necessarily work for fiction. And we are led, by this evasion of responsibility, to reëxamine the characters who come to us by way of these metaphors, as well as by way of the events that have preceded: a type of heroine, a type of blackguard, a type of gentle hero, a type of soiled woman—all of them unfolding their not very complicated natures, at enormous length, in conversation and conduct the high-minded subtlety of whose language often implies distinctions of a subtlety to be found nowhere in the text, and is liable to suggest an enervated triviality of human resources.

There are, of course, easier targets in James than *The Portrait of a Lady*. One might illustrate some of the curious uses of James's high-minded uneventful subtlety: to inflate simple antitheses that would be better reduced to aphorisms (as in "The Real Thing"); to divert our attention from the mere stupidity of a protagonist who, for the purposes of the story, must be seen as intelligent but obsessively insensitive (as in *The Beast in the Jungle*); to elevate beyond criticism the hysterical melodrama of cynical thrillers (like *The Turn of the Screw*) or of pretentious thrillers (like *The Jolly Corner*); to diffuse that reverent adolescent haze of words which James finds the ideal medium for his ideal women (as in *The Wings of the Dove*); to project that sort of pervasive and directionless irony which suggests less a capacity for discrimination than an incapacity for decision, or which may even suggest a meretricious Empsonian toying with language for the sake of implying any meaning the reader would like (a fault that is perhaps inherent in James's late manner). So that when fiction seems by its language to aspire to the precision of poetry, it may only be endeavoring to conceal the absence or the failure of its own proper powers.

The unit of fiction is the event. Dickens is a considerably less fastidious writer than James; but he is a better novelist because of his mastery of event, of movement and process. Jane Austen is quite as fastidious a writer as James, and the fastidiousness of her language is always in the service of her mastery of event. Moreover, although the unit of fiction is the event, although no writer can create memorable fiction who does not have the talent for conveying in language an immediate sense of the detail, the amplitude, the vividness, and the importance of specific human events, it is equally axiomatic that the fictional event does not terminate in itself, that its aim is to ascertain the shape and meaning of those individual lives, and of their relations with one another, that are created by, and with steadily increasing salience figure in, and may therefore ultimately be said to constitute, the total action. The distinctive talent of the writer of fiction is to make events; the mark of his maturity is to offer, by way of events, a community of individual lives in the act of defining themselves.

One of the recurring anxieties of literary critics concerns the way in which a character in drama or fiction may be said to exist. The "purist" argument—in the ascendancy nowadays among critics—points out that characters do not exist at all except insofar as they are a part of the images and events which bear and move them, that any effort to extract them from their context and to discuss them as if they are real human beings is a sentimental misunderstanding of the nature of literature. The "realistic" argument—on the defensive nowadays—insists that characters acquire, in the course of an action, a kind of independence from the events in which they live, and that they can be usefully discussed at some distance from their context. The purists have trouble with Chaucer, Shakespeare, and the great novelists, many of whose characters manifest an individual vitality which, though it incontestably springs from nowhere but dramatic or fictional events, seems so extravagantly in excess of any specifiable dramatic or fictional function as to invite further inquiry. The realists have trouble with almost all dramatists except Shakespeare, and with the writers of allegory, whose characters manifest only as much individual vitality as is necessary to suggest and to discharge their function in the events that beget and contain them. For our purpose, however, it is most notable that the purists—who are, of course, the partisans of poetry—have special trouble with characters in fiction.

The fictional character is a fairly recent invention of Christian Europe. Whether people were—or are—ever as complicatedly distinguishable from one another as the great nineteenth-century novelists would have us believe, the requirement and acceptance of such complicated uniqueness in the literary representations of human beings is almost as recent as the novel itself. No doubt it has something to do with the Renaissance, or with that still earlier turning—as in Dante and Chaucer—from the vision of man as a community of souls bent on salvation, to the more prosaic (and therefore more novelistic) fascination with the details and diversity of man's conduct on earth; a turning that Erich Auerbach (in *Mimesis*) has described as it paradoxically occurs in Dante, in the very poem that is the enduring monument of the Christian view of man:

> In our passage two of the damned are introduced in the elevated style. Their earthly character is preserved in full force in their places in the beyond. Farinata is as great and proud as ever, and Cavalcante loves the light of the world and his son Guido not less, but in his despair still more passionately, than he did on earth. So God had willed; and so these things stand in the figural realism of Christian tradition. Yet never before has this realism been carried so far; never before—scarcely even in antiquity—has so much art and so much expressive power been employed

to produce an almost painfully immediate impression of the earthly reality of human beings. It was precisely the Christian idea of the indestructibility of the entire human individual which made this possible for Dante. And it was precisely by producing this effect with such power and so much realism that he opened the way for that aspiration toward autonomy which possesses all earthly existence. In the very heart of the other world, he created a world of earthly beings and passions so powerful that it breaks bounds and proclaims its independence.

And one can observe this same process, the dissociation of the individual life from the divine scheme that has hitherto been regarded as containing and expressing it wholly, at a later and more acute stage in Chaucer and Shakespeare. Still, for the purposes of literary representation, the norm of humanity remained emblematic and typical man: Chaucer's contemporaries were Gower and Langland; Shakespeare's were Marlowe and Jonson. It is as if the individualizing power in Dante that Auerbach describes—the power to compel us to take a human being as valuable and interesting beyond his collective and eschatological value—was given only to the supreme Christian poets; until, in eighteenth-century Europe, the emergence of industrialism and the general breakdown of the sacramental view of life made the dissociation virtually complete, and opened the sources of individual conduct to general scrutiny. Prose narrative is as old as Europe; but, with several astounding exceptions (the most astounding, *The Tale of Genji,* having been written in eleventh-century Japan), the novel, that vehicle for the minute and leisurely inspection of human events and individual motives, begins in eighteenth-century Europe.

It is not surprising that in its early exuberance the novel discovered not merely the individual but the freakish, the source of whose conduct is so disablingly individual, so stamped into the very physique, as to preclude choice or even consciousness. Three of the four major eighteenth-century English novelists are caricaturists; indeed, from this standpoint, Dickens himself is perhaps the best and certainly the most fertile eighteenth-century novelist, whose proper effect—an inexhaustibly self-generating sequence of grotesque events and characters—is occasionally spoiled by a Victorian infusion of melodrama and pietistic sentimentality. By the nineteenth century however, except for Dickens, the first exuberance was played out, and had been succeeded by an interest in the representation of individual lives the sources of whose conduct suggest, more or less forcefully, personal consciousness and at least the possibility of personal choice and change. The eighteenth-century novel is characteristically episodic and optimistic; it travels and discloses, rather than develops. But Fielding's eighteenth-century definition of the novel as "a comic epic poem in prose" becomes within a century prodigiously inadequate; for if choice is possible, tragedy is possible; and the novels of Stendhal and Flaubert, of Tolstoy and Dostoevsky and Turgenev and Goncharov and Gogol, of Jane Austen and George Eliot (not to mention the *Clarissa Harlowe* of Fielding's great hostile contemporary, Richardson), are by Fielding's definition not novels at all.

In nineteenth-century fiction, the image of the individual personality emerges for the first time as an identifying feature of a literary genre. This point would be more obvious in English literature if it were not for such stunning anachronisms as Chaucer and Shakespeare; but they can also help us to make the point. The image of Chaucer's Pandarus or Pardoner, of Shakespeare's Iago or Falstaff, enforces such an impression of complex and unexhausted vitality, of other choices which might have been made and of other powers which might have been exercised, that the image survives the events whose effect and fulfillment it is.

The now universally scorned nineteenth-century commentators on Shakespeare discussed Shakespeare's characters as if they had had an historical existence independent of their dramatic function. Today we know that fictional or dramatic characters are only more or less efficient patterns of words subordinate to larger patterns; but it remains a fact that legends can gather round Hamlet as they gather round historical figures, and that a Volpone or a Piers Plowman or a Tamburlaine repels curiosity except in the work in which he assumes his own more specialized kind of vigorous life. In respect of their personages, Chaucer and Shakespeare and great fiction bear an immediate resemblance to history, to the recorded and recov-

erable past: the Antony we extrapolate from various historical
accounts (as well as from two of Shakespeare's plays!) and the
Antony of Shakespeare share a bounty of individual vitality
that lifts them dolphin-like out of the element they live in; on
the other hand, Shakespeare's Antony and Marlowe's Tamburlaine (for the comparison with Dryden's Antony would be too
easy) are related only through the imposingly fulfilled function of each as the hero of a drama; and between Marlowe's
thundering verse-reciter and the historical and legendary con-
queror, there is almost no resemblance beyond the name. Fiction is more philosophical than history, says Aristotle; but it can
also *be* history. Hamlet, or Raskolnikov, or Anna Karenina is,
finally, not only a character in a play or a novel, but a datum of
the past, a fact of history, an exemplar of the transcendence of
the individual personality as well as of its immersion in events;
a human resource like the great men of the past; history's
double face of avoidable experience. "Those who cannot remember history," said Santayana, "are condemned to repeat
it"; and the statement might be made about those who are indifferent to the human resources of fiction.

Yet, in the work of fiction, a character lives in and is an
aspect of events; and events have their own internal cause, duration, magnitude, and consequence. The events of a work of
fiction may be linear and unresonant: simply and clearly moti-
vated, of sufficient duration and magnitude to gratify expectation and sustain interest, with clear and simple consequences.
Pushkin's *The Captain's Daughter*, a novel written by a poet, is
an instance: its characters are only perfectly adequate to its
events, and its events are chosen and ordered with a precision
and inevitability analogous to the precision and inevitability
with which words are chosen and ordered in a poem. Narrative
—which is the action of a work of fiction considered exclusively as a sequence of events—is complex and resonant in direct proportion to the complexity of the individual lives whose
natures it suggests. The writer may, then, choose, as Pushkin
does, to articulate an action that in the linearity of its movement scarcely requires characters at all. In a novel-length narrative, such a choice is both rare and difficult: narrative that
proceeds beyond a certain length begins to suggest, or ulti-

mately begins to require, characters of some depth and salience (even *The Captain's Daughter* is barely long enough to be called a novel). Narratives of short-story or novella length, on the other hand, are likely to approach the conditions of poetry for the reason of length alone: the shorter the work of fiction, the more likely are its characters to be simply functions and typical manifestations of a precise and inevitable sequence of events (as the aphorisms of a poem develop, explicitly or implicitly, out of a precise and inevitable sequence of words). In a few short works of fiction, the precision and inevitability of the events, and the typicality of the characters, enact an intense and grandly single-minded vision of man's destiny on earth: of which two great instances are Tolstoy's *The Death of Ivan Ilyich* and Melville's *Billy Budd*, perhaps the two greatest short works of fiction ever written.

Such short fiction, however, is still rarer than novels like *The Captain's Daughter*. Most great fiction generates interest through those of its events which establish a community of complex individual lives; through the events which dramatize the collisions between these lives, it achieves intensity. There are no Emma Bovarys or Elizabeth Bennets in short fiction: to establish a community in which such characters can be conceived to exist requires the time and space, and the uncertainty, of a novel. The partisans of poetry point out, quite correctly, that novels have nothing like the inevitability of poems: "Anything can happen in a novel." Character, in fiction as in life, is fate, but it is also potentiality. Elizabeth Bennet would not be so memorable a character if she did not appear capable of many things she does not in fact do, or if she did not do some things that appear not quite consistent yet somehow are acceptable and enlightening. Characters are consistent: they live through an ordered sequence of events; they have motives, and their conduct has consequences. But the great fictional character also appears as a kind of primal energy, a pretext and a vindication for startling and enlightening events, which themselves are not necessarily "lifelike" or "probable" or even "possible" but which realize human potentiality. Consistency sometimes expresses only the incapacity of the novelist to create such an impression of primal energy. Even Dostoevsky, in *The Idiot*, weakens our impression of Nastasya Filippovna by making too direct and simple a connection between her earlier mistreatment by Totsky and her present suicidal capriciousness —a quality in beautiful women which, as Dostoevsky shows elsewhere, solicits and will endure no single explanation, indeed no explanation at all if the character radiates the energy and pathos of the damned and illuminates, as Nastasya Fillippovna does, all the characters fatally drawn to her.

To associate Emma Bovary and Elizabeth Bennet and Nastasya Filippovna is also to suggest a distinction within the genre of the novel itself. Both *Madame Bovary* and *Pride and Prejudice* are novels about a society. The former sardonically questions the basis of its society, the latter is genteelly mocking; but the assumption in both is that society determines and encloses the lives of its members, so that the happy ending of *Pride and Prejudice* is acceptance by a society, and the unhappy ending of *Madame Bovary* destruction by one. Nastasya Filippovna and Prince Myshkin, on the other hand, though they too exist in a recognizable society, more crucially exist in an arena of contending cosmic forces, as the figures of an epic do. *The Idiot* will have to be classified, then, under the apparently unavoidable hybrid term, "epic novel."

Ezra Pound defines an epic as "a poem containing history." We have already spoken of history in its sense of the recorded and recoverable past. If now we take it, as Pound does, in its other and more comprehensive sense of the total simultaneity of possible events, an epic novel is a novel containing history—a novel, that is, in which the characters not only function in the action but recapitulate the history of man in the cosmos. Lawrence's *The Rainbow* is a novel with history: its action not only engages and defines a community of individual lives, but measures the energy of these lives against the cyclical succession of the generations of man on earth. *War and Peace* is a perhaps too obvious instance: it has hundreds of pages of heavily interpreted history-textbook documentation, it represents a struggle of cosmic opposites under the image of a great war between two contending peoples; but much of its documentation, and most of its interpretation, are ill-tempered patriotic journalism somewhat disguised by occasional magnificent descriptive passages; and the ill-prepared, uneasy domestic epilogue allows one to suspect that Tolstoy would have liked, but was too intelligent, to accept imbecile domesticity as the merited goal of a cosmic hero's life. *The Brothers Karamazov* is a more useful instance. "The Legend of the Grand Inquisitor" recapitulates the history of Christianity in parable as Ivan and Alyosha and Father Zossima recapitulate it in life; opposing moral forces of cosmic magnitude rend the spirit of each of the major characters and make judgments and decisions, for the characters and the reader alike, terrifyingly difficult and absolutely essential. Fiction becomes history as it differentiates itself into persons, and as it synthesizes itself into a vision: Ivan Karamazov is history as a datum of the recoverable past; *The Brothers Karamazov* is history as a moment of full human consciousness. It may be unnecessary to add that epic novels are very long, and that no ordinary happy or unhappy ending under social auspices will do. An epic novel may end—all passion spent—in the exhausted but superearthly serenity of Alyosha Karamazov; or—as *The Idiot* ends—in tragedy; or—as *The Rainbow* ends—in the promise of a new cycle of history.

The epic novel is an effort to reachieve the sacramental view of life without evading or surrendering the modern secular fact of the complex personality. Society recedes, and the characters in an epic novel are accountable only to God and to the fullness of human experience (a formulation that brings to mind such bogus contemporary efforts as Camus's solemnly diagrammed allegories and Graham Greene's shrewdly calculated melodramas). In *The Idiot*, the action is of Scriptural boldness: Prince Myshkin, a Christ figure in appearance and in fact, is permitted by reason of his apparent innocuousness to penetrate a society whose ruling passions are greed and lust; and by his impossible example of Christian charity and his never quite understood exhortations to love, releases these passions from the meanness of their social confinement and allows them grandly to shatter two families, to drive a man to murder, to confirm one woman in a despair that leads her to choose a sacrificial death, to exasperate another woman into a sacrificial marriage, and to send the Prince back to the asylum from which he came. The Prince practices Christian love and, since he is impotent in the secular society that can see divine love only under the image of sexual love, betrays two women who expect him to be not only God but man; he suffers from epilepsy, the sacred disease that gives him his shining instant of total understanding just before he collapses into the pit of the unconscious forces which he seems to have been pledged to reconcile and overcome; his strong and discriminating compassion for all who think they need him embitters and alienates each one, who will accept only all the Prince's compassion; he is an idiot, since only a person of inadequate wits can ignore the conventions and mean appetites of a secular society, in order to perceive those human abysses which no society can acknowledge, and for which no redeemer is in this latter age likely to be forthcoming.

In such a novel, in which human potentiality is simultaneously baffled and liberated, limiting notions of character and event will no longer serve. Each of the characters (except Myshkin) is a complex personality firmly committed to his society, and each (except, perhaps, the rather too conventional villain, Totsky) is a primal energy capable of as many incarnations as crisis exacts. Each of the events shows distinct and opposing personalities in collision, and each releases unsuspected energies that transcend personality. Even ordinary chronology will not serve: during the first chronological day of the novel, the number of crucial events and of the characters which they introduce and develop suggests a lifetime of experience, but with such an effect of prophetic intensity as not to violate or even to rouse our sense of chronological probability. Time is transcended because Myshkin is God in human events, creator and specific suffering personality, a thorn in the side of the commonplace human beings whom he transfigures and damns before they expel him back into the pure darkness of idiocy, of unmanifested personality. *The Idiot* is a supreme instance of history, of the simultaneous manifestation of a cosmos of human resources, which Myshkin evokes in order, compassionately and unintentionally, to destroy them. Characters and events become one: personality is the sum of human resources, which manifest themselves as the sum of human events; and the tremendous action which releases and vindicates these events is nothing less than the creation and destruction of the moral universe.

Fiction, seeking words only just precise enough, begins with the single contrived event. In its successful instances, it gives the ancient and always renewable pleasure of circumstantial and articulated narrative. In its great instances, it accumulates into images of persons more particular and more complete, more prodigal of energy and more indicative of human possibility, more instructively responsive to one another in a living society, than the figures of recorded history. In its supreme instances, it accomplishes a vision of history more comprehensive than recorded history, and realizing that apocalypse of man's place in the cosmos which is the substance of wisdom, and which philosophy—the love of wisdom—delights in contemplating.

1960

IV. Contemporaries

PODHORETZ AND MRS. TRILLING:
THE HOLY FAMILY

These are both, surprisingly, first books,* by critics whose names have long been familiar to readers of the New York literary and political journals. *Doings and Undoings* is "the first book of the most brilliant young critic of our day." Podhoretz himself, taking over from the shill on the jacket, declaims in his own precocious voice that he "chooses to be a critic of the contemporary rather than a browser among masterpieces or a reverent interpreter of the classics." And again: "A literary critic ought—or so they tell me [who are "they"? the editors of the Cuyama Valley Poetry Journal?]—to regard literature as an end in itself; otherwise he has no business being a literary critic. For better or worse, however, I do not regard literature as an end in itself . . ." Podhoretz appears also to believe that his collection was not "written by a single person. How many people wrote it, then? Two, I think, or possibly three. I am one of them." This is the sort of private notion that a writer may lean against, in moments of depression, to nerve himself for the gratuitous effort of carrying on (I *am* progressing, I am *not* repeating myself, I am *too* smarter than I was); but private

* *Doings and Undoings*, Farrar, Straus; *Claremont Essays*, Harcourt, Brace & World.

notions don't necessarily coincide with ascertainable facts, and it is a fact for the reader that the same voice drones on in the same doomful, humorless, cosmopolite-social-historical-tragical tone through the vicissitudes of these occasional pieces.

Mrs. Trilling doesn't need to cheer herself up with such an avowal of serial schizophrenia; she comes right out and admits that her essays were "all written by the same person." On the other hand, she resembles Podhoretz in shrinking from the imputation of mere belletrism: "the diverse essays in this book are unified . . . by a particular point of view common to them. The point of view is perhaps best described as 'social.' Even in those essays which deal with individuals . . . I think there is always a discernible reference to the entity we call society . . ." And she has her own private notion—it might be called a regional commitment—with which to sustain herself, that the still center of the turning hub of Western civilization is a small residential neighborhood contiguous to Columbia University: "The title of this volume is taken from the small street in New York City on which I live, Claremont Avenue . . . more than a street, Claremont Avenue is a neighborhood, with all this implies of a cultural as well as geographical discreteness within the larger city scene . . ." For those who might protest that she is simply indulging a whim—a family joke, perhaps—with her title and its explanation, Mrs. Trilling is candid enough to produce a pyrotechnical eye-opener: "The Other Night at Columbia: A Report from the Academy," an essay justly celebrated as one of the most entertaining self-exposures by a public woman since Lady Godiva.

"The Other Night at Columbia" was first published in *Partisan Review* five years ago. Nominally it is an account of Mrs. Trilling's speculations about Allen Ginsberg and the Beats on the occasion of Ginsberg's reading his poetry at Columbia. Actually, it is a cosmic melodrama in one act, which takes place in a shabby anteroom of Heaven, rather like the setting in which one imagines Lucifer to have challenged God on the probity of Job; there is a Prologue in Limbo and an Epilogue in Heaven; and the Narrator and Stage Manager throughout is a spiteful and disgruntled Archangel.

In the Prologue, the Narrator rehearses Ginsberg's juvenile history as "a student of my husband's":

> I had heard about him much more than I usually hear of students for the simple reason that he got into a great deal of trouble which involved his instructors, and had to be rescued and revived and restored; eventually he had even to be kept out of jail. Of course there was always the question, should this young man be rescued, should he be restored? There was even the question, shouldn't he go to jail? We argued about it some at home. . .

Who but an Archangel, speaking to the ear of God, could temper compassion with such malicious tattling sanctimony? or brandish like a gun "my principle . . . of equal responsibility for poets and shoe clerks"? or be outraged by the disappointed "expectation that a student at Columbia, even a poet, would do his work, submit it to his teachers through the normal channels of classroom communication, stay out of jail, and, if things went right, graduate, start publishing, be reviewed, and see what developed, whether he was a success or failure"? or, having revealed that Ginsberg's mother "was in a mental institution," complain about this "unjust burden for Ginsberg to put, as he so subtly did, on those who were only the later accidents of his history"? or know, with the intuitiveness of God's deputy, that "Ginsberg had always desperately wanted to be respectable, or respected, like his instructors at Columbia"? or fret the present unilluminated with do-it-yourself exhortations that take as their model the unfallen Eden of the 'thirties: "One didn't use pathology in those days to explain or excuse or exhibit oneself and one never had to be lonely"? or with confused thunder denounce the "effectlessness" of the Beats and their bourgeois patsies: "Like the respectable established intellectual [even instructors at Columbia? even those who reside on Claremont Avenue?]—or the organization man, or the suburban matron—against whom he makes his play of protest, he conceives of himself as incapable of exerting any substantive influence against the forces that condition him. He is made by society, he cannot make society. He can only stay alive as best he can for as long as is permitted him"?

We are transported, at length, to the event itself. The ante-room of Heaven is "Columbia's poor dull McMillin Theater," tasteless enough to display "the shoddiness of an audience in which it is virtually impossible to distinguish between student and camp-follower; the always-new shock of so many young girls, so few of them pretty, and so many blackest black stock-ings; so many young men, so few of them—despite the many black beards—with any promise of masculinity." The audito-rium, however, does not "smell bad," and "there's nothing dirty about a checked shirt or a lumberjacket and blue jeans; they're standard uniform in the best nursery schools." Another Archangel, whose alias is Fred Dupee, presides over these petty damned with a steely aplomb that recalls Charles I or Walter Mitty at the block:

> "The last time I was in this theater," Dupee began quietly, "it was also to hear a poet read his works. That was T. S. Eliot." A slight alteration of inflection, from irony to mockery, from wit to condescension, and it might well have been a signal for near-riot, boos and catcalls and whistlings; the evening would have been lost to the "beats," Dupee and Columbia would have been defeated. Dupee transformed a circus into a classroom.

Ginsberg reads his poems, among them, notably, a "poem . . . addressed as well as dedicated to Lionel"; and—one more ray of hope—manifests in himself "the full tug of something close to respectability," for, "reading his verse," he "had naturally given it the iambic beat. . . . A poet . . . may choose to walk whatever zany path in his life as a man; but when it comes to mourning and mothers and such, he will be drawn into the line of tradition."

Finally, the stunning Epilogue in Heaven ("At Home with the Trillings"; or, "Great Moments on Morningside Heights"):

> There was a meeting going on at home of the pleasant profes-sional sort which, like the comfortable living room in which it usually takes place, at a certain point in a successful modern literary career confirms the writer in his sense of disciplined achievement and well-earned reward. It is of course a sense that all writers long for quite as much as they fear it; certainly it is not to be made too conscious, not ever to be spoken of except

with elaborate irony, lest it propose a life without risk and therefore without virtue. I had found myself hurrying as if I were
needed, but there was really no reason for my haste; my entrance
was an interruption, even a disturbance of the orderly scene, not
the smallest part of whose point for me lay, now, in the trou-
bling contrast it made with the world I had just come from.
Auden, alone of the eight men in the room not dressed in a
proper suit but wearing a battered old brown leather jacket, was
first to inquire about my experience. I told him I had been
moved; he answered gently that he was ashamed of me. In a
dim suffocated effort of necessary correction, I said, "It's different when it's human beings and not just a sociological phenomenon," and I can only guess, and hope, he took what I
meant. Yet as I prepared to get out of the room so that the men
could sit down again with their drinks, I felt there was something
more I had to add—it was so far from enough to leave the "beats"
as no more than human beings—and so I said, "Allen Ginsberg
read a love-poem to you, Lionel. I liked it very much." It was an
awkward thing to say in the circumstances, perhaps even a little
foolish as an attempt to bridge the unfathomable gap that was all
so quickly and meaningfully opening up between the evening
that had been and the evening that was so surely reclaiming me.
But I'm certain that Ginsberg's old teacher knew what I was
saying, and why I was impelled to say it.

Why is Auden wearing that jacket? Do all poets wear the
standard uniform of the best nursery schools? Is the Archangel
simply recording a hard inconsistent fact of experience? Just
why is Auden ashamed of her? Does he object to the young
men who so conspicuously lack "any promise of masculinity"?
Can we be certain that "Lionel" knew what she was saying?
Why didn't she ask him later, before she wrote the essay, to
make sure? Why the unexplained ambivalence toward "respectability"—Claremont Avenue's proper suit of it, the Beats' hankering after it, their bourgeois targets' ignoble possession of it?
What is the difference between the "effectless," "respectable
established intellectual" whom she despises and the writer
whose "successful modern literary career confirms [him] . . .
in his sense of disciplined achievement and well-earned reward"? Never mind. To roll and kick in such a swamp of
clonic self-assertion is its own archangelic fulfillment; and may

assist, perhaps, in exorcising one's last resistances to stone-cold comforts: "the tug of . . . respectability," "the line of tradition," the "well-earned reward."

Podhoretz deplores effectlessness too; he too takes the ceremonial whack at the Beats (in "The Know-Nothing Bohemians"); but he reserves his personal attention for the American Negro. The socko conclusion to his volume (it drew many excited, soul-searching letters to *Commentary*, where it was first published) is "My Negro Problem—and Ours."

The essay consists of an ostensibly ruthless self-scrutiny, documented with flashbacks to Podhoretz's childhood in a Brooklyn slum. He is a Jewish boy, who hates and fears Negroes: "To me, at the age of twelve, it seemed very clear that Negroes were better off than Jews—indeed, than all whites. A city boy's world is contained within three or four square blocks, and in my world it was the whites, the Italians and Jews, who feared the Negroes, not the other way around." He presents dramatically encapsulated recollections (traumatic? unforgettable?) of his childhood when he was "beaten up, robbed, and in general hated, terrorized, and humiliated." Having begun with his autobiographical testimony to this reversal of social rôles, he confesses to the ineradicable survival of his revulsion into manhood: "I know it from the insane rage that can stir in me at the thought of Negro anti-Semitism; I know it from the disgusting prurience that can stir in me at the sight of a mixed couple . . ." He infers that "we white Americans are . . . so twisted and sick in our feelings about Negroes that I despair of the present push toward integration." There is, however, a solution, shocking though it may seem (to Podhoretz): color must "*in fact* disappear: and that means not integration, it means assimilation, it means—let the brutal word come out—miscegenation." And in a highly visible anguish of spirit this patriarch pledges his women to the task: "If I were to be asked today whether I would like a daughter of mine 'to marry one,' I would have to answer: 'No, I wouldn't *like* it at all. I would rail and rave and rant and tear my hair. And then I hope I would have the courage to curse myself for raving and ranting, and to give her my blessing. How dare I withhold it at the behest of the child I once was and against the man I now have a duty to be?'"

The calculated, didactic hysteria of this essay might be more persuasive if other Jews had not had the same childhood experiences as Podhoretz. They remember the fear, the hatred, the beatings. But they also remember that every bit of information that came to them, not at twelve but from the earliest age of consciousness, out of the world at large—their parents, their older brothers and sisters at college or work, the newspapers and magazines and books and movies, every text in their schools, what they saw whenever they walked into a hotel lobby or spent a day at the beach—assured them, and the Negro, that he was dirt and the future theirs: the jobs, the blonde actresses, the power of office, the arts, the money and all the places to spend it in. And these Jews will abhor Podhoretz's *ad hoc* paradoxes, his belated and self-righteous squeals of pain; they will refuse to credit—except as a mask for other, unacknowledgeable personal problems—the image of a clever twelve-year-old Jewish city boy who didn't already know that he would be a doctor, or a university professor, living in some lily-white suburb with occasional recollections of his distaste for the Negroes of his childhood.

Mrs. Trilling and Podhoretz are both New York Jewish intellectuals. They take pride in the fact. It is the introspective material, explicit and implicit, of their more impassioned essays; they challenge the reader to hold it against them (and remind him of the six million dead); in the pages of *Partisan Review* and *Commentary* they celebrate the assumption of intellectual authority by the children and grandchildren of those hopeful dispossessed who poured into America from the pogroms of Eastern Europe at the turn of the century. Mrs. Trilling, in her essay on the Beats, celebrates it even as she mourns the loss of the idiosyncratic, communal Jewishness of the 'thirties (the comic emblem is "Michael Gold's mother, who wanted to know did her boy have to write books the whole world should know she had bedbugs"). Nobody can be more meanly intolerant, more insistent on his right to be heard whatever the quality of what he says, more confident of receiving the humbly sympathetic attention that derives from his listener's sense of collective guilt, than the member of a persecuted minority at a time when social attitudes are undergoing geological alterations (especially if, like the fly on the wheel, he considers himself the engine of these alterations). James Baldwin—not to mention eloquent representatives of the Black Muslims—addresses enlightened white audiences, who applaud wildly as he tells them how unspeakable the white man is; Baldwin is intelligent and persecuted, and they are guilty.

Meanwhile, little politburos of the insulted and injured spring up; intellectual ascendancies are established on the evidence of the loudest breast-beatings about the messiest scars on the most delicate psyches; taking the right stand on a political issue is confounded with the capacity to define, distinguish, qualify any issue at all, political, philosophical, artistic; what was once an embattled and exacerbated ghetto culture contracts into a coterie (Mrs. Trilling, says her blurb, is "deeply opposed to coterie thinking") with its own obtuse instruments of self-advertisement and self-aggrandizement, its household gods and dogma, its doctrinaire substitutes for thought, its defense-mechanisms against outsiders and traitors, its "proper suit" of Claremont Avenue respectability.

It is possible to live in New York, be of Jewish extraction, and have intellectual abilities—it is even possible to contribute to *Partisan Review* and *Commentary*—without joining the gang. The maverick is Harold Rosenberg. In "Death in the Wilderness" (one of the essays in his superb collection, *The Tradition of the New*), he makes the point that to be an American is to play a rôle: "Perhaps it is not possible to fit into American Life. American Life is a billboard; individual life in the U. S. includes something nameless that takes place in the weeds behind it." Rosenberg does not himself happen to draw the obvious inference that "the Jew" is the billboard rôle for such American deep-think specialists as Podhoretz and Mrs. Trilling; but he does amusingly trace the recent history of the proper suit they insist on:

When T. S. Eliot recited his poetry in the radical 'thirties his "clerical cut" was part of his comedy of anachronism: It also went well with his reading of Lear's nonsense verses. In those days Eliot's wit was a knife that cut both ways; he advocated The Family Reunion while exposing the paranoia of its relationships. Eliot's pose, like his poetry, contained a good dose of dada.

Later literary men who copied Eliot's representative-of-culture act missed its two edges and thought the point was to be dull. When I first encountered the gravity of Lionel Trilling I did not get the joke; it took some time to realize that there wasn't any. Pretty soon, people who could not understand Eliot began to look like Trilling.

Or, to take a longer historical perspective, Trilling's suit is a hand-me-down from Arnold and Eliot. But Arnold used that prissy superiority to enrage the Philistines; under cover of it the early Eliot infiltrated the *Times-Lit-Sup* with opinions subversive to those of all the subscribers. Trilling wears it as a skin merely, and is naked to Rosenberg's hoots of derision.

Elsewhere in the same essay, Rosenberg talks about "the cult of seriousness" among American literary intellectuals, whose "fabulous profession [is] to keep hunting the *Zeitgeist* in order to submit to its command. Perhaps, having without resistance yielded to the social sciences all the claims of literature in myth, psychology, history, morality, American writers have nothing to talk about but their own group superstitions." The Deity of this cult of seriousness—Mrs. Trilling's and Podhoretz's, the cult of the periodicals they publish in and control—is of course the "Lionel" of the pharisaic Archangel's Epilogue in Heaven. Podhoretz was (like Ginsberg!) a student of Trilling's at Columbia ("we sat at the feet of Lionel Trilling"), who unlike Ginsberg did the decent thing, stayed out of jail, graduated, started publishing, and was eventually rewarded, by the grace of God, at a very early age with the editorship of *Commentary* (on his grandson's accession, at the age of 23, to the presidency of the Ford Motor Company, Henry Ford the Elder remarked that here was still another proof of the opportunities for enterprising youth in America). Jehovah indeed! As an undergraduate Podhoretz was interested in Yiddish literature: "I remember . . . with what a sense of personal triumph I first heard that Lionel Trilling was writing an essay on Wordsworth and the Rabbis." Mrs. Trilling's second essay on

D. H. Lawrence is in the form of a cosy, eyelash-batting family letter to "Dearest Norman" ("When I saw you the other day, you asked me how my Lawrence introduction was going, whether I had finished it yet, and you forced me to the unhappy admission . . ."). For this Claremont daguerrotype, Trilling sits in his proper suit as the Heavenly Father, Mrs. Trilling makes a quick change from Archangel to Madonna, and Podhoretz—still muttering at the prospect of a mocha-colored grandchild—irritably straightens his crown of thorns.

On a single occasion in his book, Podhoretz is moved to a pitch of Voltairean indignation, to style as a quality of individual consciousness, style as the only measure of the civilization he despairs of discovering around him. It is Hannah Arendt's study of Eichmann that compels him to turn away from the examination of his Jewish navel and confront the Jewish catastrophe:

> For what is Miss Arendt really saying when she tells us that "if the Jewish people had . . . been unorganized and leaderless, there would have been chaos and plenty of misery but the total number of victims would hardly have been between four and a half and six million people." Why, she is saying that if the Jews had not been Jews, the Nazis would not have been able to kill so many of them—which is a difficult proposition to dispute. I do not think I am being unfair to Miss Arendt here. Consider: the Jews of Europe, even where they were "highly assimilated," were an organized people, and in most cases a centrally organized people. This was a fact of their condition no less surely than sovereign nationhood was a fact of the French condition. Yet I doubt that Miss Arendt would ever take it into her head to declare that if the French people had not been organized into a nation-state, they could never have been sold out to the Nazis by Pétain and Laval. Throughout this book, Miss Arendt is very nasty about Zionists and Zionism, but the only sense one can glean from her argument is a grain of retroactive Zionist sense. The Jews, she is implying, should have known that anti-Semitism rendered their position in the Diaspora untenable, and they should therefore either have set up a state of their own or renounced their communal existence altogether. She does not explain how such renunciation could have saved them from the Nuremberg Laws. Nor does she tell us why the slaughter of

Jews in occupied Russia should have been so complete even
though there was no central Jewish leadership or communal
organization in the Soviet Union.

But it is unnecessary to pursue the absurdities of Miss Arendt's
argument on this issue, just as it is unnecessary to enter once
again into the endless moral debate over the behavior of the
Jewish leaders—the endless round of apology and recrimination.
They did what they did, they were what they were, and each
was a different man. None of it mattered in the slightest to the
final result. Murderers with the power to murder descended
upon a defenseless people and murdered a large part of it. What
else is there to say?

This essay takes up the important nineteen of the 371 pages of
the volume. Otherwise, whether Podhoretz is writing literary
history, literary or pop-cult criticism, political or social
comment, all the cant and leaden metaphors of his chosen milieu crowd into his head: "New voices begin to proclaim the
birth of a new era and to clamor for . . ."; "the school that
. . . rose to dominance . . . on the shoulders of the new
wave of enthusiasm for . . ."; "only a thin line divides the human from the bestial"; "his consummate artistry"; "A renewed
sense . . . of the loss of values is beginning to impose itself
. . ."; "The dilemma today is that nothing seems to be left in
our world to set an honest man's feelings on fire": so he drifts
without a paddle up the creek of generalization, this honest
man whose feelings yearn to be set on fire (and, indeed, on one
occasion were). Podhoretz disdains to "regard literature as an
end in itself"—which is just as well, since he is an all-thumbs
literary critic, predictably swindled by that thesaurus of col-
lege-humor whimsy and lockstep liberalism, *Catch-22*, over-
whelmed by the period cynicism of Nathanael West,
thunderstruck by the most contrived style among contemporary American novelists ("Bellow is a stylist of the first order,
perhaps the greatest virtuoso of language the novel has seen
since Joyce").

It is a fact about Mrs. Trilling, though, that two decades ago
she was capable of competent literary criticism. She wrote useful reviews of novels for *The Nation;* she turned out an excellent introduction to the Viking Portable Lawrence (and much

later muddied the waters with her ungenerous, febrile recantation in the "Dearest Norman" essay). About fifteen years ago she was persuaded that her forte is social or literary-cum-social criticism; and since then she has specialized in such figures as Margaret Mead, Hiss, Oppenheimer, Profumo's Dr. Ward, Mailer, Edward Albee ("I am going to deal with Mr. Albee's play . . . only as a document of contemporary society"), Marilyn Monroe.

The essay on Dr. Mead (written in 1950) is a shrewd assessment of the condescensions and self-contradictions in the work of that formidably feminist opponent of feminism; though Mrs. Trilling can't help dragging in the Claremont commitment to the civilized and discontented Freud: "sacrifice and frustration lie at the very core of the personal and social organization—it is the great Freudian truth, of course." Discussing Hiss and Oppenheimer, Mrs. Trilling takes the opportunity to dissociate herself from the American climate of hospitality toward the Soviet Union in the 'thirties, and while summarizing the evidence offers some simplistic definitions of "totalitarianism" (once again, the antidote is Harold Rosenberg, in his essay "Couch Liberalism and the Guilty Past"). The piece on Marilyn Monroe—first printed, appropriately, in a huge-circulation women's magazine—pretends to be a magnanimous tribute to Miss Monroe as "the very embodiment of life energy," but is in fact a farrago of intrusive amateur psychoanalyzing and mealy-mouthed snobberies ("I do not know what, if anything, was read at the service, but I'd like to think it was of an elevated and literary kind, such as might be read at the funeral of a person of the first intellectual rank"). Mrs. Trilling contends— oh, that Freud!—that "our mockery" of Miss Monroe's professed "taste for Dostoevsky . . . signifies . . . our disbelief that anyone who has enough sexuality needs to read Dostoevsky." An alternative explanation, which seems not to have occurred to Mrs. Trilling, is that we laughed because (1) Miss Monroe, in her numerous pronouncements, had expressed no literary interests before, (2) she had shown no signs of education or intelligence, but some signs of a sense of humor, and (3) we have heard of press agents. It is possible, after all, to believe simultaneously in sexuality *and* Dostoevsky; even if, for at least a few in the audience, poor-butterfly and worse-actress Miss Monroe never gave the impression of being acquainted with either.

It's getting late, and, from Dostoevsky to Marilyn Monroe, the Claremont saints are dead. Still, any subject will do, so long as one can locate a *Zeitgeist* in it, a verification of one's involvement in the holy charade of historical process (Mrs. Trilling, having taken a long look in the mirror, snappishly charges "Dearest Norman" with "compulsive historicism": it seems to be a family trait). The trouble is that the *Zeitgeist* of the present (even of the past!) may be that there is no *Zeitgeist*, not even the *Zeitgeist* of Freudian determinism; and so there is no longer anything to write about except the fact that there is no longer anything to write about. Mrs. Trilling and Podhoretz have names for this narcissistic and infinitely extensible subject: "maturity," "respectability," "responsibility," "tradition," "Claremont Avenue." But that gadfly Rosenberg has the last word: "Naturally you don't develop a style by contemplating your maturity and its implications."

1964

Both Norman Mailer and William Styron are forty (a year more or less), just old enough to have been, as both were, very young servicemen during World War II. Between then and now, each of them published, in his middle twenties, a widely admired first novel; each in his thirties, after the interval of a single minor or transitional work, produced an elaborate shocker of a novel for a less enthusiastic audience; each has done—at least written—less than most of his readers must once have confidently anticipated; each has shown an inclination to sink his talents into journalism and literary politics, each apparently bent on retiring—as Cyril Connolly observed of Mailer—into public life. Each was regarded for some time, among a band of earnest critics, as the hope of American fiction; and, not without large plans for future novels, each seems to have settled into his appointed place as a fixture of the Establishment (*Esquire, Life, Playboy, Mademoiselle,* photos and interviews and panel discussions, New York cocktail parties and gossip columns: various combinations and permutations of which held—for almost three unanticipated years—promise of entrée to that central salon of the cultural establishment, Mrs. John F. Kennedy's White House).

The question is whether what they wrote—early or later—

justified any of the fuss; and the answer is that it did. To go no further than their first books, both *The Naked and the Dead* and *Lie Down in Darkness* are remarkably skilful novels, probably the outstanding virtuoso performances of postwar American fiction. Nor did Mailer and Styron suddenly afterward lose their skill, or dissipate it in some spectacular misapplication, or renounce it like Rimbaud. What happened is sadder and more complicated, and begins, for both, at the beginning.

"I may as well confess," says Mailer (in *Advertisements for Myself*), "that by December 8th or 9th of 1941, in the forty-eight hours after Pearl Harbor . . . I was worrying darkly whether it would be more likely that a great war novel would be written about Europe or the Pacific"; and he records his pragmatic conviction that "it was and is easier to write a war novel about the Pacific—you don't have to have a feeling for the culture of Europe and the collision of America upon it."

So, assisted by his eventual first-hand experience in the Pacific, Mailer wrote *The Naked and the Dead*. He had calculated the odds, as well as his own abilities, correctly: there is no big novel about the European war; *The Naked and the Dead* is the only surviving big novel about either half of World War II. No other book approaches its copious documentation of that unideological, interminable, unrelievedly ugly assault on positions and places that could serve nobody except for military advantage, in a part of the world that had nothing to say to the swarms of dull strangers who systematically ravaged it. *The Naked and the Dead* is a manual of soldiering in the tropics, a compendium of tactics and expertise, a diary reverberant with authentic details, an exposé, an angry memoir, an encyclopedia of meticulously sweated-up information, a panorama and gallery of the Pacific war; everything but a novel about it.

Mailer's skill in this book is opportunistic and timely. He does not scrutinize or shape the material but rather crams it, with the energy of unilluminated ambition, into any number of pigeonholes: war as a stimulus for fine writing about death ("It was an eloquent corpse, for there were no wounds on its body, and its hands were clenching the earth as if to ask for a last time the always futile question"); America as melting-pot

(Valsen, Gallagher, Minetta, Goldstein, Martinez, Czienwicz, Croft from Texas, Willie Brown from Oklahoma—the whole dreary spectrum of sectionalisms and nationalities that Mailer discriminates, in and out of their respective ghettoes, more doggedly but no more individually than the shoddiest patriotic movie); the detached, self-questioning, unheroic hero ("He foresaw the annoyances, the dangers, the inevitable disillusionments, but at least this was a positive action"); the villain as wicked stepfather, the General, suave, ticking like a bomb with minatory genteel mannerisms, Fascist and latent homosexual, who (Mailer hopes) will radiate satanic corruption in his approximations of deep thinking—

> The howitzer like a queen bee I suppose being nurtured by the common drones. The phallus-shell that rides through a shining vagina of steel, soars through the sky, and then ignites into the earth. The earth as the poet's image of womb-mother, I suppose.

If Mailer is seldom so inept (he means the General to sound like a first-class brain gone wrong), he nevertheless can seldom claim for his particulars anything better than the journalistic authority of unpenetrated experience. Characteristically, his style makes an effort to appear all toneless surface and thus a suitable medium or reflector of the material:

> After the night when the Japanese failed to cross the river, the first squad remained in its position for three days. On the fourth day, 1st Battalion advanced a half mile and recon moved up with A Company. Their new outpost was on the crest of a hill which looked down into a tiny valley of kunai grass; they spent the rest of the week digging new holes, stringing barbed wire, and making routine patrols. The front had become quiet.

But, as in this simulation of Hemingway deadpan, the style is characteristically synthetic and derivative, an echo-chamber of identifiable influences; whether James T. Farrell's Chicago-Irish dialogue (transported, stone-dead as ever, to the far Pacific):

GALLAGHER: Some fuggin mornings like this I wish I'd catch a bullet.

WILSON: Only goddam trouble with that is you can't pick the spot.
STANLEY: You know if you could, the Army wouldn't be keeping me long.
GALLAGHER: Aaah, there ain't a goddam place you can get a million-dollar wound that it don't hurt.
STANLEY: Sometimes I think I'd lose a leg, and call it quits.

—or Fitzgerald's never-quite-focused American daydream of youth and money:

The last summer before college is a succession of golden days, and shining beaches, the magic of electric lights on summer evenings, and the dance band at the summer bathing club, AN AIRLINE TICKET TO ROMANTIC PLACES, and the touch and smell of young girls, lipstick odor, powder odor, and the svelte lean scent of leather on the seats of convertibles. . . .

—or the face of America as the tragic mask of history, *à la* Dos Passos:

A big man with a shock of black hair and a small sharp voice, a heavy immobile face. His brown eyes, imperturbable, stared out coldly above the short blunted and slightly hooked arc of his nose. His wide thin mouth was unexpressive, a top ledge to the solid mass of his chin.

—or the blowsiness of Thomas Wolfe's geographical rant:

For a thousand, two thousand miles the roads and the earth have led up to it. The mountains have snubbed down to hills, lapsed into plains, rolled on majestically in leisurely convolutions and regroupings. No one ever really comprehends it, the vast table of America, and the pin points, the accretions, the big city and the iron trails leading to it.

—or John O'Hara's image of sex as the quotidian bourgeois alternative to murder:

Their lovemaking is fantastic for a time:
He must subdue her, absorb her, rip her apart and consume her.
This motif is concealed for a month or two, clouded over by their mutual inexperience, by the strangeness, the unfamiliarity, but it must come out eventually. And for a half year, almost a

year, they have love passages of intense fury, enraged and power-ful, which leave him sobbing from exhaustion on her breast.

—or the paid ardor of travel brochures:

> The sunset was magnificent with the intensity and brilliance that can be found only in the tropics.

—or, inescapably, the huge shadow of Papa Hemingway, whenever military routine or male self-contemplation or the natural history of the dead requires to be inspected:

> Another Japanese lay on his back a short distance away. He had a great hole in his intestines, which bunched out in a thick white cluster like the congested petals of a sea flower. The flesh of his belly was very red and his hands in their death throe had en-circled the wound. He looked as if he were calling attention to it. He had an anonymous pleasant face with small snubbed fea-tures, and he seemed quite rested in death. His legs and buttocks had swollen so that they stretched his pants until they were the skin-tight trousers of a Napoleonic dandy. Somehow he looked like a doll whose stuffing had broken forth.

The young novelist attempts also four Conradian *tours de force*, those long sections, carefully prepared and worked up, which set out to register prodigies of reluctant physical exer-tion: the dragging of the antitank guns; the reconnaissance through the jungle; carrying the mortally wounded soldier back toward the coast; the climb up Mt. Anaka. But Mailer does not achieve, as Conrad can, the very taste of numb and driven endurance; the words accumulate only into a sequence of assertions, interrupted by pretty pictures:

> In the brief moment . . . [the flare] lasted, they were caught at their guns in classic straining motions that had the form and beauty of a frieze.

This footnote to the Planting of Old Glory on Iwo Jima is neither war nor fiction; but it is the sort of plummy writing into which the novel relaxes when it does not work at being sober and factual, and it helps to explain the enormous popular success of *The Naked and the Dead*.

The literary ancestry of *Lie Down in Darkness* is much sim-pler: Faulkner; rather, one novel by Faulkner, *The Sound and* *the Fury*. The moribund and doomstruck Southern family, the Negro servants sustained by a primitive faith inaccessible to their masters, the incest-motif as the node and symbol of in-bred blood-guilt, the continuous ranging among points of view and through layers of time not to disclose something new but obsessively to circle and recapture the already stated and known—small wonder that *Lie Down in Darkness* is one of the few twentieth-century novels which Faulkner himself publicly set apart for praise.* Yet Styron draws back from Faulkner's most destructive temptation, his rhetoric. Styron's prose is open, scrupulous, limber, unplagued by echoes (most unlike the tight-lipped pastiche of *The Naked and the Dead*): it modulates easily between plain narrative and lyric evocation, it can even accommodate itself to the pyrotechnic and ominous lightnings of Peyton Loftis's conclusive monologue—

> He hocked something up, spat it out the window; in the fading afternoon two young men strolling along, one with an earring, both in silk verdigris pants. *Shall Thy wrath burn like fire?* I couldn't think again, then thought flooded over me with a rustle of feathers, scraping, katydid wings: suppose. Yes. Suppose it was not like that at all, but that he should say you just go to hell. Suppose that turned out to be. Then I should never go home, south again, but always uptown like this, always north: and he shall never come again. I couldn't help it, with Harry going: once at night at Uncle Eddie's in the mountains, it was summer and cold and upstairs alone the katydids scared me: she closed the door, sealing me in blackness, with only my child's fearsome conscience—the alarm clock at my bedside whirring away, bright with greenly evil, luminous dots and hands. I knew nothing about birds then, or guilt, but only my fear: that I should be borne away on the wings of katydids, their bewhiskered faces that nuzzled mine and brittly crackling claws that pinched my flesh, a hum of wings overhead carrying me outward and outward and outward . . .

* The praise was mild enough, to be sure ("a book . . . that I thought showed promise"); but it was the only book that Faulkner, having disclaimed competence to answer, mentioned in answer to the question (in 1957): "Mr. Faulkner, could you tell me who you think is the most promising young writer in America?" F. L. Gwynn and J. L. Blotner (editors), *Faulkner in the University*, 1959, 12f.

Nor does Styron, concerned—as in *The Sound and the Fury*
Faulkner is—to reconstitute the obstinate dimension of time,
take for a model Faulkner's rather brutal bumping together of
time-levels (as in the Benjy section, with its signpost italics).
Styron's dissolving and self-restoring chronology is in fact the
technical triumph of the book. It would have delighted the patriarch of the time-shift, Ford Madox Ford; in its seamless and
transparent intricacy it is an astonishing feat, and would alone
support a sympathetic interest in the talent and future of its
creator.

If anything similar might fairly be said about Styron's plot,
his characters, his scenes, the judgments he sees fit to provide,
Lie Down in Darkness would be an impressive and substantial
novel. But the plot is mere fate, a bloated india-rubber spider in
the toils of which the characters are these crippled buzzing
flies; the scenes congeal into melodramatic suspensions, postures, tableaux (Mailer's "form and beauty of a frieze"):

> During the instant she heard that voice it seemed that time itself
> had stopped: nothing stirred, no leaf fell; beyond the shore the
> incoming waves lay without motion in piled-up billows, sus-
> pended one behind the other in endless, furrowed procession
> around the bay, as silent and unyielding as if they had been
> carved from glass. The evening wind had frozen in the trees.
> Below, Milton and Peyton sat like statues together, and Peyton
> had one hand raised to a place where sunlight had gathered in
> her hair. There was no sound or movement anywhere, except
> for the furious quick beating of Helen's heart.

Though all the fevers and miseries of spirit are intended to
carry (and the dislocations of chronology to define) histories,
origins, motives, moments of early purity and joy, what domi-
nates and expels everything else is the savored parade of effects
—alcoholism, frigidity, self-abasements and humiliations, a
tangle of guilts and hatreds, incest or just about. It is as if there
were never anything to lapse *from*. Since there are no motives
or origins, the effects are sensational, like an exact description
of mangled bodies in an auto accident, or like Mailer's lingering
look at battlefield carrion (the intention of the look is doubtless bitterly sardonic—anti-war—but Mailer has no characters
either, and so he too commands only effects).

As for Styron's few attempts to equip his mouthpieces with prophetic optimism ("'. . . I want to paint and paint because I think that some agony is upon us. Call me a disillusioned innocent, a renegade Red, or whatever, I want to crush in my hands all that agony and make beauty come out . . .'"), they are banal enough to send us off in pursuit of mere sensation ourselves, especially when poor Peyton is made to expose the aspirations of modern youth:

> . . . I've wanted to be normal. I've wanted to be like everybody else . . . because, Bunny, you can believe me, most kids these days are not wrong or wrongdoers, they're just aimless and lost . . .

Lie Down in Darkness has nothing more to say, and says it with an extraordinary battery of fictional devices. Like *The Naked and the Dead*, it is an accomplished, even a brilliant book by a gifted and ambitious writer, who knows that to be what he is determined to be—a successful and respected novelist—it is necessary to write novels.

Certainly nothing but ambition can account for Styron's second book. *The Long March* is a novella, extended by generous type and margins into a scant volume, about an incident among Marine reserves called back into service during the Korean war. Here is a sample of the kind of women's-magazine shorthand that Styron will settle for when he feels no impulse at all, only the need to keep his name before the public:

> A flood of protest had welled up in him, for he had put the idea of war out of his mind entirely, and the brief years since Okinawa had been the richest of his life. They had produced, among lesser things, a loving, tenderly passionate wife who had passed on to their little girl some of her gentle nature and her wealth of butter-colored hair; a law degree, the fruits of which he had just begun to realize, even though somewhat impecuniously, as one of the brightest juniors in a good New York law firm; a friendly beagle named Howard whom he took for hikes in Washington Square; a cat, whom he did not deign to call by name, and despised; and a recordplayer that played Haydn, Mozart and Bach.

Mailer, who likes to comment on his contemporaries, has written that *The Long March* is "remarkably good." His only ascertainable reason must be that it is a sort of compliment to him. The whole action of the novella resembles a hasty first draft of any one of the four episodes of intolerable physical stress in *The Naked and the Dead;* as in Mailer's novel, military reality is faced up to, the messier the better ("the slick nude litter of intestine and shattered blue bones"); the villain is Mailer's General Cummings demoted to a Marine lieutenant-colonel named Templeton, who like Cummings subtly flaunts a couchful of neurotic mannerisms as he utters the starchy periods of comic-book villainy:

> "Wait a minute, Captain, wait a minute," the Colonel said. Once more the voice—as cool and as level as the marshy ground upon which they were sitting—carefully skirted any tone of reproach and was merely explicit: "I don't want you to think I'm taking it out on the Battalion merely because of you, or rather H & S Company. But they aren't reserves. They're *marines. Comprend?*" He arose from the chair. "I think," he went on flatly, almost gently . . .

Only Captain Mannix, the rebellious Jew from Brooklyn, is not out of Mailer's bag of tricks; but the virile and unpretentiously heroic Jew is a counter-cliché that Styron has already used in *Lie Down in Darkness* (Peyton's husband): the circumstances differ, and therefore the reactions, but the same type-cast actor could play both parts.

Barbary Shore, on the other hand, is a difficult and sizable effort, and in fresh directions for Mailer. At least—after the all-bets-covered caution of *The Naked and the Dead*—it may be said to have the crude look of chance-taking and exploration. Its Dostoevskian plot combines conspiratorial politics with detective-novel concealments and surprises; its ethos is the febrile and despairing utopianism of lost causes; it plunges with naïve rashness into argument, polemic, tirade, prophecy; its style has withdrawn from Mailer's early influences and is already assuming the constricted, anxious, hectoring intonation of most of Mailer's writing after *The Naked and the Dead;* its narrator, deprived by amnesia of background and blood-ties, is Mailer's new hero, the individual outside history, the unmemoried anonymous American, the orphan, the unrelated man, who starts from nowhere with nothing and must somehow manage to understand, in time, the unexampled predicament of the world. Moreover, against all these lowering clouds, Mailer comes up with Guinevere, the gorgeous sloven who daydreams in uninhibited technicolor:

> "It takes place in this city in New York State, and the main characters are a doctor, a real good-looking guy with a mustache, big you know, and his nurse, she looks like some of those blonde stars, and then he's got a girl friend, a dark-haired girl, any feature player could do that part." Guinevere lit a cigarette. "Now, this guy, the doctor, he's a pretty good guy, good heart and so forth, and he's a wow with the women. He's got the biggest whang on him in the whole town, and maybe he don't know it. He's got dozens of girl friends, and there isn't one of them who won't surrender herself to him, you know. . . ."
> . . . "The operation turns out a failure. She isn't going to have the baby any more but at the same time he does something, he makes a mistake, and the society girl can't make love any more. She looks perfectly okay, but she's crippled there, a beautiful girl, and yet she can't do it any more. Well, when she finds out, she's mad, and she's going to expose him, but the nurse who's a wonderful character convinces him he ought to marry the society girl and he does even though there can't be anything between them, and for a while they all keep living in the same town, and he keeps up his affair with the blond nurse. They're still in love, and it's gotten very chemical like it used to be with the society girl, he goes down on her and everything, and she loves him. . . ."

Having outlined this script for a smash movie she hopes the narrator will "write up" for her, Guinevere soon disappears into the turbid puzzles of the plot (unfortunately, since she might have been the heroine of a mean and brassy novel). After all, with the best of intentions, *Barbary Shore* is melodrama. Mailer's vision of the police-state in America has the necessary props and actors: the revolutionary, the disciple, the unwitting betrayer (the girl, no less! who introduced, or crazily fancies she introduced, the assassin to Trotsky), the secret policeman, the "little object" which becomes the emblem of hope for the world when the disciple—the man without a past —inherits it and so inherits a possible future. Apart from

Guinevere, however, Mailer's inventiveness is absorbed and exhausted by the scheme of his subject, which thereupon generates its own stock of platitudes. The nasty cop, for instance, is predictably identified by momentous crumbs of stage-business:

> "I wonder," Hollingsworth began, "if you have come to a favorable decision on my offer?" and expectorated neatly into his handkerchief.

And so is the revolutionary:

> With what effort he replaced his eyeglasses, adjusted them upon his nose. "It is Hollingsworth then," he whispered incomprehensibly.

The best Mailer can do to imply the anguish of the heroine is to set her adrift on currents of whimsy:

> "This morning I woke up, and I thought of all the dresses I had, and my typewriter, and all those little chains. I'm a cat. I don't want strings to my legs. I gave them away to Father Pawnbroker." She smiled. "Like Vincent I cut off my ear and gave it to my beloved and now I hear sounds I never knew before."

Nor does the politics ever distinguish itself from romantic pamphleteering:

> ". . . it is impossible for you to know the excitement I felt that night on the bridge when I heard you talk with precision enough for me to realize that here was one of the young generation with a socialist culture . . ."

Finally, the narrator-hero, for all his busy ubiquitousness, is a stick: Mailer ought perhaps to have heeded one of the ancient unwritten laws of fiction, that a first-person hero tends either to get in the way or to recede into the wallpaper (even Dickens had his troubles of perspective and proportion with the protagonist who speaks for everyone else as well as for himself).

In *The Deer Park*, Mailer has no better luck with a similar narrator-hero at the source and center of the action: again the orphan, the free and unrelated man, the voluntary agent; and again a stick. This time, though, the failure is more damaging

because the hero is seeking not a political but a personal apocalypse. The existential dynamo has shifted its base of operations
from revolutionary socialism (Mailer regards *Barbary Shore* as
his first "existential" novel) to revolutionary sex. The capital
question now is the question of personality—outward index of
the potency that must transform us all:

> Almost everybody I knew in Desert D'Or had had an unusual
> career, and it was the same for me. I grew up in a home for
> orphans. Still intact at the age of twenty-three, wearing my
> flying wings and a First Lieutenant's uniform, I arrived at the
> resort with fourteen thousand dollars, a sum I picked up via a
> poker game in a Tokyo hotel room while waiting with other
> fliers for our plane home. The curiosity is that I was never a
> gambler, I did not even like the game, but I had nothing to lose
> that night, and maybe for such a reason I accepted the luck of
> my cards. Let me leave it at that. I came out of the Air Force
> with no place to go, no family to visit, and I wandered down to
> Desert D'Or.

"Built since the Second World War," Sergius O'Shaugnessy
continues, "it is the only place I know which is all new." So the
new man takes up the challenge of the new city, which as it not
accidentally happens is the retreat and playground of the
Hollywood illustrious. There is an American myth which is a
long time dying: Fitzgerald believed it, Mailer believes it,
Styron in *Set This House on Fire* tries hard to be cynical or
wise but believes it: that Hollywood—enameled smirk and all—
holds the keys to the ultimate arcanum of sex. Sergius, then, is
the toothpaste-ad knight ("I had blond hair and blue eyes and
I was six feet one") in quest of this oldest and latest and most
American sacred mystery.

The myth is a myth of power. It rests on the assumption that
the Hollywood amalgam of forces—technical, personal, organ-
izational—which alters, distorts, reshapes, imprisons the sexual
consciousness of millions must itself be a reservoir of sexual
power, a sort of Catharist cell whose holy heretics practice
rites forbidden and unimaginable to the laity. The myth has
had much highbrow currency recently (consider the
posthumous deification of Marilyn Monroe). It was anticipated
by Fitzgerald in *The Last Tycoon*, a pretentious and sentimen-

tal fragment which fails to prove that a man who skilfully
makes bad movies can be intelligent, interesting, and a (somewhat depleted) reservoir of sexual power. Perhaps the only satisfactory fictional treatment of the myth has been Walker
Percy's *The Moviegoer.* The protagonist of this notably un-
pretentious novel is the conscious, willing, and sardonic victim
of the myth, the American who accepts the fate that for Americans the movies are realer than life:

> I am attracted to movie stars but not for the usual reasons. I
> have no desire to speak to Holden or get his autograph. It is
> their peculiar reality which astounds me.

That the convergent egos of hundreds of technicians, book-
keepers, press-agents, and ill-trained players in a film on view
in thousands of theaters will necessarily affect the dreams of
millions is obvious. Mr. Percy merely proposes that the "real-
ness" of Bill Holden and his colleagues is relative, a testimony
not to any vitality of theirs but to the national void which their
images—factitious tokens of sense, touch, unaging sinless flesh
—rush to fill. The cult of youth and of the unaging body is not
identical with—it may indeed preëmpt and nullify—the cult of
sex. It may express only the national hatred for mind, for the
past, for unillusioned love, for all the fumbling cravens—ourselves—who will never make the team, climb the ladder of
success, marry the boss's daughter. Revenge! cries the thinned
blood. Ah, to build and consummate the dreams of all our envi-
ous brothers in thousands of darkened auditoriums, as Sergius
can do in his bouts with the movie goddess, Lulu Meyers:

> I was able to discover emotions I never knew I owned, and I must
> have enjoyed it as much as Lulu. So I thought by virtue of the
> things we did I would put my mark on her forever. What she
> may have intended as a little dance was a track and field event
> to me, and I would snap the tape with burning lungs, knotted
> muscles, and mind set on the need to break a record. It was the
> only way I could catch her and for three minutes keep her. Like
> a squad of worn-out infantrymen who are fixed for the night in
> a museum, my pleasure was to slash tapestries, poke my fingers
> through nude paintings, and drop marble busts on the floor. Then
> I could feel her as something I had conquered, could listen to

her wounded breathing, and believe that no matter how she acted other times, these moments were Lulu, as if her flesh murmured words more real than her lips. To the pride of having so beautiful a girl was added the bigger pride of knowing that I took her with the cheers of millions behind me. Poor millions with their low roar. They would never have what I had now. They could shiver outside, make a shrine in their office desk or on the shelf of their olive-drab lockers, they could look at the pin-up picture of Lulu Meyers. I knew I was good when I carried a million men on my shoulder.

"Emotions I never knew I owned": what these emotions are, Sergius will not tell us. If the contest almost kills him, his consolation is that to win it would be to win everything; yet what he would win, beyond Lulu, is not clear. And, though Lulu's magnetic charms are tirelessly asserted, in illustration they soon wane: " 'Sugar, get me a small Martin' " or—"When Lulu finally came back, she perched on my lap and said in a whisper the others could hear, 'Sugar, I tried, and I couldn't make doo-doo. Isn't that awful? What should I eat?' "; or—

> We played our games. I was the photographer and she was the model; she was the movie star and I was the bellhop; she did the queen, I the slave. We even met even to even. The game she loved was to play the bobby-soxer who sat with a date in the living room and was finally convinced, always for the first time naturally enough.

Now Mailer is not writing, approvingly or satirically, about debauchery in Bel-Air. He is writing, so he plainly thinks, about a mystery, an occult ceremony, as between Eitel and Elena:

> For Eitel, who had decided more than once that when all was said, not too many women really knew how to make love, and very few indeed loved to make love, Elena was doubly and indubitably a find. He had blundered on a treasure. It was one of the best experiences of his life.

The mystery, like Lulu's charms, is never revealed but always asserted. If its practitioners—foggy vectors of unspecified energy—were otherwise entertaining or intelligent, we might credit their practice; but the rest are as pneumatically monotonous as Lulu. Potency without personality is like the smile without the Cheshire cat. Sergius himself, appointed by Mailer to survey the mystery, is a grand lacuna into which whole chapters topple and vanish. It is chiefly when Mailer forgets the mystery for a moment and does some tough local satire—on the movie producers, for instance—that the novel has the ring of at least minor truth. Marion Faye, on the other hand—pimp, diabolist, spoiled priest, dark herald of Mailer's approaching dawn of polymorphous-perverse sexuality—is so patently derived from any one of Dostoevsky's agonized nihilists that he seems a quaint keepsake rather than corrosively modern.

As for Styron (who had written to Mailer, "I don't like *The Deer Park*, but I admire sheer hell out of it"), he makes plain, in *Set This House on Fire*, that *The Deer Park* imposed on him the moral obligation to put Mailer straight about some important matters. It is true that he has his own breathless fling with the Hollywood myth:

> There was an indescribable grace and attractiveness about this man [a movie director], and there is hardly any way I can outline these qualities without feeling that I am being stale and pedestrian. . . . There was something powerfully sensual about him (I felt Rosemarie come electrically alive at his approach, somewhat I should say, like a mare) . . .

He also concocts, for his own didactic purposes, his own version of Marion Faye. Mason Flagg is comparable to Faye not only in his name; like Faye, he chooses to direct his life down a corridor of titillatingly infamous possibilities. The difference is that Styron altogether disapproves of Flagg; and of Faye, and Mailer. Mailer having been reckless enough to speak for himself—

> There was a frontier for my generation of novelists. Coming out of the orgy of the war, our sense of sex and family was torn in two. The past did not exist for us. We had to write our way out into the unspoken territories of sex—there was so much there, it was new, and the life of our talent depended upon going into the borderland . . .

and having elsewhere called sex "perhaps the last remaining frontier of the novel," Styron sets out to demonstrate that Mailer's notions are foolish and wicked; that Flagg, seductive though he is to all who meet him (if not to the reader), has no marvelous secret, heralds no future, is a mendacious and dirty-minded idler whose appropriation of Mailer's metaphor clinches his equivalence with Mailer as well as with Faye:

> "Sex meant a lot to Mason—more than any human being I ever laid eyes on. That pornography of his, for instance. What he always was talking about was the new look in morals—that's what he called it—and this business about sex being the last frontier. . . . He wanted all the arts to embrace complete, explicit sexual expression—I'm quoting him. He said that pornography was a liberating force, *épater le bourgeois*, and all that crap—though Mason was deep down the most dyed-in-the-wool bourgeois who ever walked. . . ."

Whatever the merits of Styron's argument (spoken by his purged and beatified hero), Styron's villain in his own novel is a simple machine, so instantaneously comprehensible that he poses a threat only to the reader's attention: " '. . . I've heard that a man hasn't even begun to *savor* life, until he's had one of these native girls moaning *mamma mia* to him in the sack. . . .' " Moreover, Styron's alternative to life on Mailer's frontier is rural domesticity with a wife whose womanly capacity for affection (which Styron and his hero announce at every opportunity) is matched only by her total brainlessness: " '. . . Every time I pick up the paper I read about some American hitting some Italian with his car. I think it's just a shame the way people drive around in these irresponsible American cars. . . .' " The same novelist had an earlier heroine cry out in a moment of truth: " '. . . I've wanted to be normal. I've wanted to be like everybody else. . . .' " If Styron is in search of "the most dyed-in-the-wool bourgeois who ever walked," he might look closer to home than the character (and rival novelist) he singles out.

While Styron keeps a cold eye on other people's morals, his novel slips off into iniquities of its own. In *Lie Down in Darkness*, Styron was content to be influenced principally by Faulk-

ner's theme and subject; now he deluges us with cataracts of
neo-Faulknerian rhetoric:

> . . . dreams that told him that God was not even a lie, but worse,
> that He was weaker even than the evil He created and allowed
> to reside in the soul of man, that God Himself was doomed, and
> the landscape of heaven was not gold and singing but a space of
> terror which stretched in darkness from horizon to horizon. Such
> a man knew the truth and, knowing it, would take the best way
> out. Which was to remove from this earth all mark and sign and
> stain of himself, his love and his vain hope and his pathetic crea-
> tions and his guilt, and be duped by life no longer.

If such rodomontade fails to hold our interest, Styron can always rely on novelistic chewing-gum: "In the oddest way I
was reminded . . ."; ". . . the strange thing was . . .";
"Then I saw a remarkable thing happen"; "bright ineffable
glamour"; "Her voice was incredibly sweet . . ."; "indescrib-
able grace"; "unutterably weary"; "I vaguely sensed . . .";
"for some reason . . ."; "For God knows what obscure reasons. . . ." Upon such phrases the final judgment has been
made by F. R. Leavis (speaking of a similar habit in Conrad):
that the writer "must here stand convicted of borrowing the
arts of the magazine-writer (who has borrowed his, shall we
say, from Kipling and Poe) in order to impose on his readers
and on himself, for thrilled response, a 'significance' that is
merely an emotional insistence on the presence of what he
can't produce. The insistence betrays the absence, the willed
'intensity' the nullity. He is intent on making a virtue out of
not knowing what he means." *

Styron is, it may be concluded, no great moralist. *Set This
House on Fire* is a safe and unctuous movie spectacular in the
guise of a serious novel. It leaps nimbly from sensation to sensation—a bloody auto accident, a rape, a horrible disfiguring
murder, a ghastly natural death in thrilling color, to mention a
few—for all of which there will of course be an accounting,
but oh what fun while they last, till over everything Styron
can pour his shiny final lacquer of regeneration. The novel
even has a part for an unutterably beautiful and virtuous Italian

* *The Great Tradition*, Anchor, p. 219.

peasant girl, who must die so that the hero, having dallied with her (innocently!), can return to his imbecile spouse for the happy ending. It is an ignoble book.

It is the sort of book that Mailer seems incapable of writing. His literary vices do not include sanctimoniousness. He is even insecure, he shouts at us and yearns for our approval, he is childish but not ignoble. *Advertisements for Myself* is a lumpish, blundering book full of self-pity, without a single achieved piece of writing (except for a very brief, astringent fable about Hollywood, "Great in the Hay"). It is a grotesquely self-indulgent anthology: it makes room for juvenilia that could be of interest only to a Ph.D. candidate doing a thesis on Mailer; it reprints lengthy selections from his second and third novels; it reprints a number of professionally tidy short stories in the voiceless (or many-voiced) prose of *The Naked and the Dead*; it even reprints some of Mailer's political journalism, and presumably would have reproduced his laundry bills if the publisher had not called a halt somewhere. Yet about a quarter of it—mostly the running commentary throughout and the last quarter of the text—is as fascinating page by page as it is exasperating and disappointing. Such fluency, urgency, anxiety—such an energetic compulsion to be the conscience of our time —must somehow merge into form and radiance; or so it is possible to feel as one reads.

And there are still new programs to explore. In "The White Negro" and "The Time of Her Time," the existential focus has narrowed from sex in general to the orgasm in particular. In "The White Negro," Mailer describes the pursuit of the orgasm as it evolves into the new mystery of hip, the Negro mystique liberated from the white man's tyranny over the dark places of his own psyche; the revolution from within. In "The Time of Her Time" (which according to Mailer is a fragment of a novel in progress), Mailer's by now furiously baroque prose presents, in imagery reminiscent of the dragging of the antitank guns through the jungle in *The Naked and the Dead*, the efforts of a hipster Don Juan to induce an orgasm in the frigid girl he has accepted as worthy of his talents. The prose shudders with high-minded evangelical fervor; for Mailer is a very moral writer, with his own strict ideas of heroism:

Like a child on a merry-go-round the touch of the colored ring just evaded the tips of her touch, and she heaved and she hurdled, arched and cried, clawed me, kissed me, even gave of a shriek once, and then her sweats running down and her will weak, exhausted even more than me, she felt me leave and lie beside her. Yes, I did that with a tactician's cunning, I let the depression of her failure poison what was left of her will never to let me succeed, I gave her slack to mourn the lost freedoms and hate the final virginity for which she fought, I even allowed her baffled heat to take its rest and attack her nerves once more . . .

The style—this lethal competition with one's material—defeats and parodies itself, sinks into narcissism, bellybutton lint-picking. Such puritanical zeal has not been seen in American fiction since *The Scarlet Letter*; but it was Hawthorne's subject, not his style, and he did not make the mistake of drowning in it.

What remains is the "Prologue to a Long Novel," with which Mailer ends the book, and in which he announces his most recent program: not politics, not sex, not orgasm—but orgy as the existential cul-de-sac, the brick wall against which the ego can batter itself to death and transcendence. Mailer has often expressed his admiration for Sade, and in this Prologue his self-identification with the divine Marquis is complete; or would be, if only Mailer could cease to be so nervously attentive to his readers:

> . . . that mob of readers whose experience of life is as narrow as it is poor, and worse if the truth be told . . .
>
> For those readers courage is required. My passion is to destroy innocence, and any of you who wish to hold to some part of that warm, almost fleshly tissue of lies, sentimentality, affectation and ignorance which the innocent consider love must be prepared instead for a dissection of the extreme, the obscene and the unsayable.

There follows much portentous promise of dreadful things to come, hints and warnings, extravagant premonitory images. It all provokes feelings like Tolstoy's amused reaction to the sensational stories of Andreyev. Tolstoy recalled "the story about a boy who, unable to pronounce the letter 'r,' said to his chum: "I went for a walk and suddenly I saw a wolf. . . . Are you

fwightened? Are you fwightened?' 'So Andreyev,' continued
Tolstoy, 'also keeps on asking me: "Are you fwightened?"
And I am not in the least frightened.' " *

Mailer's novel may get done and published; it may even be
good, though there seems every reason—including the two excerpts printed in *Advertisements for Myself*—to be skeptical.†
In his time Mailer may have seen a wolf or two; but anyone so
fluttery about the sensibilities of an audience is unlikely to give
a useful account of his adventures in the deep forest. Mailer's
ambition to be heard is undermined by his anxiety; it may in
fact be just another name for anxiety. *Set This House on Fire* is
ambitious too, a bad ambitious novel, anxious to inflame and
impress, full of cardboard wolves with grinning teeth. But Styron's manners—if not his methods—are much more ingratiating than Mailer's. Mailer has written angrily about Styron's
campaign to smooth the way for his shocker: "Styron . . .
spent years oiling every literary lever and power which could
help him on his way, and there are medals waiting for him in
the mass-media." Those are medals that Mailer had for a season
and still pitifully craves. It is not Styron's ambition that Mailer
deplores, but the social graces with which he pursues it: if not
in the genial valleys of mass esteem (accessible, in the twentieth century, only to a Frost or a Hemingway, and only under
very special conditions), at any rate on the peaks of the Establishment—to live as a gentleman-novelist unsoiled by one's
work, to have been called Bill by the First Lady and, during
those years, to have mingled in the Green or Blue Room with
the other certified celebrants of a New Frontier rather different from Mailer's. If only America would include *me!* cried
Mailer, in his agony of unrequitable love for the Far Princess
and the Hollywood America of his peevish dreams:

> . . . there was a way she could show us she was beginning to
> learn, it was the way of the hostess: one would offer her one's

---

* Ernest J. Simmons, *Leo Tolstoy*, Vintage Books, Vol. II, p. 347.
† *An American Dream* is not the promised novel. Mailer seems to have
attempted, in this diversion, to make indelible all the defects of his style
and imagination; it reads like Frank Sinatra's memoirs ghost-written by
Anaïs Nin. It is so absolute a fiasco that one hopes, without confidence,
that it was done only for money.

sword when Henry Miller [not to mention Norman Mailer] was
asked to the White House as often as Robert Frost . . . [and]
Archibald MacLeish. . . .

For Mailer's myth of America is the old Hollywood myth
again, a myth of power. "I want to know how power works,"
Mailer once said to his friend James Baldwin, "how it really
works, in detail." And the rejoinder that Baldwin, as a Negro,
made for himself is one that Mailer cannot accept: "Well, I
know how power works," says Baldwin, "it has worked on me,
and if I didn't know how power worked, I would be dead. And
it goes without saying, perhaps, that I have simply never been
able to afford myself any illusions concerning the manipulation
of that power. My revenge, I decided very early, would be to
achieve a power which outlasts kingdoms."

In such a power, neither Mailer nor Styron believes. Mailer's
true belief has its comic, or possibly deranged, aspect. He appears to have quite seriously contemplated running for Mayor
of New York, till a marital contretemps that made the tabloids
removed him from the race. He has written on several occasions that his article on Kennedy, which was published in *Esquire* a few weeks before the 1960 election, may well have
swung that election. In reply to a polite complimentary letter
from Mrs. Kennedy ("the Catholic wife," as he afterward rue-
fully reminded himself, "of a Catholic candidate for President"), Mailer expansively wrote that he "hoped one day . . .
to do a biography of the Marquis de Sade and the 'odd strange
honor of the man' "; and their correspondence ended. Mailer's
obsession with Mrs. Kennedy, however, did not end; he continued to write about her, and in an open letter to her husband
soon after the Cuban crisis of 1962 he demanded that the President show his good faith during any future crisis by dispatch-
ing his family to the prime target, New York: "Why not send
us a hostage? Why not let us have Jacqueline Kennedy?"

There must be power somewhere, power to do if not to do
good, in Washington and Hollywood; and Mailer has seemed
on the verge, now and then, of comprehending the relation
between these North and South Poles of the torn and convul-
sive American psyche:

Jack Kennedy understood that the most important, probably the only dynamic culture in America, the only culture to enlist the imagination and change the character of Americans, was the one we had been given by the movies. Therefore a void existed at the center of American life. No movie star had the mind, courage or force to be a national leader, and no national leader had the epic adventurous resonance of a movie star.

So the President nominated himself. He would fill the void. He would be the movie star come to life as President.

"Politics," says Mailer, "even practical politics, has roots in a mystery, in that part of the mystery which contains sex, death, dread, courage, and intimations of waste and growth." No doubt. But a mystery can be exploited, cheapened, stamped out by those who merely conduct its ceremonies. Power may, in the decrepitude of mystery, be whatever fills the void; the nominal charisma of title and office may belong to whoever, having accurately forecast the lowest ebb of the national capacity to resist, moves in to claim the unoccupied places of power; moves in, perhaps, without having heeded the unexpended public madness that, in a time of self-appointed heroes, moves with him into the great vacancy.

Perhaps the need—certainly once a possible goal—of the novelist is to have power beyond the keepers of title and office, to be the acknowledged voice and conscience of his time, like Dickens or Tolstoy; perhaps the doom of the contemporary American novelist is that at best he can sit at the tables of the mighty, scrambling for crusts. Meanwhile, he lives for the day of the big review and the months of the best-seller. Mailer tells us how he lived only on the hope that the sales of *The Deer Park* would crack one hundred thousand; and he reports that Styron was embittered by the failure of *Lie Down in Darkness* "to make him a household word in America." Dickens and Tolstoy had power; for the novelist now, only popularity is possible; and money—for the novelist, as for the movie star—is the index of popularity. A novelist presents, creates, with unprecedented detail and amplitude, the community, society, nation, collective will he lives in and has nightmares about. Is it surprising that to be ignored by what he has brought into being is an indignity which, once he has spent his arrogant youth,

mauls and unhinges his individual will? If the American novelist does his best work in his twenties and early thirties (as
Hemingway, Fitzgerald, Faulkner did; as Styron and Mailer, so
far, have done), the reason may be that there is no room for
him in the desperately unconscious and platonic country of his
invention, America, the country in which everything sooner or
later dematerializes into the abstractions of money and the
oblivions of violence and random coupling. Mailer, like other
broken idealists, is trying to pretend that the country of his
invention is also—at least in becoming, in the pure oxygen of
some pan-hipster future—the country of his desire; that it *must*
be—else what will he have to write about? and for whom will
he write? The First Lady declined to notice his Napoleonic
letter; and the public, which does not read him, will never even
learn that it is expected to reply.

Styron, defeated as a novelist, has coldly chosen the garden
path to the drawing-rooms of the Establishment. One may suspect that he knew all along where he was heading and what it
took to get there: talent, but not too vigorously exhibited;
style, without bite or intelligence; supine moralities momentarily illuminated by sulphur and brimstone. If Mailer has gone
the same way, at least he has entertained us kicking and scream-
ing and ruffling the languid nerves of his hostesses: the terrible
infant who can still offend, and may yet carry off some of the
silverware, and is therefore more attractive to those outside
than the stony proprietors and docile guests of the Establishment. For the critic, however, the distinction may not be
worth making.

1964

POSTSCRIPT 1970

Nothing pleasant comes to mind regarding either late Styron
or late Mailer. Styron spent most of the 'sixties on *The Confessions of Nat Turner*, which turns out to be what it was in-

tended to be, a compassionate and prophetic money-maker about slavery and other problematic issues. When Styron is trying to reconstruct Nat's sensibility, as in the first third or so of the book, he melts with magnolia lyricism; when he tries to deal with the available facts, he is (often simultaneously) pedestrian and melodramatic; when he ponders the bad movie that the book will make, he composes instructions aimed at tiny-tot film directors—

> Again his words fade away on my ears, and I briefly shut my eyes, half drowsing, and again I hear her voice, bell-clear on that somnolent dusty Sunday half a year past . . .

Styron is now the last of the drugstore novelists.

Mailer, on the other hand, has been very busy establishing himself as the great American writer for people who don't read. Stravinsky invented a helpful new formula for criticism when he remarked that "Wagner is the Puccini of music." By the end of the 'sixties it had become reasonable to propose that Hemingway is the Norman Mailer of literature. The Mailer career more and more desperately resembles a travesty of Hemingway's. Mailer too, as Cyril Connolly foresaw, "retired into public life" and is now a full-time political journalist and public nuisance, not just in his hot-off-the-firing-line accounts of the Pentagon march and the 1968 conventions and the jolly astronauts, but in so preposterously literary a hasty-pudding as *Why Are We in Vietnam?*, post-Joyce, post-Hemingway, post-Faulkner, post-Burroughs, post-mortem: "Herman Melville go hump Moby and wash his Dick," muses Minbad-the-Mailer's 18-year-old "well-hung" Texas scion on his way to proving— bless us!—that war is the last refuge of the supermale. For Mailer's opinions aren't even unorthodox or timely: despite all the churning-up of no-longer-dirty words and stale scraps of hippie-commune mysticism he is as automatic as a *New York Times* editorial, James Reston in fright-wig and topless bikini.

Malamud, Bellow, and Roth have taken upon themselves the job of inventing the contemporary fictional Jew. In contemporary America, where Jewishness has been more and more rapidly converging into the Wasp matrix of neutral pristine affluence, the job is almost anachronistic, almost archeology, like setting up a wailing wall in a supermarket. It is as if a Hebrew patriarch, having outlived the wife of his youth, had married the wife of his old age and fathered three sons to say *Kaddish* for him in post-ghetto America: Bernard, traditional and belated down to the self-protective ghetto humor, a pillar of the synagogue, rather prosaic maybe but steady and reliable, his father's son; then Saul, irresistible talker, promoter, last of the big-time spenders, flashy, wilful, hypnotically charming, bottomlessly cynical and sad, home only for the high holidays when he puts on the skullcap and a pious face for services; finally Philip, nervous, vulnerable, the doomed and delicate one, least committed to the past and most troubled by the future, whom all the family fusses over and is apprehensively fond of. In post-1945 America they are not unlike Faulkner of the twenties and thirties, appropriating a subject which was already slipping out of sight at the time he began to write about it. To mention Faulkner is to propose a standard which they cannot meet, but which suggests their provincialism and their seriousness. Malamud, Bellow, and Roth are, in a dry spell for American fiction, the most intelligent and the most considerable American novelists since World War II.

What a dry spell, though! with even the better novelists redoing the slick-magazine iconographies of war, of Hollywood and New York glamor, of struggle against social injustice, of existentialism or Zen or voodoo or camp, of publicity and news; until so (probably) talented a writer as Norman Mailer can publish in *Esquire* his pop-novel *An American Dream*, which regurgitates, installment by installment, all the chic pipedreams that readers of *Esquire* customarily derive from its ads and cover articles. Against such stuff, Malamud's owlish attention to every can of beans on the shelves of a failing grocery reads like Tolstoy; Roth's Martha Reganhart is Helen of Troy; Bellow's Tommy Wilhelm, Hamlet and Faust. Still, it had better be clear that the claims for Malamud, Bellow, and Roth will have to be modest enough, and that they will exclude much or most of the work. For instance, *The Natural* is a very silly novel, a comic-book sports story tricked out with sex and a moral. Much of Bellow, especially Augie and Henderson, is an obfuscatory whirlwind of juvenile pep and philosophizing (Henderson thinks, talks, and behaves—at fifty-five!—with the shy, gawky, endearingly brainless innocence of Holden Caulfield). And *Goodbye, Columbus* is a collection of stories— knowing, ironic, salted with symbols, assembled according to the best models—by the most promising member of the advanced creative writing class at State U.

Goodbye, Columbus is a characteristic false start by a bright young man. It is also, under its machined surface, vexed by emotions it can't begin to cope with. Roth, almost a generation younger than the others, was in his middle twenties when it appeared in 1959: an acclaimed volume whose twists and gimmicks are mainly at the service of Roth's never satisfactorily explained distaste for the nearly assimilated Jew. The long title story is typical—an exposé of country-club Jews with gobs of money, whose son is large enough to have played Big Ten basketball (though his name is Patimkin), whose daughter has the comparable temerity to play tennis, bob her nose (even though

her name is not Wentworth or MacDonald but *Patimkin!*),
and in the end choose her family over a penniless young Jewish
librarian as lachrymose as he is uninterruptedly self-congratu-
latory. At a critical moment, for instance, the librarian medi-
tates in St. Patrick's Cathedral—daring and ironic setting—on
whether bed with beautiful Brenda would compensate for all
the revolting, Jewish material comfort he would have to put up
with (Brenda, meanwhile, is at the doctor's being fitted with a
diaphragm):

> It wasn't much cooler inside the church, though the stillness
> and the flicker of the candles made me think it was. I took a seat
> at the rear and while I couldn't bring myself to kneel, I did lean
> forward onto the back of the bench before me, and held my
> hands together and closed my eyes. I wondered if I looked like
> a Catholic, and in my wonderment I began to make a little
> speech to myself. Can I call the self-conscious words I spoke
> prayer? At any rate, I called my audience God. God, I said, I
> am twenty-three years old. I want to make the best of things.
> Now the doctor is about to wed Brenda to me, and I am not en-
> tirely certain this is all for the best. What is it I love, Lord? Why
> have I chosen? Who is Brenda? The race is to the swift. Should
> I have stopped to think?
>
> I was getting no answers, but I went on. If we meet You at
> all, God, it's that we're carnal, and acquisitive, and thereby par-
> take of you. I am carnal, and I know You approve, I just know
> it. But how carnal can I get? I am acquisitive. Where do I turn
> now in my acquisitiveness? Where do we meet? Which prize is
> You?
>
> It was an ingenious meditation, and suddenly I felt ashamed.
> I got up and walked outside, and the noise of Fifth Avenue met
> me with an answer:
>
> Which prize do you think, *schmuck?* Gold dinnerware, sport-
> ing-goods trees, nectarines, garbage disposals, bumpless noses,
> Patimkin Sink, Bonwit Teller—
>
> But, damn it, God, that *is* You!
>
> And God only laughed, that clown.

Stephen Dedalus, another sniveling prig who detested his com-
patriots, had better reasons.

Malamud and Bellow, each almost two decades older than
Roth, grew up in the very different Jewish milieu of the De-

pression, an enclave of the poor and the unassimilated; and their earliest efforts to deal with it take no account of the fact that it had virtually disappeared by the time they began to write. Moreover, before they came to it, they made false starts in other directions. Bellow's first novel, *Dangling Man*, is an attempt to turn the plight of a man waiting to be drafted (during World War II) into an allegory of the rootlessness of modern life, a malicious and penetrating self-analysis by a new underground man; but Bellow's rhetoric, even when he's being unbearably profound—

> The sense in which Goethe was right: Continued life means expectation. Death is the abolition of choice. The more choice is limited, the closer we are to death. The greatest cruelty is to curtail expectations without taking away life completely. A life term in prison is like that. So is citizenship in some countries. The best solution would be to live as if the ordinary expectations had not been removed, not from day to day, blindly. But that requires immense self-mastery.

—amounts to little more than that people get awfully tired of waiting. As for Malamud's first novel, *The Natural* is a lamentable attempt to take baseball seriously (Ring Lardner did the best that could be done, fictionally, with the game by assuming that everybody who makes a career of it is an imbecile).

It was in their second novels that both Bellow and Malamud took up the subject of the Jew in America. Bellow's title, *The Victim*, might have been Malamud's too, and proposes their emphasis and intention. *The Victim* was published in 1947, when Buchenwald was topical enough to mask the fact that anti-Semitism would not be among the political issues of the future. Bellow was still writing allegory, and it was still very literary: this time with echoes of "The Secret Sharer" and other *Doppelgänger* stories; this time drawn out well beyond the novella length of *Dangling Man* by masses of naturalistic and symbolic detail, by thriller-like accumulations of suspense and (startlingly irrelevant) complications of plot. *Dangling Man* tries to convert the topical into allegory and literature, and so does *The Victim*. But Bellow doesn't manage to sense that aspect of the topical which will outlast the day, as, say, Dostoevsky did with the newspaper murder story that launched *The Possessed*. Indeed, Bellow stakes everything on the unimpaired survival of the topical, as if newspapers were history; so that when his inquisitor-victim, Allbee, deplores the mongrelization of America—

> "Hell, yes. Well, you look like Caliban in the first place," Allbee said, more serious than not. "But that's not all I mean. You personally, you're just one out of many. Many kinds. You wouldn't be able to see that. Sometimes I feel—and I'm saying this seriously—I feel as if I were in a sort of Egyptian darkness. You know, Moses punished the Egyptians with darkness. And that's how I often think of this. When I was born, when I was a boy, everything was different. We thought it would be daylight forever. Do you know, one of my ancestors was Governor Winthrop. Governor Winthrop!" His voice vibrated fiercely; there was a repressed laugh in it. "I'm a fine one to be talking about tradition, you must be saying. But still I was born into it. And try to imagine how New York affects me. Isn't it preposterous? It's really as if the children of Caliban were running everything. You go down in the subway and Caliban gives you two nickels for your dime. You go home and he has a candy store in the street where you were born. The old breeds are out. The streets are named after them. But what are they themselves? Just remnants."
>
> "I see how it is; you're actually an aristocrat," said Leventhal.
>
> "It may not strike you as it struck me," said Allbee. "But I go into the library once in a while, to look around, and last week I saw a book about Thoreau and Emerson by a man named Lipschitz . . ."

—when Allbee articulates his hatred, what at our distance in time we hear is not a threat and a prophecy, but a voice from a newspaper morgue. Bellow has failed to observe that, though the topical *contains* the threat, to reproduce the topical is not to isolate or identify the threat, which, to the confusion of newspaper-readers and apprentice novelists, insists on changing its habitat and appearance and therefore its name from one edition of the daily press to the next. Nor does Bellow regain our confidence at the end by losing his own, when he shrugs off the whole plot as a bad season through which Leventhal has safely passed. It meant more than that to the protagonist at the time, and to the author; and counted on meaning more than that to us.

Ten years later, and as much farther from Buchenwald, Malamud wrote his own version of *The Victim. The Assistant* also sees the Jew as allegorical, representative, and bedeviled, in a context—economic for Malamud, as it was political for Bellow—that recalls 1937 rather than 1957:

> He felt weightless, unmanned, the victim in a motion of whatever blew at his back; wind, worries, debts, Karp, holdupniks, ruin. He did not go, he was pushed. He had the will of a victim, no will to speak of.
>
> "For what I worked so hard for? Where is my youth, where did it go?"
>
> The years had passed without profit or pity. Who could he blame? What fate didn't do to him he had done to himself. The right thing was to make the right choice but he made the wrong. Even when it was right it was wrong. To understand why, you needed an education but he had none. All he knew was he wanted better but had not after all these years learned how to get it. Luck was a gift. Karp had it, a few of his old friends had it, well-to-do men with grandchildren already, while his poor daughter, made in his image, faced—if not actively sought—old-maidhood. Life was meager, the world changed for the worse. America had become too complicated. One man counted for nothing. There were too many stores, depressions, anxieties . . .

Or the view may be from outside the pale, as when the Italian assistant observes the Jewish readiness for shared misery:

> When Breitbart first came to Morris' neighborhood and dropped into the store, the grocer, seeing his fatigue, offered him a glass of tea with lemon. The peddler eased the rope off his shoulder and set his boxes on the floor. In the back he gulped the hot tea in silence, warming both hands on the glass. And though he had, besides his other troubles, the seven-year itch, which kept him awake half the night, he never complained. After ten minutes he got up, thanked the grocer, fitted the rope onto his lean and itchy shoulder and left. One day he told Morris the story of his life and they both wept.
>
> That's what they live for, Frank thought, to suffer. And the one that has got the biggest pain in the gut and can hold onto

it the longest without running to the toilet is the best Jew. No wonder they got on his nerves.

One of the differences between Bellow and Malamud is in their tutelary divinities. In his first two novels Bellow is writing with a self-conscious awareness of Conrad, of Dostoevsky, of such quasi-literary metaphysical agonists as Kierkegaard and Sartre: his allegory too easily disentangles itself from plot and aims at an independent and unprovincial *Weltanschauung*. In *The Victim* Bellow is impatient with the stereotype of the Jew, he wants the Jew to be a man, and then Man; Leventhal is recognizably enough an image of the New York Jew, but his crisis is too quickly a crisis of Western civilization, or too quickly intends to be. Moreover Bellow is handicapped in his strenuous purpose by an inert and colorless style, naturalism without its possible saving doggedness of accuracy on how people pass the days of a life; nothing like, for instance, the precision and hallucinatory intimations of Conrad's best prose; nor much like Malamud either.

Malamud embraces without reservation the provincialism he has no interest in evading: his Depression Jews, their undisplaceable identity, the dreary inventory of local impedimenta that keep them where they are, and the style that may be all too faithful an analogue of their cluttered, graceless, and wellmeaning lives. Malamud's great exemplar is Hardy. Like Hardy, he has a tin ear except for the dialectal speech of his locality; like Hardy, he is in no hurry to be cosmopolitan; like Hardy, he believes with the passion of perfect knowledge in what unexceptional people do. It is of course a question of likeness and not equality: Malamud resembles Hardy in subject, in method, in knowledge and conviction, in limitations, though not in size. But Bellow, aspiring to be Dostoevsky, achieves the master's occasional impression of melodramatic strain without suggesting either Dostoevsky's magnitude or any of his virtues.

Malamud, like Hardy, has the provincial bias. The allegorical intentions of *The Assistant*—like Hardy's cosmic backdrops to the events of heath and village—are momentous because Malamud really believes that life lived close to subsistence, close to the level of animal need (and therefore close to "na-

ture," in a setting as claustrophobic as Hardy's though urban
rather than rural), is the truest and most representative life, it
tests the spirit and insists on the most unequivocal manifestations of fortitude, loyalty, and love. Malamud's conviction
leads him to construct an allegory of expiation, prodigious labors, self-sacrifice, and what might be called—after the two
millennia of the Christian ascendancy—reconversion; and his
knowledge of the ordinariness out of which such extraordinary
manifestations must come is so patient and unsparing that the
allegory becomes simply the meaning of the events—of an
event, for example, as impersonally traditional, as mechanical,
as full of indispensable lies and omissions, as a rabbi's eulogy at
the funeral of a man he never knew:

> "My dear friends, I never had the pleasure to meet this good
> grocery man that he now lays in his coffin. He lived in a neigh-
> borhood where I didn't come in. Still and all I talked this morn-
> ing to people that knew him and I am now sorry I didn't know
> him also. I would enjoy to speak to such a man. I talked to the
> bereaved widow, who lost her dear husband. I talked to his poor
> beloved daughter Helen, who is now without a father to guide
> her. To them I talked, also to landsleit and old friends, and each
> and all told me the same, that Morris Bober, who passed away
> so untimely—he caught double pneumonia from shoveling snow
> in front of his place of business so people could pass by on the
> sidewalk—was a man who couldn't be more honest. Such a per-
> son I am sorry I didn't meet sometime in my life. If I met him
> somewhere, maybe when he came to visit in a Jewish neighbor-
> hood—maybe at Rosh Hashana or Pesach—I would say to him,
> 'God bless you, Morris Bober.' Helen, his dear daughter, remem-
> bers from when she was a small girl that her father ran two
> blocks in the snow to give back to a poor Italian lady a nickel
> that she forgot on the counter. Who runs in wintertime without
> hat or coat, without rubbers to protect his feet, two blocks in the
> snow to give back five cents that a customer forgot? Couldn't he
> wait till she comes in tomorrow? Not Morris Bober, let him rest
> in peace. He didn't want the poor woman to worry, so he ran
> after her in the snow. This is why the grocer had so many friends
> who admir-ed him . . ."

The grocer's daughter knows better: ". . . I didn't say he
had many friends who admired him. That's the rabbi's inven-

tion. People liked him, but who can admire a man passing his life in such a store? He buried himself in it; he didn't have the imagination to know what he was missing. He made himself a victim. He could, with a little more courage, have been more than he was." But the rabbi's lies are the last dignity that the corpse earned by dying; and the truths are what Frank Alpine, the hoodlum assistant, builds on with his terrible effort to transform himself into the man he robbed. Malamud's powers are not up to convincing us of the probability of Frank's ultimate decision. And the novel is more convincingly a funeral eulogy than a prospect of the future, Frank's or anybody else's. But *The Assistant* is a failure only in its terminal insistence on allegorical tidiness.

The subject of *The Assistant* is the Jew as victim and example; and it is a subject that attracts Malamud sufficiently to bring him back to it in several of his short stories: "The Mourners," for instance, "The First Seven Years," "The Death of Me," or "The Cost of Living," of which the last reads like a suicidally despondent first draft of *The Assistant*. Or the Jew is a butt, as in the farcical and sometimes very funny stories about Fidelman, the student painter in Europe, on one occasion imprisoned by an Italian thug who for the sake of an elaborate ransom scheme forces him to make a copy of the "Venus of Urbino":

What a miracle, thought Fidelman.

The golden brown-haired Venus, a woman of the real world, lay on her couch in serene beauty, her hand lightly touching her intimate mystery, the other holding red flowers, her nude body her truest accomplishment.

"I would have painted somebody in bed with her," Scarpio said.

"Shut up," said Fidelman.

Scarpio, hurt, left the gallery.

Fidelman, alone with Venus, worshipped the painting. What magnificent tones, what extraordinary flesh that can turn the body into spirit.

While Scarpio was out talking to the guard, the copyist hastily sketched the Venus, and with a Leica Angelo had borrowed from a friend for the purpose, took several new color shots.

> Afterwards he approached the picture and kissed the lady's hands, thighs, and breasts, but as he was murmuring, "I love you," a guard struck him hard on the head with both fists.

Or the Jew is a genre figure in a provincial setting that emphasizes, not the imminence of ruin, but the proliferations of custom and idiosyncrasy, as when the rabbinical student consults the matchmaker in the title story of *The Magic Barrel:*

> Salzman . . . placed the card down on the wooden table and began to read another:
> "Lily H. high school teacher. Regular. Not a substitute. Has savings and new Dodge car. Lived in Paris one year. Father is successful dentist thirty-five years. Interested in professional man. Well Americanized family. Wonderful opportunity."
> "I know her personally," said Salzman. "I wish you could see this girl. She is a doll. Also very intelligent. All day you could talk to her about books and theater and what not. She also knows current events.". . .
> ". . . but I'm not interested in . . . school teachers."
> Salzman pulled his clasped hands to his breast. Looking at the ceiling he devoutly exclaimed, "Yiddishe kinder, what can I say to somebody that he is not interested in high school teachers? So what then you are interested?"
> Leo flushed but controlled himself.
> "In what else will you be interested," Salzman went on, "if you not interested in this fine girl that she speaks four languages and has personally in the bank ten thousand dollars? Also her father guarantees further twelve thousand. Also she has a new car, wonderful clothes, talks on all subjects, and she will give you a first-class home and children. How near do we come in our life to paradise?"

There are also fantasies, in a Yiddish tradition of tales of the supernatural—encounters with angels and other emissaries of God and the Devil—a tradition of which the distinguished living exponent is Isaac Bashevis Singer; but Malamud doesn't altogether avoid the temptation which the mode offers to whimsy (as in "The Jewbird" and "Angel Levine"), or to an unvalidated presumption of superearthly issues (as in "Take Pity" and the title story of *Idiots First*). The fact is that, after *The Assistant*, Malamud's interest in the Jew as fictional subject is never so intense, so apocalyptic, it becomes increasingly ironic and remote, even exploitative. The victim and example is becoming a sad sack, a vaudeville comic down to the pratfalls and rubber nightsticks, possibly a holy innocent in a world of sharpers. The ghetto is turning into a stage.

Bellow, too, after *The Victim*, seems to have lost interest in the subject; or rather to have grown impatient with its limitations. His spectacular attempts to break it up and to break away from it are, respectively, *The Adventures of Augie March* and *Henderson the Rain King*.

In *Augie*, as in *The Victim*, the protagonist is a Jew; but in all other ways Bellow seems resolved to turn inside into out and down into up. *The Victim* is a closed system, heavily plotted, in a setting as fixed as that of *The Assistant; Augie* is open, episodic, picaresque. The hero of *The Victim* is a Jew and therefore somehow a stranger and under surveillance in America; Augie March is a Jew almost fortuitously and without consequence, but from the first sentence "an American, Chicago born," who recollects the anti-Semitic brutalities inflicted upon him in his childhood only to disclaim their influence on him:

> . . . I never had any special grief from it, or brooded, being by and large too larky and boisterous to take it to heart, and looked at it as needing no more special explanation than the stone-and-bat wars of the street gangs or the swarming on a fall evening of parish punks to rip up fences, screech and bawl at girls, and beat up strangers.

And, as the foregoing quotation suggests, Bellow has contrived a style for Augie's speaking voice that he hopes will convey a "larky and boisterous" quality as unlike the flat-footed somberness of *The Victim* as possible.

Not that Bellow abandons the Jews. What he does is transmogrify them into a great elbowing parade of the unsubduable robust (not at all the trampled and wailing ghetto pygmies); so that by page 20 the reader is near exhaustion from descriptions of consecutive giants and monsters:

> That would be Five Properties, shambling through the cottage, Anna's immense brother, long armed and humped, his head

grown off the thick band of muscle as original as a bole on his back . . .

The intention resembles Isaac Babel's in his Odessa stories. Babel's heroic desperado, Benya Krik, is not, as Babel has the narrator remark, called the King for nothing; and Babel accomplishes the *tour de force* of turning into credible giants Jews who still inhabited the Odessa ghetto. Babel is Benya's affectionate Homer, the lyrical magnifier of his fame; but Babel has a wink for the reader as well as respect for Benya's impressive deeds. Bellow's giants, though, are less agile, they are even torpid and musclebound, perhaps because there are so many of them that he can scarcely do more than describe them one to a page, perhaps also because he insists on stressing, not (as Babel does) the comic excess of their vitality, but their mere size.

Bellow's intention is to show the ghetto Jews as worthy progenitors of Augie the all-American boy, pure metal fresh from the melting pot; but his method is less to invent actions than to attack the reader with a calculated hubbub of assertions, data, objects, Whitmanic catalogues and lists, historical and philosophical references (Augie is bookish, a good Jewish trait), wry humor (issue of a good Jewish head), and that colloquial pitchmanship which will die trying or amalgamate all of these into a new (if you'll pardon the expression) Jerusalem, American style, a city of Olympic-size swimming pools and matching plaster monuments:

> William Einhorn was the first superior man I knew. He had a brain and many enterprises, real directing power, philosophical capacity, and if I were methodical enough to take thought before an important and practical decision and also (*N. B.*) if I were really his disciple and not what I am, I'd ask myself, "What would Caesar suffer in this case? What would Machiavelli advise or Ulysses do? What would Einhorn think?" I'm not kidding when I enter Einhorn in this eminent list. It was him that I knew, and what I understand of them in him. Unless you want to say that we're at the dwarf end of all times and mere children whose only share in grandeur is like a boy's share in fairy-tale kings, being of a different kind from times better and stronger than ours. But if we're comparing men and men, not men and children or men and demigods, which is just what would please Caesar

among us teeming democrats, and if we don't have any special
wish to abdicate into some different, lower form of existence
out of shame for our defects before the golden faces of these
and other old-time men, then I have the right to praise Einhorn
and not care about smiles of derogation from those who think
the race no longer has in any important degree the traits we
honor in these fabulous names . . .

—which is a fancy introduction for a man who occupies little
space in the book, and most of that taken up by descriptions of
his not infallible bent for minor-league commercial finagling.
But then, Einhorn is a fixer, a user, an operator, a man of the
world who will ceremoniously, at the right hour, conduct a
growing boy to his first prostitute; and Bellow is determined to
see such talents as, because he conceives them to be American,
primary virtues.

Bellow, through Augie, is in hot pursuit of the American
experience. He wishes to glorify and praise the inveterate
American obsession—Jefferson and Pound are two of its il-
luminati—with particulars and how to handle them, expertness,
know-how: mastery of data and process, expecially mechanical
and impersonal process, like capturing whales and carving and
boiling them up into various neat messes of merchandise; and
he equally admires the parallel obsession with grand reductive
abstractions, as in *Moby Dick* (the nineteenth-century American novel that aspires to be the great American novel and
therefore, since America is the ineluctable future, the great
novel of the world). Augie will know all things and how they
work, will use them up like paper in a flame; though out there,
always, lies a darkness still more ineluctable than America:

However, as I felt on entering Erie, Pennsylvania, there is a
darkness. It is for everyone. You don't, as perhaps some imagine,
try it, one foot into it like a barbershop "September Morn." Nor
are lowered into it with visitors' curiosity, as the old Eastern
monarch was let down into the weeds inside a glass ball to observe the fishes. Nor are lifted straight out after an unlucky
tumble, like a Napoleon from the mud of the Arcole where he
had been standing up to his thoughtful nose while the Hungarian
bullets broke the clay off the bank. Only some Greeks and admirers of theirs, in their liquid noon, where the friendship of

beauty to human things was perfect, thought they were clearly divided from this darkness. And these Greeks too were in it. But still they are the admiration of the rest of the mud-sprung, famine-knifed, street-pounding, war-rattled, difficult, painstaking, kicked in the belly, grief and cartilage mankind, the multitude, some under a coal-sucking Vesuvius of chaos smoke, some inside a heaving Calcutta midnight, who very well know where they are.

Against this darkness, Augie's boyish charm avails him not. The best he can muster against it is a sequence of girls, some palaver about love as the infinite; most modestly and persuasively, affection for his brother, the rich businessman, whom Bellow presents with a truthful audacity that he mostly fakes for the others:

> . . . Simon worked himself into a rage at Mrs. Magnus in her brown dress. He tried to read the paper and cut her—he hadn't said a word when she came in—but finally he said, and I could see the devil in him now, "Well, you lousy old miser, I see you still buy your clothes off the janitor's wife."
>
> "Let her alone," said Charlotte sharply.
>
> But suddenly Simon threw himself across the table, spilling the cherries and overturning coffee cups. He grabbed his mother-in-law's dress at the collar, thrust in his hand, and tore the cloth down to the waist. She screamed. There were her giant soft breasts wrapped in the pink band. What a great astonishment it was, all of a sudden to see them! She panted and covered the top nudity with her hands and turned away. However, her cries were also cries of laughter. How she loved Simon! He knew it too.
>
> "Hide, hide!" he said, laughing.
>
> "You crazy fool," cried Charlotte. She ran away on her high heels to bring her mother a coat and came back laughing also. They were downright proud, I guess.
>
> Simon wrote out a check and gave it to Mrs. Magnus. "Here," he said, "buy yourself something and don't come here looking like the scrubwoman." He went and kissed her on the braids, and she took his head and gave his kisses back two for one and with tremendous humor.

It is a fine and uncharacteristic moment, in a book that rings with the shrillness of unfulfilled ambitions.

The book is also very sad in its pretense of joy, the pretense of a self-reforming but unregenerate misanthrope. By the time of *Henderson the Rain King*, the pretense has become grotesque in its frantic didacticism and lack of conviction. Bellow is reduced to having his hero converse with Africans whose level of English is "I no know" or "I no bothah you" or "Me Horko"; and even when the Me-Tarzan-You-Jane dialogue is expanded for the King's quasi-Oxonian ontological ditherings about lions, Henderson continues to associate himself with such quaint locutions as "strong gift of life" and "the wisdom of life," such sudden illuminations as "I don't think the struggles of desire can ever be won," and such racy life-loving as follows: "I am a true adorer of life, and if I can't reach as high as the face of it, I plant my kiss somewhere lower down. Those who understand will require no further explanation." Bellow would like Henderson to be *truly* American, purebred old-stock Anglo-Saxon (of all things!), Paul Bunyan in an age of bad nerves; but Henderson in the pages of the book is half Augie, half catcher in the rye. One wonders whether Bellow has any notion of how much he is borrowing in postures and phony wistfulness from a writer so inferior to him as Salinger; especially at the embarrassing conclusion, when Henderson races round the plane with the child in his arms, that Salinger child (sometimes named Phoebe) who will redeem us all.

Between Augie and Henderson, Bellow produced his novella, *Seize the Day*, which is the real pastrami between two thick slices of American store bread. In *Seize the Day* Bellow comes to terms with his characteristic themes and obsessions, at least to the extent of setting them suitably down among the gross fleshy shocks of credible fictional encounters; between the derivativeness of *The Victim* and the modulated hysterias of Augie and Henderson he accomplishes, on a plateau of unharassed self-knowledge, a style that can deal honestly with the agonies he is elsewhere content to gloss over with solemn or breezy rhetoric. The wise man, for example, is a recurrent figure in Bellow: Schlossberg in *The Victim*, Einhorn in *Augie*, Dahfu in *Henderson*—none of whom, however, survives Bellow's insistence on the blaring unambiguous singleness of power and wisdom, the last golden words we must come to and stop at. His great discovery, in *Seize the Day*, is the duplicity and chanciness of wisdom, the charlatanry of power, the ungraspable difficulty and slipperiness of both; and his great illustration is the connection between the poor slob, the genuine baffled victim, Tommy Wilhelm, and the quicksilver conman, Dr. Tamkin:

> "I want to tell you about this boy and his dad. It's highly absorbing. The father was a nudist. Everybody went naked in the house. Maybe the woman found men *with* clothes attractive. Her husband didn't believe in cutting his hair, either. He practiced dentistry. In his office he wore riding pants and a pair of boots, and he wore a green eyeshade."
>
> "Oh, come off it," said Wilhelm.
>
> "This is a true case history."
>
> Without warning, Wilhelm began to laugh. He himself had had no premonition of his change of humor. His face became warm and pleasant, and he forgot his father, his anxieties; he panted bearlike, happily, through his teeth. "This sounds like a horse-dentist. He wouldn't have to put on pants to treat a horse. Now what else are you going to tell me? Did the wife play the mandolin? Does the boy join the cavalry? Oh, Tamkin, you really are a killer-diller."
>
> "Oh, you think I'm trying to amuse you," said Tamkin. "That's because you aren't familiar with my outlook. I deal in facts. Facts always are sensational. I'll say that a second time. Facts *always!* are sensational."

So they are; but Bellow has in other books impersonated Dr. Tamkin rather than understood him, this model of the contemporary mind, ragbag of public and private facts and fancies lavishly scattered like farts in a windstorm, as miscellaneous and unassemblable as amputated legs and arms, tumbling outward toward horizons of meaninglessness:

> "Her brother. He's under my care, too. He has some terrible tendencies, which are to be expected when you have an epileptic sibling. I came into their lives when they needed help desperately, and took hold of them. A certain man forty years older than she had her in his control and used to give her fits by suggestion whenever she tried to leave him. If you only knew one per cent of what goes on in the city of New York. You see, I

understand what it is when the lonely person begins to feel like
an animal. When the night comes and he feels like howling from
his window like a wolf. I'm taking complete care of that young
fellow and his sister. I have to steady him down or he'll go from
Brazil to Australia the next day. The way I keep him in the
here-and-now is by teaching him Greek."

This was a complete surprise! "What, do you know Greek?"

"A friend of mine taught me when I was in Cairo. I studied
Aristotle with him to keep from being idle."

Wilhelm tried to take in these new claims and examine them.
Howling from the window like a wolf when night comes
sounded genuine to him. That was something really to think
about. But the Greek! He realized that Tamkin was watching
to see how he took it. More elements were continually being
added. A few days ago Tamkin had hinted that he had once been
in the underworld, one of the Detroit Purple Gang. He was once
head of a mental clinic in Toledo. He had worked with a Polish
inventor on an unsinkable ship. He was a technical consultant
in the field of television. In the life of a man of genius, all of
these things might happen. But had they happened to Tamkin?
Was he a genius? He often said that he had attended some of
the Egyptian royal family as a psychiatrist. "But everybody is
alike, common or aristocrat," he told Wilhelm. "The aristocrat
knows less about life."

An Egyptian princess whom he had treated in California, for
horrible disorders he had described to Wilhelm, retained him
to come back to the old country with her, and there he had had
many of her friends and relatives under his care. They turned
over a villa on the Nile to him. "For ethical reasons, I can't tell
you many of the details about them," he said—but Wilhelm had
already heard all these details, and strange and shocking they
were, if true. *If* true—he could not be free from doubt. For instance, the general who had to wear ladies' silk stockings and
stand otherwise naked before the mirror—and all the rest. Listening to the doctor when he was so strangely factual, Wilhelm had
to translate his words into his own language, and he could not
translate fast enough or find terms to fit what he heard.

Wisdom may, after all, turn out to be nothing more than somebody else's cockeyed and circumstantial dreams of glory:

"Those Egyptian big shots invested in the market, too, for the
heck of it. What did they need extra money for? By association,

I almost became a millionaire myself, and if I had played it smart there's no telling what might have happened. I could have been the ambassador." The American? The Egyptian ambassador? "A friend of mine tipped me off on the cotton. I made a heavy purchase of it. I didn't have that kind of money, but everybody there knew me. It never entered their minds that a person of their social circle didn't have dough. The sale was made on the phone. Then, while the cotton shipment was at sea, the price tripled. When the stuff suddenly became so valuable all hell broke loose on the world cotton market, they looked to see who was the owner of this big shipment. Me! They investigated my credit and found out I was a mere doctor, and they canceled. This was illegal. I sued them. But as I didn't have the money to fight them I sold the suit to a Wall Street lawyer for twenty thousand dollars. He fought it and was winning. They settled with him out of court for more than a million. But on the way back from Cairo, flying, there was a crash. All on board died. I have this guilt on my conscience, of being the murderer of that lawyer. Although he was a crook."

Wilhelm thought, I must be a real jerk to sit and listen to such impossible stories. I guess I am a sucker for people who talk about the deeper things of life, even the way he does.

What's more, Tamkin is a poet; and here is the second stanza of his poem, "Mechanism Vs Functionalism: Ism Vs Hism":

> *Why-forth then dost thou tarry*
> *And partake thee only of the crust*
> *And skim the earth's surface narry*
> *When all creations art thy just?*

Wilhelm's father, the ironic and self-contained Dr. Adler—all cold vanity—is an equally if less surprisingly solid character. And Wilhelm himself—at the mercy of his fears, his cannibalistic wife, his father, Dr. Tamkin, the stock market, the world —is, till the last scene, everybody's most exasperated secret image of himself, the Jew unmasked and un-Judaized, Everyman drowning in the shoreless multitudinousness of America. At the end, unluckily, Bellow thinks he has nowhere to go but up, up, up into the firmament of wishful allegory (so did Malamud at the end of *The Assistant*); and the funeral, which induces Wilhelm's presumptively clarifying tears, doesn't work.

But *Seize the Day* is Bellow's triumph, and a large, distinctively American achievement.

Herzog, on the other hand, might well have been a disaster: this shapeless lament of an ill-tempered, narcissistic, misogynistic, megalomaniacal, pontificating, endlessly self-pitying middle-aged Jewish professor, lifelong patsy to wife and friends and now disgorging a lifetime of ineffectual spite at the very names of his betrayers:

> Should he have been a plain, unambitious Herzog? No. And Madeleine would never have married such a type. What she had been looking for, high and low, was precisely an ambitious Herzog. In order to trip him, bring him low, knock him sprawling and kick out his brains with a murderous bitch foot.

It is nevertheless, as this savaging of Madeleine indicates, an interesting and hectically energetic book. It has the energy and candor of a man too tired to put on customary masks, the wizard novelist's or Henderson's or Augie's: "the way you try to sound rough or reckless . . . ," says Ramona, Herzog's mistress, "like a guy from Chicago . . . It's an act. Swagger. It's not really you." Herzog may occasionally play Augie for Ramona; but for us and himself he is Augie punctured, the swagger is out of him. Only humiliation and deep loathing, and the memories that reconstitute them hourly, are his present and future:

> "Oh, balls! So now, we're going to hear how you SAVED me. Let's hear it again. What a frightened puppy I was. How I wasn't strong enough to face life. But you gave me LOVE, from your big heart, and rescued me from the priests. Yes, cured me of menstrual cramps by servicing me so good. You SAVED me. You SACRIFICED your freedom. I took you away from Daisy and your son, and your Japanese screw. Your important time and money and attention." Her wild blue glare was so intense that her eyes seemed twisted.
> "Madeleine!"
> "Oh—shit!"
> "Just think a minute."
> "Think? What do you know about thinking?"
> "Maybe I married you to improve my mind!" said Herzog. "I'm learning."

"Well, I'll teach you, don't worry!" said the beautiful, pregnant Madeleine between her teeth.

His love is for the irrecoverable pre-American ghetto past, out of his pain he submerges into the delusion of completeness and unattempted potencies:

> Napoleon Street, rotten, toylike, crazy and filthy, riddled, flogged with harsh weather—the bootlegger's boys reciting ancient prayers. To this Moses' heart was attached with great power. Here was a wider range of human feelings than he had ever again been able to find. The children of the race, by a never-failing miracle, opened their eyes on one strange world after another, age after age, and uttered the same prayer in each, eagerly loving what they found. What was wrong with Napoleon Street? thought Herzog. All he ever wanted was there. His mother did the wash, and mourned. His father was desperate and frightened, but obstinately fighting. His brother Shura with staring disingenuous eyes was plotting to master the world, to become a millionaire. His brother Willie struggled with asthmatic fits. Trying to breathe he gripped the table and rose on his toes like a cock about to crow. His sister Helen had long white gloves which she washed in thick suds. She wore them to her lessons at the conservatory, carrying a leather music roll. Her diploma hung in a frame. *Mlle. Hélène Herzog . . . avec distinction.* His soft prim sister who played the piano.

Back! cries poor Herzog (and Bellow seems to be crying it too), back to the racial—if not the maternal—womb. It is a sincere cry, the sentimentality of the damned, and one hesitates to laugh at it.

The novel ought to be titled *Who Killed Herzog?* or, *Placing the Blame Squarely on Anybody Else's Shoulders*. The Jewish-American writer is at last bereft of his familiar incubus: anti-Semitism is no longer there to lean one's justly suffering soul against; and Bellow relies on what he calls the "Jewish art of tears" to make the case: "Herzog wrote, *Will never understand what women want. What do they want? They eat green salad and drink human blood.*" Yet whenever the case isn't being made, and often when it is, the weary and compulsive straightforwardness of the statement makes for a kind of authenticity which Bellow nowhere else approaches except in

Seize the Day, and which—engaging a more complex or at least
a more disorderly protagonist—keeps alive and unconsum-
mated a promise of bigger fish than Tommy Wilhelm or even
Dr. Tamkin. Herzog's unmailed letters, taking up chapters in
this self-indulgent novel, are hot air left over from Augie and
Henderson; and Herzog's "equilibrium" at the end, which Bellow seems to regard as an Oriental calm of perfect awareness, is
just brute apathy after unendurable exertions of the spirit, before the old rationalizations and remorses build up their necessary steam again. If only Bellow knew what he was seeing! But
most of the time, in *Herzog*, he doesn't. Nor does he much
care either; and so he makes only token efforts to get in the
way of what he's seeing, which is the modern comedy of the
exhausted and undefeatable ego.

Malamud's Jewish hero has no such traumas to struggle
through since he doesn't begin with such a dose of hubris as
Bellow's. When Malamud's Jew leaves the ghetto, he becomes
not a displaced person but—as a number of the short stories
have already made clear—a tourist. In Europe he has an American passport, glories in the scenery, does his best to sample the
women. In Cascadia, the Northwestern locale of *A New Life*,
he has the graduate school's passport to a college teaching job:
his name is Levin. He is Malamud's holy innocent again, a
timid, fumbling, yearning young idealist. Infants he politely
picks up urinate over him, thwarted rivals steal his clothes
while he is trying to make love (some day a scholarly article
will be published on how many times in Malamud's fiction
somebody's coitus is interrupted), his first day in class is a sensation but only because he has neglected to close his fly, auto-
mobiles are mysteries to him and turn his pleasure trip into a
nightmare. Like Fidelman in love with a painted nude, he is
always grateful for beauty—the beauty of the scenery for instance:

> They were driving along an almost deserted highway, in a broad
> farm-filled valley between distant mountain ranges laden with
> forests, the vast sky piled high with towering masses of golden
> clouds. The trees softly clustered on the river side of the road
> were for the most part deciduous; those crawling over the green
> hills to the south and west were spear-tipped fir.

My God, the West, Levin thought. He imagined the pioneers in covered wagons entering this valley for the first time, and found it a moving thought. Although he had lived little in nature Levin had always loved it, and the sense of having done the right thing in leaving New York was renewed in him. He shuddered at his good fortune.

—and, of course, the beauty of women:

"Why can't we take one of the blankets off a cow?" Levin asked. "We'll put it back later."

"If you look good you'll see the cows don't sleep with blankets on them. They'd get sick if they did."

Laverne spread the horse blanket on the ground, and standing on it began to undress. She was neat with her clothes, folding each thing and putting it down on a hay bale nearby. Levin placed his hat, trousers, and shoes stuffed with socks and garters, next to her things. He kept his shorts on.

Watching the girl undress in the shadowy light of the lamp in the stall, Levin felt for her an irresistible desire. Ah, the miraculous beauty of women. He considered falling in love with her but gave up the idea. He embraced Laverne and they kissed passionately.

"Your breasts," he murmured, "smell like hay."

"I always wash well," she said.

"I meant it as a compliment."

Ah, women! especially when they're not hanging around all the time to spoil that instant of beauty which is like a fading coal. While Levin is having an affair with a married woman, who has a family to get back to and a gift for quick orgasm, he experiences a bachelor's vision of the earthly paradise:

She visited him not often but often enough. One of her "meetings" was a good enough excuse for a night out. And Gilley assisted by teaching a winter-term weekly extension course for teachers, in Marathon. Usually Pauline walked the dozen blocks to Levin's. When she had the car she parked it about two blocks from the house. Gilley was home from Marathon by eleven. She had left Levin's room at ten-thirty, short but sweet. He could read afterwards without a stray thought, a great convenience. He envisioned a new Utopia, everyone over eighteen sexually satisfied, aggression reduced, peace in the world.

If Malamud had been content to go on and on in this idyllic vein, *A New Life* might have done for Cascadia what *Typee* did for the South Seas: Come to the great state of Cascadia, admire our mountains, climb our wives. But Malamud is writing—worse luck—one of those academic novels, in which every professional type since Aristotle must be described, for the benefit of the book-club subscribers, in stupefyingly predictable detail down to the last wart, as if every college were a zoo of unheard-of beasts rather than just another enclosure for the same old fictional lapdogs, tabbies, and pet rats: the elderly stuffed prune of a chairman, the unworthy claimant, the snappish recluse, the departmental nymphomaniac, even the ghost of a departed young Turk who once threatened the whole establishment. The contest for the chairmanship fairly makes one's flesh crawl: Will evil be routed and good prevail? Will Levin get caught rifling everybody else's files? Will Levin's mistress muck up everything, as women usually do?

The trouble is that Malamud himself, through Levin, has notions about life on earth which, though more wistful and appealing than, say, Augie's, are not less extraneous to the action of the novel. Malamud really believes, when his shrewdness deserts him for the moment, that life is a contest between good and evil, or at least between readily distinguishable good and evil impulses:

> Good was as if man's spirit had produced art in life. Levin felt that the main source of conscious morality was love of life, anybody's life. Morality was a way of giving value to other lives through assuring human rights. As you valued men's lives yours received value. You earned what you sold, got what you gave. That, if not entirely true, ought to be. Our days are short, thought Levin, our bodies frail. The universe is unknown, remorseless. We have no certain understanding of Nature's intentions, nor God's if he intends. We know the meagerness, ignorance, cruelty of too many men and too many societies. We must protect the human, the good, the innocent. Those who had discovered their own moral courage or created it, must join others who are moral; these must lead, without fanaticism. Any act of good is a diminution of evil in the world.

In the context of the novel, these moony speculations are provoked by Levin's feelings of guilt about his adulterous affair with a woman whom he understands very well:

> She had caused herself to love out of discontent, although her discontents were tolerable. Gilley was good to her; she had a better than average home, kids she loved. Maybe she was bored but she wasn't desperate; she probably could go on living with him forever. If diversion was what she had wanted, a little love on the side, she wasn't made for it, the pleasure butchered by anxiety and shame. She wasn't the type who could give "all" for love. And he doubted he could inspire such love, the limits of her passion conditioned by the man he was.

The most surprisingly effective scene in the novel is Levin's last confrontation with the husband, who confirms with sheaves of blood-curdling evidence what his wife (any wife?) is like:

> . . . She was born dissatisfied . . . you'll wake up at six A.M. to hear her already going on about her life and how it didn't pan out as she wanted it to. When you ask her what she had expected, all she can tell you is that she wanted to be a better person than she is . . . Then you will hear in long detail everything she thinks she has done wrong, or those things she tried to do and had to give up, or everything she now does and does badly. She will never once tell you what she does well, which can get pretty monotonous. After that she'll blame you for as much as she blames herself, because you married her . . . and didn't do what she calls 'bring me out,' meaning make out of her something she couldn't make out of herself though you may have broken your back trying to think up new ways to do it . . .

Moreover, according to Gilley's inexorable testimony, she's a rotten housekeeper and cook, has constipation and female ailments, is afraid of doctors, and lacks the moral capacity to be grateful for past pleasures. When Levin, notwithstanding, persists in his decision to carry her off,

> Gilley stared at him. "You expect to go on with this after what I've told you?"
> Levin laughed badly.

So does the reader, not only badly but incredulously, as Levin the gentle boob, deprived of job and illusions, long since deprived of love ("Was it a guilty response to experience he should have accepted as one accepts sunlight? Why must he forever insist on paying for being alive?"), drives off into the sunset with somebody else's pregnant wife and children. Maybe Jews are just born to suffer; though we had better hopes at the outset for Levin the starry-eyed scenery-buff, shy pursuer of pretty students, and happy home-wrecker. As for the novel, from an often amusing travelogue it abruptly collapses into one more allegory of self-crucifixion. But Levin is no Frank Alpine. And Malamud may have nowhere else to take his hero except on trips to each of the other forty-nine states or to Europe again; or back to the primordial ghetto.

The question is, now that the twentieth century is two-thirds finished, Whatever became of the Jew in America? In Malamud's fiction he survives as a tourist without a past; in Bellow's, barely and sourly as a displaced person, an alien tolerated and unloved, hankering after vanished patriarchal simplicities. In *Letting Go*, he is altogether absorbed into a culture he despises as much as he despises the culture from which he sprang. Whereas in *Goodbye, Columbus* Roth is unintentionally disagreeable (or, in several of the shorter stories, condescendingly sentimental) about a past that shames and exasperates him, in *Letting Go* he is intentionally and unrelentingly disagreeable about a present whose disgusts and anxieties play no favorites among the egos they feed on. After Libby's abortion, she and Paul come home to face another nightmare scene, in which the elderly Korngold, having been bilked by the equally elderly con-man, the reptilian Levy, appeals to Paul for help. Paul helps by almost strangling Levy, who eventually escapes and discharges his venom:

> But Levy was now in the doorway, slicing the air with his cane. Everyone jumped back as he made a vicious X with his weapon. "Disgusting! Killer!" he cried, slashing away. "Scraping life down sewers! I only make my way in the world, an old shit-on old man. I only want to live, but a murderer, *never!* This is your friend, Korngold," announced Levy. "This is your friend and accomplice, takes a seventeen-year-old girl and cuts her *life* out!

Risks her life! Commits abortions! Commits *horrors!*" He gagged, clutched his heart, and ran from the room.

Paul, almost out of his head for fear of disgrace and prison,

> . . . sat up all night in the chair. Near four—or perhaps later, for the buses were running—he walked into the hall. He hammered twice on Levy's door.
> "Levy!"
> No answer.
> "Levy, do you hear me?" He kicked five distinct times on the door. He started to turn the knob but, at the last moment, decided not to. From the darkness behind the door might not Levy bring down a cane on his head?
> "Levy—listen to me, Levy. You never open your mouth. You never in your life say one word to anybody. Never! I'll kill you, Levy. I'll strangle you to death! Never—understand, you filthy son of a bitch! I'll kill you and leave you for the rats! You filth!"
> And that last word did not leave him; it hung suspended within the hollow of his being through the rest of the night, until at last it was white cold daylight.

Nor do Jews, elderly or young, have a corner on nastiness. The same day, Paul visits the young doctor who, apparently from the kindness of his heart, directed him to the abortionist:

> Had everything worked out? Wife all right? Satisfied? Fine— he did not mean to pry. Only one had to check on Smitty. He fed the osteopath patients—almost one a month—but still it was wise to keep an eye on the fellow. Every once in a while Doctor Tom seemed to forget about slipping Dr. Esposito his few bucks. You know what I mean? Not an entirely professional group, osteopaths . . .

Most of the novel is a shuddering recoil against the horrors of human contact; for *Letting Go* is a novel about attachment, relationship, of which the intensest and most destructive instance is marriage. Paul and Libby make each other miserable in all the ways possible to husband and wife. By the end of the novel, Paul is impotent and Libby has settled into numbed and parasitic housewifery with an adopted child. Throughout the novel, Paul is helpless in practical matters, emergencies, love, anger, friendship; Libby is such a pitiable gorgon of stupid hysterical messiness that the reader can only wonder how any man could fall for her and stick with her:

> "I think I'm going to go out this afternoon," Libby said, picking at her orange.
> "Just dress warmly."
> "Don't you want to know where I'm going?"
> "Out. For a walk . . ." he said. "I thought you said you were going out."
> "If you're not interested . . ."
> "Libby, don't be petulant first thing in the morning."
> "Well, don't be angry at me for last night."
> "Who said anything about last night?"
> "That's the whole thing—you won't even bring it up. Well, I didn't behave so badly, and don't think I did."
> "That's over and done with. You were provoked. That's all right. That's finished."
> She did not then ask him who had provoked her; she's just began cloudily to accept that she had been.
> "Where are you going?" he asked.
> "When?" Now she *was* petulant, perhaps because she no longer considered it necessary to feel guilty about last night . . .

Roth's talent for dramatizing at murderous length the most squalid and irresolvable quarrels, especially between husband and wife, is exercised with bleak frequency in the novel. If it isn't Paul and Libby, it's Gabe and Libby, or Gabe and Martha. *Letting Go* intends to be almost as much about a *ménage à trois*—Paul-Libby-Gabe—as about a marriage; and in fact about four relationships that fail: Paul-Libby, Gabe-Libby, Paul-Gabe, and Gabe-Martha. The alternative to the success that eludes them is "letting go": madness, or impotence and despair. There are only two characters who do not seem created chiefly to be crammed into the gloomy design of the novel: Martha, who has enough animal vitality to enjoy herself when she can and to survive the wreckage with poise and humor; and Paul's Uncle Asher, the ancient Chorus, free outsider, who delivers the ancestral warning to his nephew before the marriage:

> ". . . Paulie, kiss the girl, caress her, stick it right up in her, but for Christ's sake do me a favor and wait a year. You're an artistic

type, a serious observer of life, why kill your talent? You'll sap yourself with worry, you'll die of a hard-on in the streets. Other women will tantalize you some day and you and your conscience will wrestle till you choke . . . Listen to Uncle Schmuck, will you? Things come and go, and you have got to be a receptacle, let them pass right through. Otherwise death will be a misery for you, boy; I'd hate to see it. What are you going to grow up to be, a canner of experience? You going to stick plugs in at either end of your life? Let it flow, let it go. Wait and accept and learn to pull the hand away. *Don't clutch!* What is marriage, what is it but a pissy form of greed, a terrible, disgusting ambitiousness . . ."

Uncle Asher makes his point much later too, for a chastened Paul possibly in sight of suicide:

". . . what I'm in favor of is getting back in tune a little bit with nature. All this emphasis on charity and fucking. Disgusting."

"But you've always had women, Asher. You told me that too, remember? A Chinese woman and so on. That's all you talked about last time we met. You made it sound as though I was leaving a harem for marriage. Let's be serious, if we're going to have discussions."

"You misunderstood. Ass is no panacea. Not even the highest quality."

"Then why do you pursue it?"

"One, I got needs and prefer ladies to queers. Number two, I told you, I'm the child of the age. I want to understand what all the movies and billboards are about. Three, you still haven't got what I'm talking about. I'm talking about taking a nice Oriental attitude for yourself. Pre-Chiang Kai-Shek. Ungrasping. Undesperate. Tragic. Private. Proportioned. So on down the line. I only want to leave you with one thought, Paulie, because I've got to get out of here and I don't want to find you dead when I get back. Nobody owes nobody nothing. That's the slogan over the Garden of Eden. That's what's stamped on all our cells. Body cells, what makes us. There's your nature of man . . ."

Uncle Asher stands in the wings; but nobody in the action of the novel is susceptible to his philosophy of non-attachment. Indeed, the most substantial and admirable character in the novel is Martha Reganhart, who practices with spontaneous piety the doctrine of love and touch even at the price of pride, who has "a natural instinct for sharing pleasure"; the harassed, puzzled, hard-working, slovenly, man-hungry wise-cracking divorcee with two kids she worries about and a roomer to help pay the rent:

> She planted a kiss on her son's neck and he drew a purple line across the bridge of her nose. "Bang! Bang!" he shouted into her ear, and she left him to his drawing.
> "What's the matter with your nose?" Sissy asked. "You look like you've just been shat upon."
> "Could you control your language in my house?"
> "What are you coming on so salty again for?"
> "I don't want my children saying shat, do you mind? And put on a bathrobe. My son's earliest memory is going to be of your ass."
> "Now who's filthy?"
> "I happen to be their mother. I support them. Please, Sissy, *don't* walk around here half-naked, will you?"

The only love and passion in the novel is between Martha and Gabe, as on one occasion when Gabe is too ill for anything but pleasure:

> "Oh Gabe," she said, "my Gabe—"
> I left her there alone, just lips, just hands, and was consumed not in sensation, but in a limpness so total and blinding, that I was no more than a wire of consciousness stretched across a void. Martha's hair came raking up over me; she moved over my chest, my face, and I saw her now, her jaw set, her eyes demanding, and beneath my numb exterior, I was tickled by something slatternly, some slovenliness in the heavy form that pinned me down. I reached out for it, to *touch* the slovenliness—
> "Just lie still," I heard her say, "don't touch, just still—"
> She showed neither mercy then, nor tenderness, nor softness, nothing she had ever shown before; and yet, dull as I was, cut off in my tent of fever and fatigue, I felt a strange and separate pleasure. I felt cared for, labored over; I felt used . . .

The affair between Martha and Gabe develops so promisingly, in fact, that it takes all of Gabe's motiveless *Angst*, plus an outrageous trick of plot, to separate them forever and reinstate the novel's atmosphere of seamless wretchedness. For Roth is determined to keep everybody wretched, or to prove out wretchedness as the norm and pleasure as a passing aberration. He will use all his skill to show that nothing works.

The skill has protracted and damaging lapses. One of these has already been mentioned: Roth is never able to indicate why Paul marries Libby or stays married to her; or why Gabe, far more improbably, continues throughout the novel to find Libby fascinating. In general, the novel is weak on motivation: a weakness that would count little if it were not for Roth's insistence on the finicky motive-hunting by Gabe the sophisticated narrator. Gabe's "ironic" discriminations between chalk and cheese are as tedious and false as Nick Carraway's in *The Great Gatsby;* and Roth indulges him at length in his bad habit. As for Roth's own motive here, it may be that he is trying to achieve some distance from a subject too close for comfort; but he is a better novelist when he just gives up and hugs it to him unironically, letting the knifelike cross-purposes of his dialogue cut him up a bit.

Malamud and Bellow are in their fifties, each with an uneven but important *oeuvre* behind him; each, however, pretty clearly in need of new subjects now that the American Jew has disappeared into their novels. Roth is in his early thirties, a *Wunderkind*, having produced in his twenties a big novel that registers the disappearance of the American Jew not only into fiction, but into the featureless and solipsistic emotional landscapes of contemporary America. Something to have done in a first novel! Now, having put the headstone on the subject that he and Malamud and Bellow worked to death, he may be in the same fix as the others. Still it is difficult not to be hopeful about all of them, in the impasse to which their energies have rashly carried them. At least Bellow has finally given up on style; and, besides, been tempered into a wary respect for the women of America, those hard facts that Malamud and Roth also are acquainted with and astounded by.

The Jew is dead: Libby killed Paul; Pauline killed Levin; Madeleine killed Herzog. The Jew was done in by the American bitch who closed his ears against the admonitory an-

cestral voices. At his tomb three novelists meditate, trying to
conceive an American sequel to the myth of Eden.

1966

POSTSCRIPT 1970

Bellow's first book after *Herzog* was *Mosby's Memoirs &
Other Stories*, about which I wrote that "Bellow's astonishing
eclecticism looks very odd in a collection: the stories are related to one another only in the sleight-of-hand virtuosity
with which each one manipulates the special style that Bellow
chooses for it. Every style of Bellow's suffers from a chronic
chill of pedantry and remoteness except the Herzog style,
which is probably as close as we'll ever get to hearing Bellow
himself. The best, if a rather slight, story is the only one in the
Herzog style, 'A Father-to-Be'. . . . 'The Old System' is
Augie March in a funereal mood; 'Looking for Mr. Green' is
Depression naturalism, more supple than Farrell or Dos Passos;
'The Gonzaga Manuscripts' is the product of Bellow's unaccountable impulse to redo 'The Aspern Papers'; 'Leaving the
Yellow House' may have compassionate intentions but it's an
iceberg of a story, a demoralizing account of the nullity of a
down-and-out old woman; 'Mosby's Memoirs' is in Bellow's
latest brilliant, showy, dense, protective manner behind which
the reader is not admitted." *

Mr. Sammler's Planet, looking for a while rather like *Herzog*
in late middle age, lacks the latter's electrifying hatred of its
hero's enemies and so lacks everything. It is an earnest, nervous, inert jeremiad against contemporary America (material-
ism; the cult of revolutionary youth; Bellow's capital sinner
the American woman, who this time is indicted for bad smells
and alleged to be "smearing all with her female fluids"). It is a
disappointing book. "I am extremely skeptical of explanations,

* "Must We Burn Mme. de Beauvoir?" *The Hudson Review*, XXI,
Winter 1968–69, pp. 755f.

rationalistic practices," austerely declares Mr. Sammler, Bellow's spokesman, pausing after two hundred pages of expository and rationalistic monologue, and about to wow a small
rapt audience with his bookworm reasons for the world's troubles. The novel is at least unfashionable in a fashionable time, it
disapproves of much; but its notions are defensive, despairing,
and not very interesting ("Violence might subside, exalted ideas
might recover importance"). Characteristically in Bellow's novels, his narrative keeps threatening to recede into allegory and
opinion: in *Mr. Sammler's Planet* Auschwitz and the 1967
Arab-Israeli war are big ideas, pretexts for Hollywood flashbacks, but they are never events or foreshadowings of events;
and the present is only the immediate pretext for the author's
moral dyspepsia. Mr. Sammler is a seventy-two-year-old refu-
gee: Bellow expects us to make every allowance for old age,
foreignness, fussiness, platitude, and any other plausible defect
in his protagonist. The author, however, is inexcusable, having
finally condemned himself to his cosmos of Air-Wick (exalted
ideas) and bad smells (reality).

I was impressed enough by *When She Was Good,* Roth's
first book after *Letting Go,* to use it for the concluding exhibit
in a review concerned till that point with French and American practitioners of the *nouveau roman:*

> *When She Was Good* . . . is in effect a posthumous Dreiser
> novel, with much family-album verisimilitude ("Edward's bron-
> chitis had lingered nearly three weeks") and some acutely ob-
> served American domesticity. Roth continues, clumsily and
> anachronistically, to be gnawed—as he was in that underrated
> novel *Letting Go*—by the problems of sin and responsibility.
> Why do destructive people behave as they do? How do they
> persuade themselves that they are good? How does it *feel* to be
> bad? Roth cares about such questions, stumbling along in the
> burlap sack of his prose:

>> This battle, too, she had fought and this battle, too, she had
>> won, and yet it seemed that she had never in her life been
>> miserable in the way that she was miserable now. Yes, all that
>> she had wanted had come to be, but the illusion she had, as
>> they drove home through the storm, was that she was never
>> going to die—she was going to live forever in this new world

she had made, and never die, and never have the chance not just to be right, but to be happy.

Roth can even, under the stimulus of a climactic scene, revive such questions for his readers, he can hear every vibration of the terrible small voice of righteousness confronting an unworthy adversary:

> She got up and went into the bathroom. Into the mirror she said,
> "Twenty-two. I am only twenty-two."
> When she came back into the living room the radio was playing.
> "How you feeling?" he asked.
> "Fine."
> "Aren't you all right, Lucy?"
> "I'm feeling *fine*."
> "Look, I didn't mean I'm going to *publish* a book even if I could."
> "If you want to publish a book, Roy, publish a book!"
> "Well, I won't! I was just having some fun. Jee—*zuz*." He picked up one of his family's old copies of *Life* and began leafing through it. He slumped into his chair, threw back his head and said, "Wow."
> "What?"
> "The radio. Hear that? 'It Might As Well Be Spring.' You know who that was my song with? Bev Collison. Boy. Skinny Bev. I wonder whatever happened to her."
> "How would I know?"
> "Who said you'd know? I was only reminded of her by the song. Well, what's wrong with that?" he asked. "Boy, this is really some Valentine's Day night!"
> A little later he pulled open the sofa, and they laid out the blanket and pillows. When the lights were off and they were in bed, he said that she had been looking tired, and probably she would feel better in the morning. He said he understood.
> *Understood what? Feel better why?*

Righteousness has its own sheer cliffs.

When She Was Good is, most of it, hopelessly old-fashioned, and it is an interesting novel. Why not? The novel, of all artifacts, remains the one least divisible from its artificer, whose idiosyncrasies and judgments may prevail over the demands of the genre itself. Roth's mind, besieged by archaic American drearinesses, is more interesting than Barthelme's or Burroughs'. Novels are too long, the novelist can't get away with gimmicks or momentary flashes; he has to disclose substance and continuity somewhere, perhaps in himself.*

The most startling fact about *Portnoy's Complaint*, however, is Roth's absence from it. The feeble pun of the title is a portent: the book's organization is rudimentary; there are maybe a half-dozen amusing pages (some of the whacking-off rhetoric; several outbursts by The Monkey; Portnoy's attempt on the virtue of the tractor-sized kibbutz heroine); and the otherwise uninterrupted cornball-ethnic witlessness comes close to proving that "Philip Roth" is a clever pseudonym for this title page or all the others. "Doctor, *please*," cries Portnoy, "I can't live any more in a world given its meaning and dimension by some vulgar nightclub clown." It's a horrid fate all right, and Roth or "Roth" ought to wipe off the greasepaint and apologize.

Malamud continues to be an honorable and conscientious writer, even in so ambitious a book as *The Fixer*. But the best part of the book is the least ambitious, the long opening section, which creates and places the promisingly irritable and disillusioned hero among the commonplaces of Jewish experience in pre-1914 Eastern Europe. When Bok is arrested, the subject-matter abruptly changes from Yiddish to Russian: it's no disgrace that Malamud is not so competent as Dostoevsky was to prove on our nerves the whole metaphysical cycle of capture, terror, torment, endurance, and redemption; at any rate, Malamud is ambitious enough to try, and skilful enough to make the details (though never their historical resonance) convincing.

* "Sarraute, Duras, Burroughs, Barthelme, and a Postscript," *The Hudson Review*, XX, Autumn 1967, pp. 485f.

THE LISTENER AND MR. HAGGIN

Twenty years ago B. H. Haggin began contributing to *The Nation* his weekly review of phonograph records; a page of condensed, specific, checkable comment that happened to be the first serious acknowledgment of what might fairly be called the Gutenberg era in the history of music. For the first time, recordings of at least the standard repertory of the concert hall, performed by excellent musicians, were being turned out in quantity by electronic methods that reproduced with recognizable approximation the sounds of live performance; one company advertised, with noteworthy accuracy, "Music You Want When You Want It"; symphonies were becoming as accessible on records as novels in printed books; and the frequent reëxperiencing, in performance, of a large number and variety of musical works—possible, till then, only for professional musicians—became, suddenly, a commonplace for the musical amateur. Mass production had unprecedentedly opened an entire art to a huge naïve audience; and it was to this audience that twenty years ago, in a situation of unexampled difficulty for criticism, Mr. Haggin at once addressed his taste, his honesty, and his awareness of the critic's responsibility:

First let me help the editors of *The Nation* solve a problem. It is the problem that confronts a newspaper editor: He can have a

concert written up by a layman, who would write of what a
layman would hear at the concert and what everyone who reads
the paper will understand. Or if he wants authoritative appraisal
he can use an expert, who will talk about things which most of
the audience would not hear and most readers will not understand. In this situation the editor likes to believe that if only the
expert will use different words everyone will understand him;
but the difficulty is not with the words, it is with the things the
words refer to: if the reader has not experienced them, there
are no words that he will understand. However, for the editors
of *The Nation* the problem is solved by the fact that I am discussing phonograph records; for when I speak of qualities of
music and performance which some readers know nothing about,
they can listen to the records and hear what I refer to.

For example, in Mozart's early Violin Concerto in G (K. 216)
they can hear what is already the true Mozart style and thought
without the richness and subtlety of its maturity; they are, then,
the better able to perceive, in the high-spirited first movement,
the truth of Tovey's observation that Mozart wrote in the language of operatic comedy; but even in the melodic passages about
1¼ inches from the first groove and about ⅜ inch before the
last groove of the first record they can perceive the fact that he
had something to say which transcended this language. They can
also hear that these qualities of the work are admirably realized
in the performance of Huberman with the Vienna Philharmonic
under Dobrowen. I must, however, warn readers not to be re-
pelled by first impressions of Huberman's playing: once they
bring themselves to ignore its lack of sensuous attractiveness
(which the Viennese recording engineers do less than nothing
about) they will hear, in more subtle qualities of inflection and
continuity, a wonderful feeling for the phrase. The warning is
the more necessary because the stuff that Columbia puts into the
grooves of its records generally spoils the results of the first few
playings. . . .

Twenty years later, in this age of LP's, when the sales and
sheer volume of new records have made record-reviewing a
business that engrosses whole sections of popular magazines,
and engages the full-time energies of numerous second-string
music critics with the standard seventeen-word vocabulary of
uncheckable cliché, Mr. Haggin's taste and honesty and heroically scrupulous attention to what is before him decline to be

swamped or intimidated; they are in fact more singular, salient, unsubduable, and useful than ever.

The critic who attempts such a lonely job for so unpracticed an audience is frequently confronted, of course, by evidence of its uncomprehending hostility:

> . . . if the critic may not impose his greater insights on the reader, neither may the reader impose lesser insights on the critic.
>
> The reader who tries to do this . . . is someone who, because he cannot hear something, does not believe anyone else can. One could say that he doesn't credit even the critic with insights greater than his own; but the truth is that he isn't aware of insights being involved. . . . He has no understanding of what sort of personal resources—of mind, emotion, character, experience—are involved, along with mere facility in sound, in the creation of good music; or of such personal resources being involved, along with mere facility of fingers, in good performance. And he has no understanding of the fact that an equipment of the same professional caliber—both in sensitiveness to the medium and in personal resources—is involved in good criticism. That is why he is shocked by the critic's disrespect for a composer or violinist, but feels free to be arrogant to the critic.
>
> It is also why he is shocked by the critic's intensity about what he thinks good or bad. That is, he doesn't realize it is the intensity of the professional who cares deeply about his art. Toscanini becomes enraged when a phrase is not as it should be, because that phrase is something he cares about.

And his job is even lonelier because most of his fellow critics, especially in the newspapers and popular magazines, are either, like John Briggs, self-proclaimed cringing partisans of insensibility—

> [The critic] is the mouthpiece for the great submerged mass of concert goers who have opinions but no way of expressing them, . . . [he] must share the tastes, viewpoint, enthusiasms and prejudices of his readers, . . . [and] he might well share their limitations also.

or, like the egregious Professor Paul Henry Lang (who has come to his reward, and is now a newspaper critic), musicologists in the Germanic scholarly tradition that equates every fact with every other fact, and that in extreme instances afflicts fact-mongers with the moon-madness to presume that philology equals insight and grants immunity from correction—

> A man with a muddled mind [says Mr. Haggin of Professor Lang] which enables him first to suppress the essential part of an argument of Ernest Newman and misrepresent the part he answers, and then to see in a demonstration of this shocking inaccuracy only a "railing at music scholars." Or to scream in the *American Scholar* once against the type of music criticism concerned with "the amorous adventures of singers and virtuosi" which "in our day . . . appears in so-called biographies (*cf.* Ernest Newman's *Liszt*)," and himself to publish in the *Saturday Review of Literature* recently a vulgar account of Liszt's amorous adventures. A man with a muddled, inaccurate mind, whose job at a great university is to teach students in musico-historical research rigor and accuracy.

or most commonly, like the busiest present arbiter of popular taste in classical music, Irving Kolodin of the *Saturday Review*, low-comedy practitioners of "the meaningless jargon of newspaper concert-reviewing"; as for example in Mr. Kolodin's recent *complete* report of a cellist's performance—

> Rostropovich impressed these ears more than he had at his recital, partially because he showed himself capable of rising to a demanding occasion, partially because he seemed, after a while, to lose himself in the performance-problem, thus conveying more of his basic artistic personality, which is an appealing one.

To spotlight the *Saturday Review* is neither accidental nor unjust. This dogmatically middlebrow magazine relaxed long enough, several years ago, from its popgun assault on modern poetry to initiate an imposing monthly Recordings Section, run by Mr. Kolodin, and eked out with pages of small-print multiple-column diagrammatic reviews that imply scholarly diligence and critical succinctness. Since 1949 Mr. Kolodin has been listed on the Editorial Board of the *Saturday Review*, and within a few years after that date—the Year One of the age of LP's—his pretensions to exhaustiveness, as well as the middlebrow circulation of the magazine, had guaranteed his influence over an audience that is very wide indeed, and far more vulnerable than the audience for modern poetry. No wonder, then, that Mr. Haggin has taken the trouble to point out the careless- ness of Mr. Kolodin (who once wrote with knowing familiar- ity about performances that had never occurred), his inability to hear what is in the performances and on the records he *does* listen to, his corresponding inability to produce anything but a fuzzy mush of performance-problems and appealing basic ar- tistic personalities. No wonder, also, that in the year of Mr. Kolodin's ascension Mr. Haggin's book *Music in the Nation,* a selection of his most precisely discriminating comments on music and performance and music critics (including Mr. Kolo- din), was entrusted by the *Saturday Review* to a hack re- viewer, who was permitted (encouraged?) to give this account of the book:

> On the strength of Mr. Haggin's title one would naturally expect to encounter a sympathetic, informed concern with the creative impulses, representative institutions and personalities, and quali- ties of taste and appreciation that characterize the musical life of the country. Instead, he is confronted by a tight little world of the author's own imagining—a world dominated by a handful of subject deities and a rather larger group of alleged frauds, nihilists, ungifted pretenders, and members of the great un- washed.

That Mr. Haggin considers it his job to discuss not only music, but music critics, will continue to be deplored by partisans of insensibility, musicologists who have tasted blood, hack jour- nalists who shovel out parody criticism of phantom perform- ances, dilettantes who require from the critic not perceptions but poetry, and—unhappily—many bewildered members of the very public to whom Mr. Haggin has continuously ad- dressed himself.

For this public he has written his weekly articles (of which *Music in the Nation* is a selection); and in 1944 he published on its behalf an explicitly introductory book. *Music for the Man Who Enjoys "Hamlet"* is a remarkable pioneer attempt at mak- ing use of phonograph records to introduce the inexperienced listener to the structures and effects of the very greatest music: one of the most remarkable facts about this adult primer being its refusal to avoid masterpieces ordinarily regarded as "difficult" and "forbidding" (the first work to be discussed is Beethoven's Sonata Opus 111). By the same point-to-point method of musical quotation and accompanying comment that Tovey employed with such illuminating epigrammatic grace, Mr. Haggin presents, examines, describes, and evaluates with his own force and precision what the reader is presumably following in the musical symbols and on the record. If the program of the book seems, nevertheless, too schematic, too austere, and too demanding for the naïve listener (reminding one of Mr. Haggin's early obligatory austerities—pre-LP and pre-diamond-stylus—which forbade record-changers altogether and insisted on a new needle for every record side, and which therefore protected the unfortunate novice's records but deprived him of the sense of continuity in the music that he may have needed more than unimpaired records)—if the book seems somehow unrealistic in its aims, it may be, in part at least, because the image of the naïve listener that Mr. Haggin begins with has itself a startling unreality:

> You reach home, let us say, with expectations of a quiet dinner, of slippers, easy chair, a much read copy of *Hamlet* to take your mind far from the wearying details and arguments and vexations of the long day at the office. And you learn with dismay that this is the night of the third concert of the city's major series, that your wife is going, and you are going with her.

The much read copy of *Hamlet* and the innocence about music may constellate in some personality somewhere; but, even with slippers and a hard day at the office (Mr. Haggin is not at his best when he essays the homely-ingratiating), they do not make up any recognizable representative listener—a listener who is likely to be more generally sophisticated or more generally illiterate than Mr. Haggin's construction, and who needs less help or far more than Mr. Haggin offers, or help of a different kind.

The trouble is that no particular work of art—especially a very great one—can be experienced in isolation from a general sense of the potentialities of its medium, from a sustained peripheral awareness of the simultaneous existence of other great works by the same artist and other artists in the same medium. The paradox of all pedagogy in the arts is that the teacher must often try to give his students a persuasive impression of the magnitude and complexity of a single work, most of whose qualities are in fact undemonstrable to minds ignorant of other works and artists and what they have been able to realize in the same medium. So that the teacher prevents restiveness and alarm in the classroom, and insures that his impression will be received as securely as possible for future deliberation, by means of fill-in lectures and illustrations and asides which provide his students with the temporary, essential illusion of a diversity of direct aesthetic experiences.

Mr. Haggin's handicap, in *Music for the Man Who Enjoys "Hamlet,"* was of course not merely self-imposed and theoretical, it was also economic: 78-rpm records were expensive to produce and to market, there were only two companies producing virtually all classical recordings issued in this country, and safe investment was the first consideration. Since the major companies steered clear of works outside the standard safe repertory of symphony orchestras and solo virtuosi, and since Mr. Haggin's pedagogic method required him to assume the accessibility only of music already on records (even so, he had to cheat a bit by including "to-be-issued" recordings that were never issued), his "bibliography" of masterpieces was necessarily meager, he could give no comparative idea of the magnitude and complexity of the works he did consider, and he gave no recorded documentation whatever of the composers'—not to mention the medium's—resourcefulness and fertility in works other than the few analyzed.

LP's, unlike 78-rpm records, are inexpensive to produce and to market. Out of this fact has come the stupendous expansion in the recording industry and in the library of recorded music; so that during the past half-dozen years almost every work of every composer of any consequence since Bach—as well as much pre-Bach music—has been finding, among the (by recent count) 373 recording companies, some engineer and the right number of musicians to tape it and put it up for sale to the public, on records that permit uninterrupted listening and that more and more closely approximate the sounds of live performance. What this aesthetic-technological flood-tide has done for Mr. Haggin is to make practical, even for beginners, his method of point-to-point analysis of masterpieces with the aid of recordings; it has enabled him to enrich and vindicate this method by supplementing it with brief comments, in the incisive terminology of the analyses, on many other works by the same and other composers, all available on records; he has the records themselves—the qualities of performance and of sound —to consider; and the result is his new book, *The Listener's Musical Companion.*

The very plan of the book has an engaging directness, economy, and logic. Beginning with remarks on the association between reader and critic—

> The critic is a music-lover and listener like his readers: he is the expert and professional listener, who is assumed to have greater powers of perception and judgment than the amateur, and therefore to be able to make his readers aware of things in the music which they mightn't notice by themselves. He functions as a sort of guidepost, saying in effect: "I hear this happening at this point"—after which his reader listens and may say: "Yes, I hear it too." But he also may say: "No, I hear *this*." That is, the critic uses his powers to animate those of his reader—but only to animate, not to dictate: what he says about a piece of music is true for the reader only if it is confirmed by the reader's own ears. And each critic writes for the group of people who have found his perceptions and evaluations sufficiently confirmed by their own experience.

—it moves in logical progression to a chapter on "the meaning of music," in which historical or biographical or even critical talk about music is split off from the music itself ("if you don't get the meaning of Beethoven's statement from the statement, you won't get it from anything else"); and, concluding the introductory section, it leads the reader by point-to-point analysis through a succession of musical forms of increasing intricacy, as these are embodied in masterpieces that demonstrate not only the mechanical utilization of a pattern, but some of the ways in which masterpieces exploit ready-made patterns and conventional procedures to achieve their own unique effects. Then, chapters on composers; a chapter on performance, in

which the insights of Casals, Schnabel, Toscanini are distinguished from the beautiful sounds, expressive of nothing but
the performer's virtuosity, produced by Heifetz, Horowitz,
Koussevitsky, Stokowski; a chapter on jazz; a chapter, with
justifying quotations, on the music critics who *do* have valuable things to say; and, finally, a section of more than one hundred pages of condensed analytic comment on recorded
performances of all the works mentioned in the book.

For Mr. Haggin's admirers, there are special satisfactions: a
mastery of method, a sufficiency and unimpeachable discretion
of comment and illustration, a continuous sense of refreshed
specific discoveries among the crowding presences of many
dissimilar masterpieces, even a relaxation that seems to flow
from the confidence of mastery without blurring any intensity
or acuteness of response. So many works by so many composers newly accessible on records seem to give Mr. Haggin too
many *good* things to talk about; in any case, this is the complete adult primer that *Music for the Man Who Enjoys "Hamlet"* could not be.

Everything is arranged as part of a total developing
experience. The order of chapters on composers, for example,
is neither chronological nor merely honorific: it presupposes a
naïve listener and it assumes that certain qualities, not necessarily less than the greatest, of great music are more immediately
appreciable than others. Mr. Haggin begins with Beethoven
(explosive power and spacious meditativeness in large forms,
and a lifetime of music that shows, like Shakespeare, an unimpeded growth in resources of spirit as well as resources of tech-
nique); goes on to Schubert (melodic loveliness magnificently
elaborated in large dramatic forms); then to Mozart ("subtlety in the expression of powerful meanings . . . emotions
expressed with an economy and conciseness analogous to what
the mathematician calls elegance") and the related idiom of
Haydn; then to Berlioz (Mozartian elegance in the use of the
medium, tact and fastidiousness in the handling of even the
most gigantic orchestral forces); and so on.

The generalized observations on composers are often vigorously heterodox (and always preceded or followed by documentation from the music itself). Brahms is a talented com-

poser in small forms but an unconvincing, arid craftsman in most of his large-scale works; Tchaikovsky, a composer of intensity, grace, and dramatic power whose qualities have been falsified by the traditional Tchaikovskian performance that distorts, exaggerates, "makes every *p* a *ppp*, every *f* a *fff*"; Bach, a great master in whom "one hears always the operation of prodigious powers . . . but frequently an operation that is not as expressive as it is accomplished"; Wagner, a magician whose extraordinary musical powers are exercised only sporadically and only as interruptions to the "quasi-hypnotic spell" of gorgeous sound to which he sets his cosmically bombastic libretti; Verdi, on the other hand, a working composer who "set to music not philosophically pretentious dramas about gods and heroes of Teutonic mythology, but melodramas about passionate Italians and Spaniards," and who created operas—especially *Otello* and *Falstaff*, but even parts of his earliest, most fervidly melodramatic works—in which the melodic invention of vocal writing and expressive refinements of orchestral texture are comparable to Mozart's; Mahler, a creator of monumental symphonic structures whose

> . . . employment of . . . huge orchestras is not the opulent daubing of Strauss; rather it resembles Berlioz's practice in the fastidiousness, precision and originality of its use, frequently, of now only these few instruments and now only those few to produce contrapuntal textures as clear as they are complex. Mahler's use of the orchestra is in fact only one part of an entire operation that resembles Berlioz's in the fact that nothing in the music is perfunctory or mechanical: if an instrument plays or an inner voice moves, the activity is never a routine instrumental doubling or filling in of texture, but always something done with attention, thought and purpose. And this evidence of a mind always working—working, moreover, in unexpected, individual, original and fascinating ways—holds interest even through one of Mahler's long-winded twenty-minute symphony movements.

Point-to-point analysis is used only sparingly in these chapters, but at decisive moments: as, for example, to contend against academic opinion of Berlioz as a meretricious thunderer by demonstrating the bold, always unexpected, exquisite phrasing of his setting of Gautier's words in *Nuits d'Eté*, and the transcendent delicacy of melody and orchestral texture in the Love Scene of his *Romeo and Juliet*. There is in these chapters, however, another sort of point-to-point method that is quite new for the author, made possible by the almost limitless new library of recorded music: what gives the book its unique character and pedagogic value is, not just the quality of the insights (many of which we have come across before in his articles and his other books: Mr. Haggin is a critic, not an aesthete, and he has no objection to repeating statements of his own that seem to him definitive of his views), but their sustained and exhaustive discriminating variety—page after page of descriptive comment in which he distinguishes, with his customary unawed directness that invites (and rewards) checking, among an exhaustive variety of works, down to single movements, arias, themes, even turns of phrase:

> [Mozart's Piano Concerto] K.466 . . . begins with what is perhaps the most powerful of Mozart's instrumental movements. The power of the hushed D-minor opening passage is an example of effect on the mind out of all proportion to the impingement on the senses: it is achieved by nothing more than the agitated syncopations of violins and violas, the quiet eruptions of cellos and basses, with not even one of the kettledrum-strokes that punctuate those eruptions in the orchestral outburst a moment later. . . .

> I mentioned earlier—as against the expansiveness of the *Eroica* Symphony—the concentration in the first movement of the Fifth; and other examples are the powerfully concise *Coriolan* and *Egmont* Overtures; the fiercely concise opening movement of the Quartet Op. 95. . . . But there are also remarkable examples of expansiveness to take note of: the endlessly and delightfully inventive second movement of the Quartet Op. 59 No. 1; the second movement of the Quartet Op. 59 No. 3, with a strangeness in its poignancy that leads Sullivan to speak of its "remote and frozen anguish."

The operation of the same unceasingly attentive critical mind is manifested—most uniquely, with an honesty and directness of idiom that Mr. Haggin may be said to have invented, and that takes the reader always back to the object—in the characteristically concise and full concluding section on recorded performances. There is, first of all, Mr. Haggin's unrelenting presentation, detail by detail, of the heartbreaking facts about the post-war Toscanini recordings: their dry, hard, unresonant, though usually at least clear sound; the monstrous perversions and distortions introduced into many of these recordings by the "enhancement" processes of RCA-Victor's incredible engineers, as in the last "improved" version of the *Eroica—*

> . . . the violin sound is changed into a liquid stream of electronic gloss; and there is a similar liquefying and blurring all the way down, which dissolves the solidity and clean definition of chords, drum-beats, and bass-notes into a mush of rumble. Moreover, with treble peaked and bass down the sound is much brighter but shallower, and the timbres of some of the instruments are altered: the horn sounds more like a trumpet; the trumpet's sound is sharpened, and may spread or split; the change from dark to light and from dry to glossy makes the cellos unrecognizable; the gloss similarly falsifies the sound of the clarinet, the bassoon. . . .

—the same perversions and distortions introduced even into many later, superb Toscanini recordings by the same botchers (one of whom had the effrontery to state, in a recently published reverential article about Toscanini and recording, that the one thing Toscanini has *never* permitted engineers to do is to alter the quality of the original auditorium sound!). And there are pleasanter facts, noted with the same clarity that equally invites the reader to find out for himself:

> Nat's performance of [Chopin's Sonata] Op. 35 . . . gives us the work undistorted and unsentimentalized by the usual exaggerated rubato—with, instead, inflections of pace governed by a sense for continuity and coherence. I would therefore choose it even though he uses a piano whose insufficiently resonant sound is poorly reproduced.

> In the Toscanini broadcasts of Verdi's operas issued by Victor the inadequacies of some of the singing and the defects of the reproduced sound are negligible in comparison with what the performances give. . . . We have . . . never . . . heard the or-

chestral parts played with such exquisite modeling of phrase, such balance of sonorities and clarity of texture, such plastic coherence, such hair-raising power in the climaxes, contributed by an orchestra of symphonic caliber not often heard in performances of Verdi. And it is literally true that we have never heard the orchestral parts with the effect they have when played this way. . . .

"Each critic," says Mr. Haggin, "writes for the group of people who have found his perceptions and evaluations sufficiently confirmed by their own experience." It is reasonable to hope that the group for whom Mr. Haggin writes will grow very much larger, by the stimulus of this inexhaustible book which describes, defines, and sums up a whole new era of musical history and in a crucial sense the whole history of music. For one of his readers, at any rate, this is the best introductory text, and the best listener's book, on music ever written.

1957

POSTSCRIPT 1970

Thirteen years later Mr. Haggin continues to produce the only readable and valuable music chronicles: his reviews of new recordings for *The Yale Review*; the Music and Ballet Chronicle for *The Hudson Review* (his comments on ballet, on Balanchine especially, are as pure, responsive, and unprecedented as his comments on music). Since *The Listener's Musical Companion* (revised and brought up to date in 1967 as *The New Listener's Companion and Record Guide*), he has published *Music Observed*, an indispensable sequel to *Music in the Nation*, his first collection of indispensable articles, and two superb books on Toscanini: *Conversations with Toscanini*, and *The Toscanini Musicians Knew*. The last is a book that must be read to be believed: Mr. Haggin's editorial labor of love and magic that arranges a series of statements about Toscanini, by musicians who worked with him, into pieces individually and most of all collectively so touching and definitive as to seem beyond the powers of even the intelligent musicians whose words are the whole book. Read it and believe.

HAROLD ROSENBERG: STUDYING THE TIME

Abrupt as daylight, Harold Rosenberg is an antidote to trends, Mosaic dicta, and the gloom of specialization. Such impudence! it's like being alive. He tells us, in one of these essays, that Baudelaire was "bent toward studying the time through its creative minds": so is Rosenberg, who has never failed to examine politics and the arts and the mass-media as attentively as if everywhere there were minds as unstinting and exuberant as his own.

*Artworks and Packages** sets out to report on contemporary painting and sculpture (most of the pieces are reprinted from Rosenberg's Art Chronicle in *The New Yorker,* against whose superincumbent chic they lean like a herd of good-humored buffalo); but the author can't help noticing everything, including "the young museum director" who vanishes into one of Aesop's fables: "To praise a work, a critic will now speak of 'the power of its presence on the environment,' whether that power is exercised by a gray box silently posed in an empty hall or by a blinking, squawking contraption as hard to evade as a nagging nerve. According to a catalogue statement by a young museum director, a wedge-shaped construction of sheets of plastic makes the room 'lose its boundaries. The lines of the

* Harold Rosenberg, *Artworks and Packages,* Horizon Press.

248

room . . . find a symbolic end-point in the sculpture; this turns the room in on the sculpture and makes it part of the sculpture. By absorbing the lines of the room, the sculpture becomes a tension-filled object, energizing the whole room.' Apparently, the sculpture swallows the room, blowing itself up like Aesop's bullfrog and making the room jump inside it. This may be difficult to grasp, but it indicates the new need to think of art Environmentally, even if the 'energizing' has to be done by the critic's prose."

Rosenberg's comic villain is the young (in heart as least) museum director, for whom "the museum has lost its character of a tomb and has taken on that of an educational institution and a distribution agency—as well as of a community center and a public relations bureau. . . . Art manufactured for the museum enters not into eternity but into the market." Because fashion and change are essential to the activity of the market, the used-car salesman pushes Camaros this week and demotes Mustangs to the back lot. Thus the Museum of Modern Art excluded from "The 1960s" painters who did not, in the opinion of its functionaries, "illustrate the contemporary movements, styles, and the forms of expression which seem most characteristic of the current decade." Rosenberg discovered, by inquiry, that "artists like Gottlieb and de Kooning . . . were typical of the nineteen-fifties rather than of the sixties, and their work was on display in another part of the building. . . . Not so long ago these painters stood large in the sunlight, but though they continue to produce works and exhibit them, they—like spirits in Hades—no longer cast a shadow. Nor was it the relentless stream of time that brought them to this pass, for other artists, of the same age group and even older—Reinhardt, Calder, Nevelson, Fontana—were represented in the exhibition. It was their affiliation with the 'styles and forms of expression' that the Museum now judged to be obsolete that deprived them of relevance to the living."

Or the same museum (as Rosenberg points out in "MOMA Dada"), launched on its "ambitious academic hijacking adventure" of an exhibition entitled "Dada, Surrealism and Their Heritage," adjusts the facts in order to verify its ascendancy over artists and historical truth: "I can think of only one pur-

pose for . . . [this] exhibition—to knock out the philosophical
underpinnings of modern art. The show is a remarkable, if not
epoch-making, instance of a museum openly intruding into current art history as an active partisan force by posing its own
conception of value and its own will regarding the future
against the will and ideas of the artists it is displaying. In the
Dada-Surrealist exhibition the Museum of Modern Art has become a kind of corporate artist using other people's pictures to
produce its own collage and parody. This, too," Rosenberg
concludes as MOMA disappears into its own faked version of
art history, "is a heritage of Dada."

When the museums aren't busy redoing the past, present,
and future, they're a-chortle with *Hair*-style entertainments:
Jan van der Marck, director of the Chicago Museum of Contemporary Art, "is convinced that 'the arts have exploded all
over the place' . . . and he is prepared to place his institution
behind experiments in music, the underground film, and poetry
readings 'perhaps accompanied by electronic effects with tapes
and lighting. . . . I'm not concerned,' he says, . . . 'with art
that has already proved its point.'" But Rosenberg wonders
whether it's possible "to eliminate art itself and yet continue to
count on the presence of artists. The 'seekers and imaginers of
elements' invoked by . . . [a group of Environmentalists] can
come into being only through the experience of a more profound reality than that conceived by current technology and
the mass public. Their orientation would have to be toward the
actual living environment rather than toward a décor constructed of lights, double images, goofy sounds, and other
twentieth-century artifacts."

No doubt in the arts anything goes. The trouble is that the
motive of calling into question the quasi-religious pretensions
of traditional art is liable to perpetrate merely goofy effects or,
as among the Dadaists, icons so purely religious that they don't
even have to be there: "The spade signed by Duchamp owes its
existence as art to the original *event* introduced by the artist
into art history in exhibiting it. . . . In this act timing is decisive; the object itself is a mere souvenir of an occasion.

"Duchamp's signing . . . inaugurates a new art history, that
in which the signature-bearing spade mocks the hierarchy of

forms by which art had sought to elevate itself above the crafts, and in which the artist's act . . . enters into the web of creative acts, regardless of when performed, the totality of which constitutes the identity of art. It is as the token of the attainment of a new stage in the history of human fabrication that Duchamp's 'ready mades' stand out from among the mass-produced duplicates among which they originated. As visual objects their value is exactly equal to that of similar urinals and spades in the hardware store. As symbols commemorating the end of the separate existence of art objects they are unique and impossible to duplicate. To understand the signed spade is to grasp an intrinsic development in human culture; to contemplate the spade is senseless—that museums exhibit Duchamp's spade, or an exact reproduction of it, as a work of art is typical of the fatuousness of an institution that has lost its bearings."

As an alternative to urinals Rosenberg proposes Action painting's creation *ex nihilo*: Pollock, Hofmann, de Kooning, Newman "have shared a concept of creation based on the intuition that there is nothing worth painting. No object, but also no idea. The activity of the artist became, in their opinion, primary. In this activity, Pollock sought what he called 'contact'—that is to say, a certain state in which the artist is guided by the image he is in the course of producing, with neither object nor preconceived image as aim. But the act of the artist *might* (the 'might' is essential, since one could not be certain)— the act of the artist *might* produce an image worth seeing. 'I paint in order to have something to look at,' said Newman." Another of Rosenberg's terms for it is " 'transformal' art—the only kind of art that is consistent with the recognition of the present formless state of our culture, on the one hand, and of the indispensability of form for human consciousness, on the other. The transformal art of Action painting stands between the sterile formal exercises of academic modernism and the liquidation of art into data and into aimless spontaneity."

The fate of any kind of art is to keep deteriorating into its repeatable and rationalizable elements: techniques, formulas. A movement like Constructivism goes so far as to reduce itself to geometry, "knowledge that can be shared, as in scholarly research, while its workshop spirit breaks down creation into a

sequence of processes as transmissible as a recipe." The media,
omnivorous mechanical appetites, aren't content with a single
set of classifiable processes, but spread out in a cluster of random expropriations, inventory without identity, "the 'double'
of the arts, able to bring into play every aesthetic element
whose function can be rationalized. Whatever art has conceived the media can re-conceive in endless variations—it may
well be that, taking into account all the art works of different
times and places brought to the surface in the twentieth century, enough art has already been accumulated to keep the
media active for the next millennium." Meanwhile, though, art
has been taking its latest unpredicted step, and the media never
quite catch up. The fate of the media (as Rosenberg's optimism
implies) is to be always barely out of date.

Artworks and Packages has wonderful set-pieces, whether
Rosenberg is considering some of his particular heroes (Pollock, de Kooning, Klee, Kline, Newman, Gottlieb, Cornell)
or Duchamp's spade or the nearly irresistible media or the
reasons why political revolutions turn out to be aesthetic-
ally reactionary or the exhaustibility of just about everything
except the artist's consciousness. Rosenberg's formal arguments, grand and lucid (suitable to anthologies compiled by art
historians and young museum directors), are less wonderful
only than his unprofessional ease and generosity, his sense of
art as something humane and comprehensive, his wit (" 'Mini-
mal' art, if the Soviets had any, would be art for the retarded
or for midgets"), his talkativeness, the range of his curiosity,
his eagerness to include the world and the rest of us. If there
were anybody else around like him, it might even be possible
to read the art journals.

                                                        1970